8 Bit Stori

I0055389

Home Computers in 1980s Britain

(1980-1988)

By Michael John Nurney.

© 2024 mjnurney

Revision 3.

Another visitor?
Stay a while…
Stay forever!

01010100 01101111 00100000 01001010 01100001 01100011
01101011 00101110

PRAISE FOR
THE ROAD TO AUM

"Sandra Powers Murphy's new book is a must-read for any investment manager struggling to attract new clients, regardless of time in market. *The Road to AUM* is a clearly written step-by-step playbook for money managers looking to grow their business. The *Words to Drive By* sections should be mandatory reading for anyone in the investment management industry."

– STEVE RUBENSTEIN, FOUNDER, ARROW PARTNERS

"Sandra Powers Murphy brings her long-distance champion's spirit, intelligence, faith in managers, and diverse and skilled experience, to readers. Great roadmap! Those taking the trip with Sandra will be rewarded."

– JOHN AHERN, CO-FOUNDER, COMPASS CAPITAL CORPORATION

"Finally, a resource for business owners and investment managers seeking to grow institutional market share. *The Road to AUM* is the quintessential tool for those who are new to the business as well as those, such as myself, who have been in the financial services industry for their entire career. I would highly recommend it for anyone seeking insight into this business. It is truly like none other."

– DONNA DIMARIA, FOUNDER, PRINCIPAL CEO, CCO, TESSERA CAPITAL PARTNERS, LLC

"It was impossible to read this without a pen and notebook as there are so many tangible takeaways. The ideas and interactive nature of the book is superb. This book provides takeaways that I was able to use immediately and tools that I will apply for the long-term. This is the playbook that will be on my desk as I think about my business; I am confident I will take it out often to read chapter by chapter or to flip to specific sections based on what I am struggling with. This is an excellent reference guide for business owners. Thank you for mapping out *The Road to AUM!*"

– JONATHAN POYER, DIRECTOR, KEY ACCOUNTS, M FUND DISTRIBUTORS

"Sandra Powers Murphy's passion for this topic is palpable, as is her deep commitment to process. Sandra's experience allows her to boil down complex topics to their essence, making the information accessible and actionable. *The Road to AUM* integrates years of insights and critical thinking into one well-written 'go to' volume which is a great gift for managers."

– SUSAN DAHL, CEO, LEVATUS WEALTH SERVICES

"*The Road to AUM* is the step by step guide on how best to approach your business through the marketing and sales lens. The reader can use this book as a tool to ask the tough questions that need to be asked on how and why the business is not growing and then use the advice and insight of experienced professionals who have seen it all to accomplish a growth strategy. Sandra Powers Murphy's connections and the direct feedback of asset allocators are unique to this book. It is a must read for business professionals."

– SUSAN KELLER, FOUNDER ENTREPRENEURIAL EXECUTIVES AND CEO ATLAS

"Sandra Powers Murphy clearly understands the institutional marketplace as she draws a compelling roadmap for asset managers wishing to control their destiny. *The Road to AUM* offers a comprehensive and systematic look at the art and science of raising institutional assets. The book outlines the marketing and sales priorities that matter most through the *Resource Prioritization Matrix*. This is a must read for firms wishing to grow their assets."
– BRIAN FITZGIBBON, CEO, FITZGIBBON TOIGO & CO LLC

"*The Road to AUM* is an indispensable guide for every money manager, whether large or small, established or emerging. Paying close attention to the details can make all the difference between a successful fundraising effort and a failed one. This book gives managers the tools to substantially skew the odds in their favor. It is a transformational opportunity for firms willing to do the hard work necessary to get on the right path to institutional asset growth."
– SCOTT NANCE, CAIA, HEAD OF BUSINESS DEVELOPMENT, IMPACTASSETS

"Anyone seeking to market an institutional investment strategy should read Sandra Powers Murphy's book to understand what hiring firms are really looking for on behalf of their clients and why."
– COVENTRY EDWARDS-PITT, CFA, CFP®, CHIEF WEALTH ADVISORY OFFICER, BALLENTINE PARTNERS, LLC; AUTHOR OF *RAISED HEALTHY, WEALTHY & WISE* AND *AGED HEALTHY, WEALTHY & WISE*

"Sandra Powers Murphy goes underneath the hood of what it takes to build and grow an institutional asset management business and allows readers to decide for themselves how to best use the knowledge provided to chart their course to success. Incredibly in-depth, *The Road to AUM* provides a 360-degree view of what it takes to build a successful firm. This is no average marketing strategy book."
– MATTHEW MCCUE, CO-FOUNDER & MANAGING PARTNER, FINANCIAL INVESTMENT NEWS

"Long-term relationships between institutional investors can lead to significant performance advantages over time. This book shares deep and relevant insight for managers interested in laying the groundwork and building those productive relationships with asset owners."
– SARAH KEOHANE WILLIAMSON, CAIA, CFA; CHIEF EXECUTIVE OFFICER, FCLTGLOBAL

"Sandra Powers Murphy has created a comprehensive marketing and sales handbook for managers that is equally valuable for any service business—small or large. The toolkits presented in *The Road to AUM* should be a must-read for anyone just starting out or seeking to accelerate growth in the professional services environment."
– SUSAN LOCONTO PENTA, MANAGING PARTNER & CO-FOUNDER, MIDIOR CONSULTING; EXECUTIVE PROFESSOR, NORTHEASTERN UNIVERSITY

Contents

Acknowledgements   i

Introduction, Second Edition   1

Part I Out of the Weeds: The Institutional Investor Perspective

Chapter 1   Methodology   15

Chapter 2   The Institutional Lens   23

Part II Stepping Back: Getting in Position to Win

Chapter 3   The Institutional Asset Gathering Marathon   33

Chapter 4   Firm First: A Pre-Launch Puzzle   41

Chapter 5   Understanding Prospects   65

Chapter 6   Redefining the Competition   73

Part III Stepping In: Driving Context and Contact

Chapter 7   The Firm's Oeuvre: Creating the Content Library   89

Chapter 8   Core Collateral   111

Chapter 9   Due Diligence and Databases   121

Chapter 10 Digital Marketing   135

Chapter 11 A Successful Introduction   161

Chapter 12 Face Time: The Live Meeting   175

Chapter 13 Tech in the Room   207

Part IV Stepping Up: Staying the Course

Chapter 14 Establishing Active Voice with Commentary   217

Chapter 15 Adding Value through Ongoing Communications   229

Chapter 16 The Institutional Research and Funding Process   247

Chapter 17 Resource Management   269

Part V Stepping Out: Overdrive

Chapter 18 Games Managers Play   291

Chapter 19 Recommendations from the Road   307

Chapter 20 The Road to AUM: A Game Plan for Asset Gathering   323

About the Author   338

The Roadmap to AUM   339

Resources   349

All opinions expressed herein are purely that if the author unless otherwise detailed. While every attempt has been made to prevent errors and omissions. Any errors will be rectified in future editions.

Dedicated to my mother, Jeanette.

1936-2008

And my loving wife, Angie.

Without whom, I would not have finished this book.

www.mvtcomputers.com

Towcester, Northamptonshire, England.

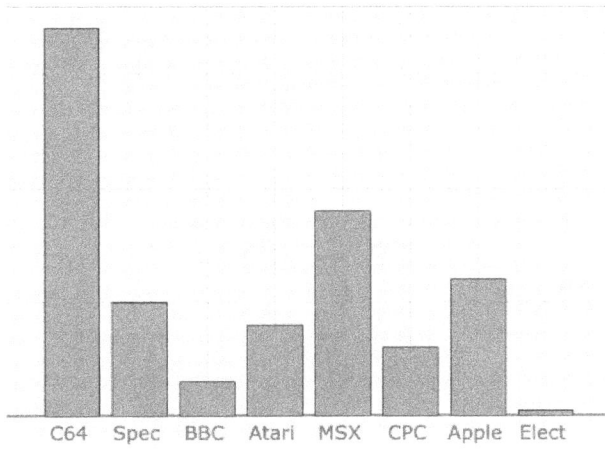

Global sales comparison. (Estimated)

Authors notes:

Thank you for buying 8-bit stories, this is my first published book, and I am very proud of it. It was a huge undertaking! Over the course of three years, a global pandemic and enforced lock downs I researched and read huge amounts about the glory years of the 8-bit computers...I wrote down most of it. In fact, my original manuscript was cut down from over a thousand pages to a more manageable 400 or so. Besides, I needed to finish it before I shuffle off this mortal coil. Having said that, I'm already working on part two - 16-bit stories.

I have talked to many people, some of whom were involved in the industry and I have heard lots of gossip and telling of tall tales. Some of which are included but sadly some of which aren't included as I simply cannot repeat some of the comments. Double dealings, theft and even the ruination of careers...it all happened in the 1980s. One day I might get permission to repeat some of the more salacious stories, maybe or maybe not. You are now reading revision three of 8-Bit Stories, revised why? A good question. I had missed numerous spelling and grammatical errors in the previous drafts, but these have now (hopefully) been corrected.

I do hope you enjoy your time here.

Michael J Nurney

Table of Contents

Authors notes: 6

Glossary 9

Introduction 11

Chapter 1 - Are friends electric? 13

Chapter 2 - Computers in every home 26

Chapter 3 - Mum, can I have one? 36

Chapter 4 - An Obsession in computing. 52

Chapter 5 -1980 67

Chapter 6 - 1981.. 79

Chapter 7 - 1982.. 100

Chapter 8 - 1983.. 127

Chapter 9 - 1984.. 144

Chapter 10 -1985.. 180

Chapter 11 - 1986... 202

Chapter 12 - 1987... 228

Chapter 13 - 1988 and on... 240

Chapter 14 - The School Playground 251

Chapter 15 - Sales Figures 267

Chapter 16 - What went wrong? 274

Chapter 17 - Games! 290

Chapter 18 - End of an Era. 327

Further Reading. 332

Index... 341

Source material... 354

Glossary

- BASIC

Beginners All Purpose Symbolic Instruction Code is a programming language that was created at Dartmouth College in the 1960`s. It is an uncomplicated way to program computers with English like instructions.

- Bit

The smallest piece of information that can be processed by a computer. It is the equivalent to a on or off instruction. Most of the computers mentioned in this book are 8-bit, except for the Ti99/4 which is 16-bit.

- Byte

Is the amount of memory needed to code a character (a number, letter, or symbol). Each byte is made up of eight bits.

- Disk drive

Usually an optional high speed data storage system. Many times, faster than loading from cassette. Disk drives allowed multiple files to be stored on one disk. 5.25- and 3.5-inch disks were the most common sizes of media used in these devices during the 1980's & 1990's.

- I/O

Input/Output of data to and from the computer, this can include Disk Drives or Keyboards.

- Modem

Modems are used to communicate with remote computers, these serial devices often used RS232 as a communication protocol and a plugged into the computer, usually software needs to load into the computer to operate the modem.

- RAM

This is a temporary storage area for programs, all of which is lost when the power is turned off. RAM is where cassette and disk programs are loaded into when the computer is in use. Memory is finite, once full it cannot be usually added to – unless extra hardware is fitted to the computer. For example, a ZX80 or 81 with only 1kb of ram can be expanded to 16kb or 32kb ram with a plug-in ram pack.

- ROM

Read Only Memory is used as a permanent storage by the computer, often to store system critical information like BASIC and System I/O protocols. It cannot the overwritten or erased – even when the power is removed.

- Hardware.

A tangible something that can be used, plugged in to or operated by the computer. Computer hardware includes the physical parts of a computer, such as the central processing unit (CPU), random access memory (RAM), motherboard, computer data storage, graphics card, sound card, and computer case. It also includes external devices such as a monitor, mouse, keyboard, printer and speakers.

- Software.

Usually, written code that is saved on cassette / disk or cartridge for loading later, purchased programs are software. Handwritten programs become software once they are saved on to a media for later retrieval on a cassette or disk. Software consists of computer programs that instruct the execution of a computer. The history of software is closely tied to the development of digital computers in the mid-20th century. Early programs were written in the machine language specific to the hardware. The introduction of high-level programming languages in 1958 allowed for more human-readable instructions, making software development easier and more portable across different computer architectures. BASIC is an example of this.

Introduction

What is 8-bit? To most people of a certain age, it is the first batch of home computers that invaded our homes in the 1980s. Familiar names like Sinclair, Atari, Commodore, and Texas Instruments all feature highly in the memory of anyone who was around at that time.

The Americans, the British and the Japanese all had a concentrated attack on our minds and wallets from 1980 and into the 1990s with the advent of the home computer. Some were much more successful than others, but the best technology didn't always win the battle. How could the little Sinclair ZX81 sell 500,000 units? It was colourless, mute and had the most hideous keyboard ever designed. The answer? Well, it was cheap and available and satisfied an itch – the computer itch.

So, what drove this devotion to the computer? Apart from writing rude words on the computers displayed at Dixons or Curry's, it Is probably down to the ZX80, ZX81 and the humble ZX Spectrum from Sinclair. They were so cheap that we had to buy them, even if we didn't know why. Advertisements relentlessly told us that we needed a computer to further our education, we needed to understand BASIC and binary, coding and how to keep grandma's recipes safe on a C15 cassette from WH-Smiths.

All admirable stuff but was it true? Did buying a Commodore VIC-20 or C64 really improve your skills at school or in the workplace? Would knowing how to load a machine code program on the BBC Mirco really help in the job interview at the local Barclays bank? I have yet to have an interview where the interviewer asked about my knowledge of Commodore BASIC version 2. Was it all pointless?

Indeed, it would seem so but what about games? Let's not kid ourselves, we all wanted to play Star-Trek, Pac-Man or Jet Set Willy.

Move on some forty years or so and we now inhabit a strange world where electrical capacitors are discussed at length. A world where white plastic cases are mysteriously turning yellow and power supplies may be starting to ripple or even explode! Perhaps causing untold damage to your mint condition Enterprise 128KB computer. But surely the old computers are now gathering dust in lofts across the UK or have long since been relegated to landfill? The Commodore plus4 and ORIC computers must have all vanished by now? Well, no, not at all.

These days I can be found at vintage shows packed with hundreds of people up and down our pleasant land. Looking thoughtfully at computers and software that not so long ago was being thrown in to skips (dumpsters) from a great height. But now we find that these very same items are not only nostalgic but valuable too.

A recent show attracted something near to a thousand attendees over a long weekend and that harks back to the old days when Sinclair had their trade shows in London and Commodore held their World of Commodore shows. In truth the shows never really stopped happening they just became less popular and became lower key.

These stories, dates, and facts included here-in are plucked from magazines of the day, online archives and many late-night conversations with engineers, designers and managers who worked at some of the biggest companies of the day. I really hope you enjoy you time here, it's taken a long time to write this down. One thing I did notice on my travels back through magazines and interviews is just how often facts are mis-quoted or are simply wrong. I hope to correct a few of those errors.

Michael J Nurney

Chapter 1 - Are friends electric?

Imagine a world where a powerful computer costs just £99.95![i] Imagine a world where this computer is just as fast or faster than anything else on sale. Was it the best? well no, of course not but it was cheap, powerful and in 1980 you could buy a 3.25 MHZ computer and take it home. Just take a moment to think about this, in 1980 you could buy a home computer and take it home for less than £100. For the first time in human history!

Before 1980 this wasn't possible, usually you would have to spend four or five times that amount and then you would have to build it yourself on the kitchen table. There were, of course some exceptions but most pre-assembled computers were for commercial or scientific use, and they were expensive.

Governments could buy the Freon cooled Kray supercomputer in 1976 for only $10 million and it would take a team of engineers a year to assemble it.[ii]More affordable was the Altair computer which was released in the U.S at a modest $395[iii], however this was equipped with rows of switches and lights, it was almost incomprehensible to use, needing boot sequences and memory locations to be selected by mechanical switches. This would never catch on.

What was needed, was a lower cost computer that used a cheap CPU. One that could undercut Intel and Motorola. Driving prices down would be the only option to start the revolution. In 1976 Intel[iv] and Zilog[v] introduced new microprocessors that were faster than their predecessors and the new Intel 8080 could address a massive 64 kilobytes of memory.

While the Zilog Z80 could run any program written for the 8080, it was faster and cheaper, but it was still expensive for home computers. Meanwhile MOS technologies 6502 microprocessor was launched in San Francisco at the low cost of only $25[vi], far less than any comparable processors from Intel and Motorola, leading some attendees to the show to believe that the CPUs were faulty. Not that it mattered, what MOS had done at the show was to humiliate Intel and Motorola. In return both companies cut their retail prices to compete with MOS Technology. This was the dawn of the new 8-bit era, a cheaper era that would enable and empower the average person to own a computer – eventually.

Meanwhile the Texas Instruments Ti99/4 would use a powerful 16bit processor (TMS9900) but disastrously, it ended up being connected to the rest of the computer via a slow 8-bit data bus. Imagine a very fast 16 lane motorway (freeway) suddenly being reduced into an 8 lane motorway…. At best the data was slowed by half but in fact the computer was slowed down by more than that. TI were forced to use the more expensive 16bit TMS9900[vii] CPU rather than the new and cheaper, CPU that TI had designed but wasn't working yet.

What is an 8-bit computer or processor? Listed below are a few of the most common variations of the CPU or processor that helped start the computer revolution, they would be used in many of the home computers that were popular during the 1970s and 1980s.

Not every processor is listed but the more common ones are, there are exceptions as both 16 and 32bit processors were available in the 1970s and 1980s they were often prohibitively expensive or were custom designs for specific applications.

The bizarre thing about these CPU's is that almost all the ones designed in the 1970s, are still being manufactured and used today but rather than controlling the latest home computer, they are probably controlling the ECU in your car or the heating in your home rather than a Manic Miner.

Manufacturer.	Model.	Release date.	Common Application.
Intel	8008	1972	First 8-bit CPU
Intel	8080/8085	1974	IBM PC, TRS100
Motorola	6800	1974	Altair 8800
MOS Technology	6502	1975	Atari, Acorn, Apple, CBM, Nintendo.
Zilog	Z80	1976	HealthKit, ZX80/81, ZX Spectrum 16/48,128, CBM C128, TRS-80
Motorola	6809	1978	TRS-80 Colour, Fujitsu FM-7, Dragon32/64, CBM Super Pet.
MOS Technology / Commodore	6510	1982	CBM 64, Commodore 1551 (6520T)
MOS Technology / Commodore	7501	1984	Commodore C16, C116, Plus4

What is 8-bit anyway? 8-bit usually refers to the computer's ability to transfer eight bits of data at the same time. 8-bit integers, memory addresses or other data units are those that are 8 bits (1 octet or 1 Byte) wide – for those who really need to know. Perhaps a brief history is needed, after all many of the people and companies included in this book may have been influenced by some these earlier historical events or perhaps maybe not.

While it's arguably true that Commodores Jack Tramiel had a personal battle with Texas Instruments, and it is said that Tramiel did study Sinclair's business model and Jack wanted this market share in Europe's low-end market for Commodore. In turn Sinclair fought his former employees at Acorn, as Acorns Electron computer sought to kill the ZX Spectrums UK sales. Sinclair's own engineers left to form new companies, which then competed with Sinclair, mostly with dire results. Commodore engineers walked out to help form Atari Corporation and Atari engineers left to join Commodore and Apple. It's such a tangled web of intrigue, but this cross pollination of employees did provide technological leak-through as designs and ideas passed from one company to another. Often with mixed results.

Engineers had a grievance with Motorola and then quit to form MOS[viii] and visa-versa (lawsuits ensued). Rivalry existed between teams that were often in the same company, never mind at competing manufacturers. This can often lead to walkouts, resignations, lawsuits, or even secret projects within a company that may or may not ever have seen the light of day.

But why did the boom in computers start in the 1970s and why did it lead to the saturation of home computers in the 1980s? Cost played a major role in this, as did availability but ultimately it all came down to MOS and its 6502.

And then it takes some time.
>wait.

A brief history of time.

- 1822 British mathematician Charles Babbage conceives of a steam-driven calculating machine that would be able to compute tables of numbers. The initial version didn't work but a revised model was designed later that did.[ix]

- 1936 As with a lot of inventions, it would take a war to accelerate feverish productivity. World War 2 gave rise to Alan Turing presenting the idea of a universal calculating machine, later called the Turing machine, capable of computing anything that is computable. Turing went on to join the Government Code and Cypher School, with the outbreak of war with Germany in September 1939 and moved to Bletchley Park. Turing helped to design a code-breaking machine known as the Bombe. The bombe was designed to crack the secret German Enigma code.[x]

- 1944 With a World War in full flow two University of Pennsylvania professors, John Mauchly and J. Presper Eckert designed a computer, it filled a 20-foot by 40-foot room and had 18,000 vacuum tubes. It is regarded as the first electronic computer and was used to calculate artillery firing tables for the U.S Military.[xi]

- 1958 In the U.S Jack Kilby and Robert Noyce unveil the integrated circuit. Robert Noyce would later become known as the father of Silicon Valley. Both Kilby and Noyce are credited with inventing the integrated circuit.[xii]

- 1958, Jack Tramiel and Manfred Kapp incorporated Commodore Portable Typewriter Ltd which became Commodore international, for a time, the largest global computer manufacturer. Jack Tramiel, was a Polish born survivor of the Nazi concentration camps.[xiii]

- 1964 Douglas Engelbart shows a prototype of the modern computer, with a mouse and a graphical user interface. This marks the evolution of the computer from a specialised machine for scientists and mathematicians to a technology that is much easier to use. The computer mouse is US Patent 3,541,541 which describes it as an X-Y positioner.[xiv]

- 1971 Alan Shugart leads a team of IBM engineers who invent the "floppy disk," allowing data to be shared among computers using a removable magnetic floppy diskette.[xv]

- 1972 Atari is formed by Nolan Bushnell and Ted Dabney – briefly known as Syzygy but that name was taken, so they chose the name Atari. Atari comes from a 'move' from the ancient Chinese game GO or Welchi. [xvi]

- 1975 Clive Sinclair launches the Black digital watch. Until this, Sinclair was known for creating calculators, electrical test equipment and audio amplifiers. The world's first mass market digital watch which used LED display technology and small hearing aid type batteries combined to power it. Unfortunately, poor reliability hindered its success.

- 1975 Sphere Computers USA released the first all in one computer with a monitor screen and keyboard. Priced at $860 it used a Motorola 6800 CPU and contained 4KB of RAM. An all-in-one computer as we would call it today. Creator Michael Wise needed a way to clear the computer RAM while it was powered on, without needing to power down the whole computer. So, he created a way which was unlikely to be accidentally activated by the user. He chose the key combination Control-Alt-Delete.[xvii]

- 1976 MOS Technology (Metal Oxide Semiconductor) released the KIM Single board computer created by Chuck Peddle. The KIM-1, short for Keyboard Input Monitor, it was a small 6502-based microcomputer. The KIM-1 consisted of a single printed circuit board with all the components on one side.

- 1976 Commodore international buy MOS Technology, a Chip Manufacturer in Audubon, Pennsylvania. All MOS assets transfer to Commodore, including staff – and CPU designer Chuck Peddle and his team.[xviii]

- 1976   Steve Jobs, Steve Wozniack and Ron Wayne create Apple Computers with venture capitalist funding on April the 1st 1976. Steve Wozniak's Apple 1 was unveiled at the Homebrew computer club in July 1976. The caseless computer was popular – selling at $666.66. Production was discontinued on September 30th, 1977.[xix]

- 1977 Commodore unveil the all-in-one PET computer designed by Chuck Peddle. Starting the companies move away from calculators.

- 1977 Apple show the Apple II at the first West Coast [xx]Computer Fair. It offers colour graphics, 4K of RAM and initially uses a cassette drive for storage.

- 1977 Sinclair Instruments is renamed to Science of Cambridge [xxi]

- 1978 VisiCalc is released for the Apple II and is a major boost to the slow selling Apple II. The Apple II starts to sell in increasing numbers because of VisiCalc. VisiCalc (visible calculator) by Dan Bricklin is the first spreadsheet computer program for personal computers. Often called the Apple II's killer application, selling over 700,000 copies in six years, making the optional Apple disk drive essential.[xxii]

- 1978 Science of Cambridge (Sinclair) launched its MK14 microcomputer in kit form. Ian Williamson approached Clive Sinclair and Chris Curry with a computer design, which evolved into the MK14. A remarkably similar concept to the KIM1 from Commodore.

• 1979 Texas Instruments enter the computer market with a powerful 16bit home computer, TI99/4 it is the first 16bit home computer in the world but priced much higher than the current competition. Rival manufacturers wait for TI to dominate the home computer sector, but concern turns to joy as the expected sales boom doesn't happen.[xxiii]

• 1980 Commodore release the first million selling computer in history, the VIC-20. A huge advertising campaign starts, starring William Shatner with a bunch of cheap video games. The VIC-20 was released in the USA in 1980 and Europe 1981.[xxiv]

• 1980 Tim Berners-Lee at the CERN physics laboratory creates Enquire, a concept of what would eventually become an internet web browser using hypertext, which we all use now in the more common form of Internet Explorer or Safari.[xxv]

Electronic?

I can remember a time when there were no computers at all in the home. A bank or an office were the only occasion when you might see a computer. I can still remember draughtsmen busily drawing on large easels in the drawing office and this was in 1987 and not a single computer in sight. In the home, an alarm clock with blinding LEDs were popular in the early 80s, they might have word - electronic emblazoned on to it.

The mighty VHS or Betamax video player would have a digital display of some sort but the most common item with digital or electronic written on it would be the Casio watch, closely followed by the microwave! And that would be about it.

You may possibly have had a handheld game with a vacuum display that ate batteries at an astonishing rate or perhaps a portable cassette radio player that might come equipped with Stereo. Radio One broadcast in stereo in 1973…

The Atari VCS appeared in the U.S in 1977 but it would not be generally available in the UK until 1978[xxvi] and at £180.00 it wasn't a cheap option but for some lucky kids in 1978 it was a great Christmas present.

We would have to wait until 1980 to anything from Clive Sinclair or 1981 to get something chunky and American from Jack Tramiel.

So, what options did we have? Would we be forever trapped in front of the television watching Larry Hagman in Dallas. No, as good as Dallas was, it would not be too long before the humble computer made it to our living room and then everything changed. Who did shoot JR?

What could you play? And what did people want to play?

PONG on the Atari 2600 arrived on a whopping 2KB plug-in cartridge, a somewhat simplistic game that would become a world-wide craze. A square block of light (a ball? Really?) bounces across a TV screen and you must knock it with your bat. Simple stuff to us now but back then we had seen nothing like this, and it was a new world of wonder. Atari created the game called Pong, but wait a minute, didn't Magnavox create an earlier game called Ping-Pong? A lawsuit promptly followed...[xxvii] So, what if you cannot afford the new Atari 2600? Well then you need a clone machine or copy if you prefer.

Clone makers were everywhere in the late 1970s and 80s, and a simple Pong home console could be yours for only £20 with no option of adding any cartridge games later. Most Pong consoles came with half a dozen variations of the Pong game, often optimistically called Soccer, Tennis or Hockey whilst managing to look almost identical. Portable hand-held games that required huge stocks of batteries were extremely popular in 1980 and would remain so for a few more years until home computer gaming became a thing and handhelds became rather pointless. It would take the Nintendo Gameboy to reinvigorate the rather stale handheld market but that is far in the future.

However, the cheap and often tacky handheld electronic games were great for portable entertainment on the go but only if the batteries held up, they usually didn't – only lasting about 3 hours or so. But were these games any good? Were they worth playing? The answer is usually no. A few of the more expensive Space Invader clones or better yet Galaxians were interesting, but the simple versions were ultimately dull and uninteresting, but it was all that we had back then. These units usually featured LCDs, LEDs, or vacuum fluorescent displays (VFDs) for screen display, which meant they could usually only play one pre-programmed game as the graphics were etched into the glass. LCD was the only real exception to this rule. LED and VFD displays lit up or activated when a certain event happened in a game such as a player or enemy movement, a shot fired, or a life is lost. Sound was relegated to a mini speaker and a few beeps or an ear-splitting tune when the unit was first turned on. These games were hugely popular and cheap, but the better ones or licensed ones often carried a premium price, Frogger, Donkey Kong, Space Invaders, Scramble, PAC-MAN and so on.

The evolution of displays advanced very quickly and VFD display quickly vanished from store shelves. LCD became the low power winner and was much more versatile too. The single game handheld systems lasted up until the early 1990s after which the universal appeal of Nintendo and Sega with the ability to change games as you wanted sealed their fate.

Quiz Wiz from Fisher £13.79
1001 quiz questions to challenge you.[xxviii]

Logic5 from MB games £13.79 Generates 3,4- or 5-digit numbers for you to figure out![xxix]

Merlin from Palitoy £20.99 Try to beat Merlin in 6 fascinating light games.[xxx]

Speak and Spell from TI £41.49
Hours of fun learning how to spell.[xxxi]

While Atari may have created the pong game in the arcades and later flooded the market with its console and in the process caused a sensation, it would be left to the clone systems to really make an impact across the world in those early days. Binatone – a Japanese manufacturer would be an ever-present part of the 1980s. The kids all wanted electronic games, and the clone makers provided them with plenty of knock-off console type systems. They sold well too as we were bored with Tonka toys and Tin-Can-Alley.

1980 would prove pivotal in-home console and computer technology. Commodore released the VIC-20 home computer with 3.5KB of usable memory as the successor to the Commodore PET. The VIC-20 was cheap and phenomenally successful, becoming the first computer to sell more than a million units in the world.

Bill Gates and Paul Allen buy the (D.O.S) Disk Operating System from Seattle Computer Products for $75,000 to use as the operating system for their new IBM contract. It became commonly known as just DOS. DOS was also known as QDOS or the Quick & Dirty Operating System. It was originally written by Tim Paterson.

Clive Sinclair created the ZX80, a very small home computer available in the UK as a kit for £79 or as an assembled computer for £99.[xxxii] A Z80 microprocessor and a ROM based BASIC language. The computer would become a huge sales success for Clive, but this had the problem of creating a waiting list and a long one at that!

Finally, the arcade sensation Pac-Man is released[xxxiii]. The billion-dollar game that had kids pumping money in to arcade machines across the world. Developed by Namco by programmer Toru Iwatani, the idea came to him when he cut a pizza slice and studied the shape, or so he said.

What drove all this innovation in the 1970s and 1980s? well it was the microprocessor, and in some ways, it was down to a few technology giants. The mighty Intel, Motorola and MOS Technology to name a few. Others designed and built microchips such as Texas Instrument's, DEC with the VAX workstation and many more too. MOS was part of the Commodore group at this time and were part of Jack Tramiel's vertical integration master plan. Surely only the most advanced or financially secure would survive the race that was about to begin.

But what is a microprocessor? It is any type of miniature electronic device that contains the arithmetic or logic and a control circuitry necessary to perform the functions of computer's central processing unit. In effect, it can interpret and execute program instructions as well as handle arithmetic operations. All these abilities combine to create what we call a CPU or microprocessor and every computer has one.

The introduction of large-scale integration (LSI) fabrication makes it possible to pack thousands of transistors and resistors onto a silicon wafer. This silicon wafer led to the development of the microprocessor, the first one was the Intel 4004[xxxiv], which was developed in 1971. Motorola and MOS quickly followed with their own versions of processors. Each company would create ever faster, smaller, and more efficient processors as time went on but with each passing year the technology and costs to fabricate these microchips became a problem.

Chapter 2 - Computers in every home

"There is no reason why anyone would want a computer in their home."

- Ken Olson (Founder of Digital Equipment Corporation) at the Convention of the World Future Society in Boston in 1977

Home computers in the 1970s were a hugely different entity to that of the 1980s. Few computer systems came housed in a case, or with keyboards or even an option for a video display. A common option would be to buy a PCB (printed circuit board) with or without wires and maybe a mains power supply to connect to it. Some computers even required the DIY wiring of the power supply. Bearded and bespectacled men in brown floral-patterned kitchens would be busily soldering together 240-volt power packs. A rather frightening consideration but it was not an uncommon pastime in those days. You see it all started with DIY TV set repair, CB-radio construction and then eventually circuit board designs became featured in the magazines of the 1970s.

Things become a little more civilised when pre-assembled computers arrived from the likes of Sinclair, Acorn, and Commodore. MOS technology would still supply PCB computers or SBC which are single board computers. These devices were designed for the very technically minded and certainly not for the home user, but these early foundations often led to further advancements, and they did.

MOS technologies KIM-1 SBC led to the Commodore PET computer, Acorn and Sinclair did almost the same thing and indeed they led on to the Sinclair ZX80 and the Acorn Proton.

Britain was and remains extremely technical. The British crusade into computers was starting to gain traction with numerous companies either being created or changing their production lines to include computers, often starting with simple designs like electronic calculators.

British company RM was started by two friends, Mike Fischer and Mike O'Regan. In 1973 they decided to enter the electronics business, that company was to be Research Machines - computers to be used for research. The rather catchy name aside, they had ambitions to become somewhat like a British IBM.

"We worked out we had enough money to buy parts for 200-250 computers so that is what we did. We planned to sell 250 computers in the first year, and that is what we did too," Mike Fischer remembers.

Source (https://en.wikipedia.org/wiki/RM_plc)

Nascom 1[xxxv]

The Nascom (1 and 2) were computer kits from the UK based Nasco, would later become Lucas.

- 4 MHZ Z80A processor,
- 1 KB static RAM (extendable to 8 KB, or 16 KB.
- 2 KB Monitor (NAS-SYS 1),
- 8 KB Microsoft BASIC,
- 48x16 video interface to attach to a standard TV,
- serial in/out, selectable between cassette tape, RS-232.

The Nascom computers were particularly useful for learning about microcomputer hardware and through the available documentation, learning about BASIC programming. All electronic schematics, datasheets of special components and the complete source code of the monitor were available from NASCOM.

The first and most successful of the "big board" computers was the NASCOM 1. The project started in the summer of 1977. Although the company selling the NASCOM 1 was Lynx Electronics, the UK subsidiary of North American Semiconductor (NASCO) the design was subcontracted to Shelton Instruments a London based company.

John Marshall, head of NASCO, had noticed that the UK wasn't well served by the higher priced US products and had decided that a special product was needed, the NASCOM-1. The NASCOM-1 was based on the Z80 and was targeted to be less than £200 ($300). The computer took the form of a single large PCB which contained the Z80, 1KByte of EPROM, and 2KBytes of RAM. What made it special was that for not much more than a price of a microprocessor trainer it included a TV display and full keyboard. The minimum configuration featured 2 KB RAM and 1 KB ROM monitor, but the Nascom could be gradually extended into a system that was powerful enough to compete with many home computers of the time like the CBM Pet, Apple ii, or Tandy TRS-80.

A complete range of peripherals and expansions were available from independent suppliers, as well as a vast range of software from user groups. Several magazines were dedicated to the Nascom and its relatives, called the Gemini computers, were published. Many languages were available including BASIC, PASCAL, C, FORTH, etc.*Science of Cambridge MK14[xxxvi]*The MK14 (1978) is a superb example of just how far these products went to achieve a rock bottom price. Although it was a late arrival on the scene, the low cost meant that it was a popular option. Made by Science of Cambridge which was a Clive Sinclair company, which then morphed into Sinclair Research in 1979 soon after Sinclair Radionics went out of business.

Sinclair Research went on to produce the ZX family of home computers which includes the ZX Spectrum. So, in this sense the MK14 was a forerunner of the ZX Spectrum and later machines. The kit consisted of a single PCB with a membrane Hex keypad on its lower half and a segment display which functioned as the user display. The memory was a "huge" 512-byte PROM containing a simple executive program and 256 bytes of RAM. The MK14 allowed you to enter an address in Hex, then enter a data byte as two more Hex values. Once you had entered a program byte-by-byte in this way you pressed "Go" and watched the eight-digit display show you the result. As you can imagine programming was extremely limited and thinking up something that was impressive was a big problem. All users of such systems were adept at making words up from the few symbols on a Hex display - even if it involved turning the display upside down.

Flashing displays and symbols moving from one side to the other very slowly were the order of the day.

It was very frustrating to have a general-purpose computer in your hand and yet not be able to make it do much because it didn't have any I/O facilities. Most MK14 users ended up dreaming of adding peripherals such as a full keyboard and a TV display but most just played with the few example programs in the manual. You may think that no one would buy such a machine, but they did because it was a relatively risk free £39.95 (around $50).

A lot of people learned a lot about the inner workings of microprocessors courtesy of the MK14 and comparable products - if only there was something like it on the market today! Perhaps the closest we have now is the Raspberry PI. It eventually sold over 50,000 units.

Source: Getting to grips with the MK-14", Practical Computing, December 1979.

UK101^{xxxvii}

Source: https://www.computinghistory.org.uk/det/20372/Compukit-UK101-(2)

The number of single-board computers being developed at around the £200 ($300) marked the start of the personal computer revolution in the UK, even to the extent that the general press and TV started to run stories about the "computer craze" that was sweeping the nation.

The single-board computers started the move away from kits that only the electronics enthusiast would consider building to machines that could be bought just for the fun of programming. For example, the UK101 came complete with 8K Microsoft BASIC in ROM. You simply added a TV set and cassette recorder, switched the machine on and started programming.

For a few pounds more the manufacturers could have put them into pretty boxes and had a low-cost competitor to the Apple II or the Commodore PET which where both on the market at about the same time. I can only speculate, that to be recognized as a low-cost computer; a product had to look as unadorned as possible. As well as being as cheap as possible.

Another reason may have been that, to start a company building a PCB based computer didn't take a huge investment of capital but the cost of manufacturing the enclosure to put it in and the to add a keyboard, a monitor - it suddenly it became very expensive indeed.

What is clear is that the number of single board computers that were designed and built in the UK at the end of 1979 created a market quite unlike that in the US. With lots of small companies no having experience of designing personal computers it was inevitable that each one of these companies would attempt to design a mark II model to capture a larger share of a market. The rise of the computer was coming but it was still a hobbyist market with DIY kits selling well but fully built machines, are still too expensive and limited in their appeal for the home user.

But why? The main reason was cost.

As time went by it became apparent that computers were too expensive for the average UK user. Schools had Commodore PETs, some had the Apple II but the home user was out of luck unless someone could create a cheaper alternative. The dream to have a computer at home was probably unrealistic unless you built it yourself or if you were wealthy enough then a new Atari 400 / 800 might suit your needs. Perhaps the new Ti99/4 might be better? These were home computers, built for the consumer and not just a college or school environment.

In late 1979, riding on the success of its VCS console, Atari released the Atari 400[xxxviii] (Candy) and the Atari 800[xxxix] (Colleen). The 400 was intended as a starter computer, while the 800 was to be a high-end model for the more professional user.

For U.S buyers with $1,150 you could buy the TI-99/4 computer and a matching colour monitor. The computer has a polished metal trim, giving it an expensive appearance. The planned RF modulator which would allow plugging the Ti99 into your own TV set was not yet FCC approved and therefore could not be included in the sale. Therefore, a custom designed monitor screen was included at huge extra cost.

Jim Bagley, a gaming legend in the UK, has left an indelible mark on the video game industry, especially in the UK. His remarkable career spans decades, and he's known for his impressive programming skills and contributions to various gaming platforms.

Jim Bagley recalls his school years.

"At my high school they had a sharp MZ80k and a BBC micro. I didn't know much about computers except that I could play games on them. I grew up by the seaside, so I used to visit the arcades a lot and I wanted to play games. I didn't start writing games until I was 13, I used to program the sharp MZ as the queue to use the BBC micros was too long."

Throne Of Fire:- Spectrum :- Sole Programmer

Road Runner:- Spectrum :- Sole Programmer

Street Sports Basketball:- Spectrum :- Sole Programmer

World Class Leaderboard:- Spectrum :- Sole Programmer

Gutz :- Spectrum :- Sole Programmer

Batman Caped Crusader: - Amstrad :- Sole Programmer

Red Heat:- Spectrum :- Sole Programmer

Red Heat:- Amstrad :- Sole Programmer

Cabal :- Spectrum :- Sole Programmer

Cabal :- Amstrad :- Sole Programmer

Midnight resistance:- Spectrum :- Sole Programmer

Midnight resistance:- Amstrad :- Sole Programmer

Hudson Hawk :- Spectrum :- Sole Programmer

Hudson Hawk :- Amstrad :- Sole Programmer

Source: https://en.wikipedia.org/wiki/Home_computer

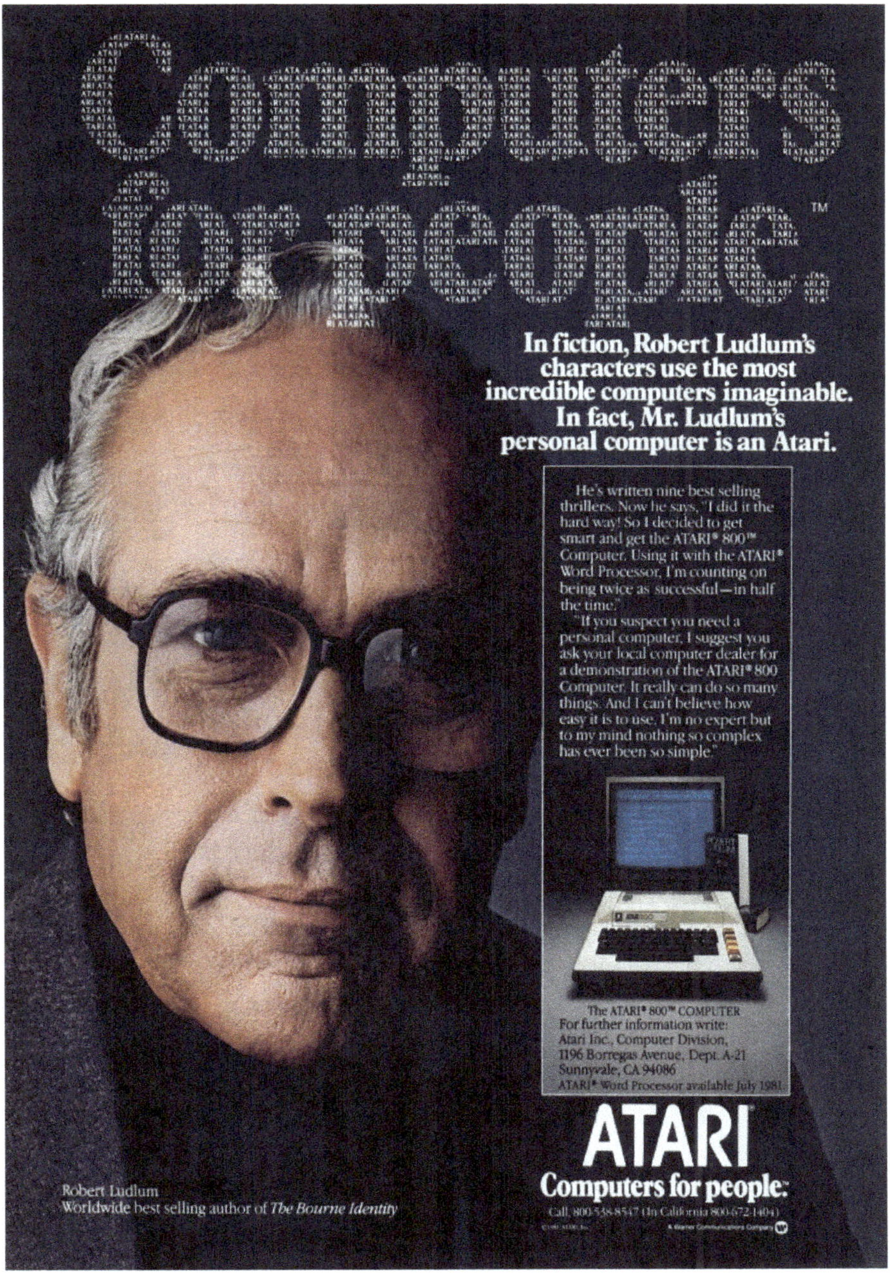

Source: Playboy magazine: Robert Ludlum 1981

Chapter 3 - Mum, can I have one?

In the beginning, computers could balance your cheque book, run a power station, or even print off a school report (should you have a thermal printer) – but would you want to wait that long? For the wealthier among us, it could connect to a BBS (the early internet) to download information, read the news and check your stocks and shares. It could provide you with up-to-date weather details, but it also plays games and that's what 99.9% of computers were used for until the dawn of the internet arrived and then we discovered mp3, warez and a whole abundance of adult material.

My first encounter with video games was at the arcade and as I mentioned earlier, I played a handful of them while on holiday in the early '80s. Arcades were the only way to play games apart from the bat and ball (tennis) or pong TV games that filled the UK market in late 70s. They were usually black and white with no sound and extremely simplistic but later ones branched out in to colour and had sound effects too. Then the Atari VCS arrived, and I played that in 82 or 83 at a friend's house but I never did own one, I fancied a computer.

You see I always thought that a console was a dumb way to play games, one button and a joystick! That is rubbish, to do anything useful you needed a keyboard and what happens when you are bored of games? How do you create anything? The answer is of course that you cannot, I thought it then and I think it now, a console is a dumb way to play games. You are just a consumer.

Later, I did end up with a pong console (It may have been a Binatone console?) that was dreadful, it had a light gun with it, and it kept me occupied for literally minutes before the entertainment wore thin and I was bored. It was time to move on and this is where the holidays mattered and more importantly my birthday too (which was during the school holidays).

The first handheld game I had, was bought for my birthday and I may have been in Scotland and very possibly Aviemore, but I digress, the game in question was "Race`N`Chase" by Bambino and it looked fantastic with the box having large, coloured artwork with police cars chasing robbers at high speed. This was going to be fantastic. It wasn't of course, it was extremely difficult and repetitious but still it was mine and I would use many a "D" cell batteries over the summer holidays playing that thing. However, that was not the game I really wanted. The game I wanted was called Galaxy Invader 1000 by CGL, the very next summer I managed to ask mum for it, and I remember going into a toy shop to buy it, it had pride of place on the top shelf of the store. Galaxy Invader was a space invader knock off and it played well, and I remember playing it endlessly. It was much more fun than Race`N`Chase which was by then discarded into a toy box. American readers may remember it as being called 'Fire Away' by Tandy.

I was lucky enough to have a mother who both listened to and grew tired of my moaning in equal amounts, although she did possess a skill in which she would dismiss and allay any of my needs or wants at the same time. Delayed promises were always a possibility.

Computers were the big thing and as we had just received a classroom full of BBC computers at school, it seemed only fair that I should have one at home.

"Mum, can I have a computer?"

"NO!" she said,

"Why not?" I begged.

"How much are they?" she decried.

"Cheap" said I.

"Maybe for your birthday" and I was dismissed.

"Ok" I smiled…

That was pretty much how the conversation went as I recall it and I'm sure it's not far off. We were not what you would call wealthy by any stretch of the imagination and looking back now I can see; just how lucky I was. I was brought up in a coal mining village in the 70s and 80s and it was not exactly a happening place in the I.T world, not once have I heard Google or Microsoft say that they were looking at Yorkshire, England as a base of operations. But none of that troubled my teenage mind. I wanted; no, I needed a computer to make it in the world and 1983 would be my year. I knew nothing of the wider picture, the companies behind the names, the people or the vast industry that enabled a circuit board with a plastic cover to sit beside our TV. All I knew was that the newspapers had large advertisements in them and the TV played endless loops of Christmas advertisements carrying the Sinclair, Commodore, and Atari names in flashing lights with `sale` now on in big letters. It was complete and utter nonsense to my parents they didn't know what RAM, CPU and data recorders were or what they were for. It meant nothing to them, and I get that now, but to me it was a world of wonder, and I wanted in.

My main source of information other than the daily newspaper, was the grim cold and often rain soaked playground, we didn't talk much in the classroom and if we did then a large wooden blackboard eraser would come hurtling in your general direct at something approaching light speed or worse still, the humiliation of being told to stand up and share with the class, what it was that was so important? Was it that, Algebra didn't matter? Well, I can tell you now that it doesn't matter, I have never used Algebra and as Billy Connolly said, I too have no intention of going there!A few other kids that I knew, had computers in mid-1983 such as Lee, the posh kid with a Commodore 64 and he had a pretty girlfriend too. Another kid had a BBC micro because his dad was a teacher, and other kids had ZX Spectrum 48K computers with sound so bad you wanted to cut your ears off and that was about it.

The Atari 1450XLD – The amazing Atari that was never released. (Cancelled - August 1983) due to Atari's financial problems.

Class is a thing.

I didn't know what class was at that age, but computers introduced me into the world of class. You may ask what the hell I am talking about but it's true, let me explain. The middle-class kids (wealthy parents) had computers early on their life cycle and that's good. The less well-off kids, well we had the bargain basement computers, the Ti99, Vic-20 or ZX81 and perhaps the ZX Spectrum 16k. The more well-to-do kids on the other hand, well they had Atari 800, BBC B or the Commodore 64 and dare I say it… with a disk drive, also early on in its life cycle. I would later align myself to the Spectrum gang, while keeping an eye on the cool Commodore kids too. The Commodore 64 was too expensive for us in 1983, I had to wait just a little longer.

In mid-August 1983, which is my birthday I was asked what I wanted? I naturally said a computer and I was presented with the biggest newspaper created on Earth. The Barnsley Chronicle, it was, and I kid you not gargantuan in size, its mighty pages spanned the kitchen table like a tablecloth and beckoned you in. However, the thing I was interested in was at the back and I had been ringing circles in blue biro pen every Friday for the last few months. It was the second-hand section or classifieds as it was called then.

The problem was and I mentioned this earlier, we didn't have much money and certainly not much to spend on a pointless computer and so I was given a budget. A lofty budget of £30 which if you adjust it for inflation, probably works out to £102.38 in today's money. Not a problem I thought and scanned the paper with renewed vigour. I wish I could remember the computers that were for sale but sadly I cannot, it was after 30+ years ago but I do remember what I bought and roughly were it came from.

Armed with £30 in cash the 12-year-old me was taken in the dark to a strangers house some twenty or so minutes' drive from home. It was both dark, cold when my step farther and mum dropped me at this stranger's address. My stepdad and I walked down the garden path, around the rear of the house and knocked on the kitchen door. As I remember it a lady who answered, and we were ushered inside, and the door promptly closed – it was cold.

"Someone's here for the computer" she bellowed, and we were escorted into the low-lit living room and there on the TV set was a computer game, I can remember it like it was yesterday. "You're not playing that aeroplane game again, are you?" and she wondered off into another room. Now what I do not remember was what the chap looked like, but it does not matter. He looked at me and said, "I just cannot get games for it "I grinned in anticipation and said, "I can, I can get them from a place in Devon." He nodded and showed me how to plug the leads in and what games it had with it. He boxed it up and the £30 was handed over, I was now a computer owner!

I had bought the mighty Texas Instruments TI99/4a personal home computer.

I must stress that, the 1980s was a hugely different time. We had to buy magazines to acquire any information about the computer systems we liked and no sooner had one model arrived, it was discontinued, and another one popped up. Sometimes it was from the same manufacturer, and sometimes not and that was my fate. You see I had just bought the only computer in the newspaper that was £30 and had games with it, a most important feature I deduced.

The term home computer just means any computer that's aimed at the home user, it could be a PC like device rather like the computers we use today but back in the 80s, it usually meant low spec, cheap computers that were usually thought of as toys. IBM joked that they would never enter the home computer market as it was a bit of a fad. Commodore saw them as a consumer product to be sold like a toaster, Sinclair didn't want anything to with it after the MK14, until Chris Curry and Acorn changed his mind. It was a wild west era of incompatible computers from different manufacturers that could be released and abandoned in weeks as the parent company collapsed, and all these companies tried to get a share of the market.

Sinclair's ZX80, ZX81, ZX Spectrum, Commodores PET, VIC-20, C64. Genie Mark 1, Acorn BBC A, B, Electron. Microbee. Grundy New Brain. Microprofessor. Dragon32. Colour Genie. Jupiter ACE. ORIC 1. Sord M5. Camputers Lynx. Vtech Laser. Memotech MTX. Mattel Aquarius. Tandy MC-10. Atari 600/800XL and believe it or not, many more too were on sale in the UK.

Arriving home meant feverish opening of the Ti99/4a's black shiny box, manuals and assorted literature packed inside. The excitement was so great that I think I even glanced through the manual which is a trait that I no longer possess. The spaghetti of cables that a computer can employ is amazing and where do they fit? A power-pack, a modulator for the TV and finally the computer its-self. You would think that plugging the leads into a computer would be easy and it was, kind of.

The TV modulator only fit in one socket, the power supply only fit into another but there were two 9 pin din plug sockets, and I had nothing to plug in to them, do I need to? And why don't the sockets have labels or markings of any kind on them? I needed to look in the manual again!

However, my excitement was cut dramatically short by the single biggest problem of the 1980s. We only had one TV, and my parents were now watching TV! No problem I said mumbling and moaning under my breath, and I set about reading the game manuals and associated paperwork that comes with a second-hand 1980s computer. I had the computer manual too– big and professionally written, with illustrations and good, helpful guides. I had a glossy brochure from TI with Mr Bill Cosby smiling at a TI99/4a with a pile of software and that was about it, apart from game manuals printed on extremely high-quality glossy paper. There were the obligatory warranty and service paperwork that no one reads too. The TI99/4A was an expensive and classy machine I deduced at that moment, and I was right to think that, after all these years I still think it is one of the best made computer systems; if not the best designed.

I had a bountiful supply of both cassettes and cartridge games, or modules as Texas Instruments called them and I can probably list them from memory. Gaming on the Ti99 was both fun and disappointing, in that some of the games were fantastic fun to play but most were horrible and slow, and you didn't know which was which until you bought them. Alarmingly I had no cassette lead with the computer so I couldn't load the cassette games just yet. There were other cassettes too, copies with handwritten labels like 'car race' which must be awesome with a name like that, but I had another problem too, I had no cassette player. In fact, we only had one in the house and that was an Amstrad HI-FI system which had no obvious way of connecting to the Ti99/4a. Of course, it did but I didn't know how to do that, I was a kid, and my knowledge was extremely limited.

School beckoned the following Monday morning, and I ran to school boasting about my new shiny stainless steel covered wonder computer. I then found out that no one had heard of it, and no one owned one. I was slightly crest fallen but undaunted I continued to expel the virtues of my computer which was the best one of course! My friends were sceptical to say the least and they arranged to come back to my mum's house after school and have a look. After a brief tour of the intro screen – bright blue with two rows of multi-coloured block and a quick game of Parsec they universally agreed that it was good but not as good as a ZX Spectrum as I hand only a dozen or so games. I disagreed but what did I know?

I didn't know the difference as I had never seen a ZX Spectrum, but I disagreed and said mine was best, this led to numerous arguments and name calling, a similar thing would prevail throughout my school and college days as we argued whose computer was the best and best usually meant a Commodore C64 as they had colourful graphics and great sound. No one had an Atari 800.

After a week or so I became apparent that my half a dozen or so games would not keep me fully occupied and I started to look at other ways to acquire more games. It wasn't easy; the Ti99 had been orphaned and abandoned in the marketplace after Texas Instruments had lost millions of dollars and dumped the machine. Again, I didn't know this at the time and continued to read the newspaper and flick through the magazines that came with the computer.

As luck would have, I found a discovery akin to Tutankhamun! In the back pages of a beaten up and much unloved Computer & Video Games magazine that I found during a math lesson at School, I saw an advert from Parco Electrics in Devon, a mail order company that had it all for the Ti99. They had hardware and software galore, all I needed to do was send of a SAE (stamped addressed envelope) and they would send me a catalogue in the next few days. True to their word, a poorly photocopied catalogue on A3 paper arrived shortly after with a whole new world of hardware and software on it, for some reason it was in blue ink and slight off centre. This added to the charm I thought but looking back it was pretty heath-Robinson and probably a one-man operation in a shed.

Atari games, TI utility software, disk software, cassettes and magazines, books and so on. They did indeed have it all. Prices ranged from £4.99 for a cassette game that you have never heard of, to £30 or more for Pole Position from Atarisoft. I would need to sweet mum to get some more games but in the meantime, I needed a cassette player and as luck would have it, we were visiting the market town of Northampton in a few weeks, not only that but we were visiting a large open market. That could mean I might be able to blag a cassette player if I tried hard.

After an age wondering about looking at stalls, I managed to find electronics stand with knock off Walkman's, cassettes, and HI-FI stereos suitable for any local ghetto. What they did have was a cheap silver cassette player for £12, a quality item this was not but it would do. Mum dutifully paid up and I was happy as a clam.

What followed were endless battles with cassette loading errors and tweaking of volume and tone levels. Eventually a sweet spot would be found where the C15 from WHSmith's would load to reveal some handwritten BASIC game that ran at a snail's pace. None the less I had a cassette loading system ready for action. OLD CS1 would be typed a million times in the next twelve months I owned the Ti99 and that cassette loading command is etched in my mind for ever more. After a few months my collection of games had increased, a few favourites had emerged and even my brother was playing them too. We constantly battled at Yahtzee; the loser had to make a cup of tea. A humiliation best avoided at all costs and the battles often raged into the night, especially if he lost.

Other favourites included Parco golf at £7.95, Robopods £4.95, Fun-Pac 1 for £4.95, MASH £17.50, Donkey Kong £20 and so on. Parco Electric of Honiton, Devon was a life saver in those days. Parco were selling the Ti99/4a for £89.00, TI Joysticks for £19.75 and the cassette lead for £9.95 which I needed too. I remember having a see-through dust cover and a blue plastic cassette storage case as well at one point.

One of the first purchases from Parco Electrics was a cassette lead and I did find out which 9 pin socket it fitted in to (I read the manual again), the other 9-pin D-Sub socket was for the Joysticks, but TI never felt the need to label any of the ports on theTi99...

Talking of joysticks, the Ti99 had 9 pin D-Sub Atari style joystick sockets, but Atari joysticks did not work correctly as the wiring is slightly different. That led to my first Quick shot Joystick being a pointless purchase a few months later.

I never told mum it didn't work as she had just spent £10.00 at Woolworths, and I didn't want to disappoint her, but it never worked on my Ti99/4a.

I didn't know it at the time, but various adapters were made that did allow the Ti99 to use Atari style joysticks like the QuickShot and the like. Some companies did make Ti99 compatible joysticks, but these disappeared from the shops almost as quickly as they arrived. Fortunately, PARSEC worked just as well or perhaps even better with the keyboard controls.

Parco Electrics introduced me to many game genres that I had never heard of before like, Adventure, RPG even simulation. This was fantastic and, in some ways, the limited game selection of software on the Ti99 made me try games that I never would do on later machines. The Fun-Pac games collections from Virgin games, they were a pack of three cassettes and each one had a collection of games written in BASIC on it. Classics like Escape the mugger, Sea-wolf and Gunfight - some of these quickly became favourites due to the TEXT input and the open world element they contained. Gunfight is a text-based action game, difficult to believe but bear with me here. In the game you have a descriptive text and then an action input prompt. The objective is to kill all of the villains in this Wild West themed game. It sounds simple doesn't it; the game layout is something like this...

WILD BILL STANDS BEFORE YOU

AND CHALLENGES YOU TO A DRAW!

DO YOU?

"D-DRAW/F-FIGHT/R-RUN"?

Now I appreciate that it doesn't look too exciting, but the twist is that you are only given a few seconds to respond before the computer takes over and decides your fate. If memory serves me correctly there were a dozen bad men to dispose of and the game gets faster after every turn. You have to be quick!

If that was a little too fast then, what about the text adventure game Starship-supernova? It was a much gentler paced game, as with most adventure games this one awaited your input before deciding on its next move. In Nuclear Disaster, which we talked about earlier the game had another kind of peril, the need to save people rather than killing them, a much more civilised prospect I think you would agree. The premise is simple; a radiation leak is escaping from a nuclear core and into the reactor room where, for some reason half a dozen scientists are trapped and unconscious. A time limit is included in the game and the radiation will fill the screen in all its 8-bit blocky, pixel glory. Games about nuclear disasters were very popular in the 1980s!

Hand typing a game in the BASIC language was a thing in the 1980's and I, like many others had the joy of typing and correcting mistyped and error prone listings from magazines. After what would usually be a few hours, the Ti99 would turn from blue to yellow and go blank for a few seconds while it processes the code I had just entered.

If you were in luck a READY? cursor would greet you but more often, it would emit a dull beep and "Incorrect Statement in line xxxx" an error would be flashed urgently on the screen. With something like that indicating an error in the code on line 160 or whatever. Of course, you do not know what the error was or if the error is linked to another line of code before that. It was a total nightmare and would consume of hundreds of hours, and yet it reaped little to no reward at all.

That reminds me of another story and possibly my first mistaken game purchase (certainly not my last). Whilst on my summer holiday in sunny France, I had been bewitched by an arcade game called – MACH-1. MACH-1 was an arcade combat aircraft game. The game was a 3D jet fighter in a chase view, flying across a rolling landscape. What I failed to realise is that the game was a laser disc powered affair which used real photography as the rolling landscape. Complete with stereo sound and fast paced dog fights, it was a feast for the eyes and ears. Could I play this game at home on my computer?

But I had a Ti99/4a with 16KB of ram...

However, all was not lost! In my latest Parco Electrics flyer, direct from Honiton, Devon I could just make out a slightly smudged offer.

- MACH from twentieth century fox - £19.99

I instantly pestered mum who gave me the money, which I then gave to my brother Christopher – who then wrote me a cheque which I posted via Royal Mail. A slightly complex routine but pretty normal in those days. My excitement was palpable, I would soon be playing a fast arcade game on my Ti99/4a. What could possibly go wrong...

A week or two later a package arrived! I unwrapped it eagerly and I was somewhat bemused by the artwork on the box. Strange I thought... I don't remember helicopters. But it can't be wrong, the name was the same as the arcade game. MASH, or was it?

Puzzled by the purchase in my hand, I was brought back to reality by the calls from mum. I had to go shopping with mum – this was a Saturday, and I had to go. So as a compromise I read the manual in the car, and this is when a problem became clear. I had bought MASH not MACH-3.

I was devastated, I have even boasted to my brothers about the arcade game on its way, no more crappy games on the TI! This was the big time...

M.A.S.H was based on the popular 1970s comedy TV show and as funny as it was, it certainly was not a laser-disk combat flight aircraft sim, I would like to say that I learned a valuable lesson that day but alas I did not. I still buy the wrong games now and probably always will, excitement and eagerness have given way to bad eyesight and the malaise of being middle aged gamer. I did play M.A.S.H on the TI99 and I pretended to enjoy it, but it was very repetitive and nothing like what I wanted to play…I'm sorry Alan Alda but I never enjoyed flying that stupid helicopter.

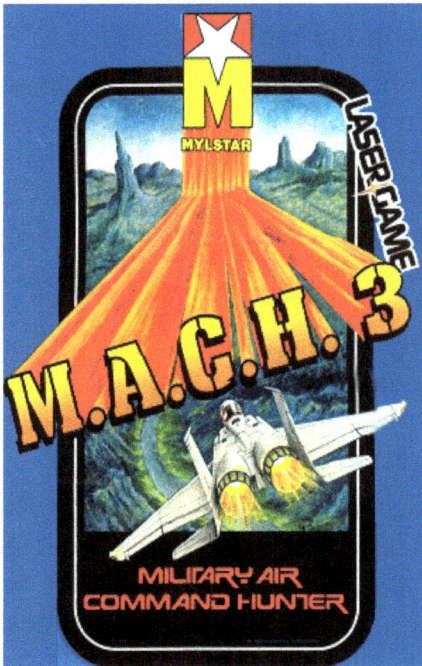

I have many fond memories of these computing days, of playing games and getting games to work but little of this interested my stepfather. My stepfather was an ex-WW2 soldier who served in the Royal Engineers, he was Rolls Royce trained and extremely clever – his mental mathematical speed was incredible, but he had no interest in games other than watching me play and no doubt enjoying the fact that it kept me quiet.

However, on a visit to see my brother in Milton Keynes one weekend while I had the TI99/4a and just before the announcement of Texas Instruments withdrawal from the computer scene. We decided to play PARSEC, a traditional defender like space shooting game, fly right and shoot anything that moves. Its fast and colourful and great fun.

On this Saturday night my brother piloted the spaceship with the keys E,S,D and X – the four directions of travel. My stepfather – Geoff hit the fire button as instructed by my brother David. A simple task but to two grown men that never really played video games before, this was hilarious, and they proceeded to play in fits of giggles so hard that my stepfather's false teeth almost fell out! While Parsec is an incredible game it may have been too fast for the family to play, fortunately I was armed with extremely fast reflexes back then and I enjoyed the game very much. I once managed more than 100,000 on the high score table! A task that would be impossible now that I am fifty!

PARSEC wasn't my only game; one absolute gem was Road Race. A TI BASIC game on a C15 cassette… Road race depicted a semi first person view of a car driving along a road with oncoming cars appearing on the horizon. The problem is that they may well be on your side of the road and heading straight for you! While this may sound exciting as a video game, imagine the game looking like the cars are made of blocks of Lego. The roadside was yellow, and devoid of detail and the refresh rate is so slow that the cars appear to flash their headlights as they approach you! This is not clever coding in BASIC but a result of the BASIC being too slow to redraw the screen. The Ti99/4a almost gives up and stops each time it redraws the screen graphics. Yes, it was every bit as bad as a flickering ZX81 game but somehow created on a 16KB 16-bit computer. The mind boggles. That's not to say it wasn't fun, it was, and I recently found a copy on eBay in Italy. It seems the Italians have impeccable taste in games too…

Golf would become the sports game for the boys in our family and the Ti99 provided two examples of this beloved grassy sport. Mr Finkell would provide a 16KB golf game in BASIC and yes it was basic, extremely basic indeed. It appeared to be created by someone who knew absolutely nothing about golf. To say that it was a poor game is not really doing it justice. It was awful but it was the only sports game that I had, and software was hard to come by.

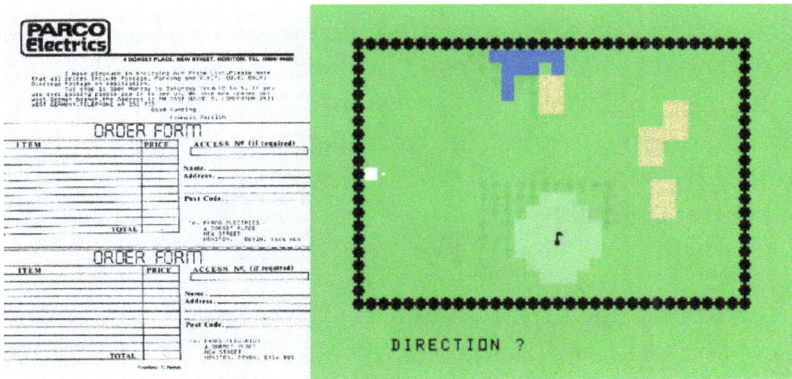

Screenshot supplied by mjnurney.

Parco Golf (1984) 16k Ext Basic. (no its not GoldenTee…)

Chapter 4 - An Obsession in computing.

Personal home computers, a relatively modern invention that arguably changed the world and created the entertainment model that is more popular now than when it appeared. I can say with some confidence that the XBOX console might not exist without IBM contracting Micro-soft in 1980 to create a BASIC for their new personal computer. The Sony PlayStation would not of had some of the high-quality software that it had, if Commodore had not bought the Amiga from Hi-Torro, providing Psygnosis (formed after the Imagine software company failed) with the graphical power that they needed for immersive gameplay. Atari would probably have collapsed in financial ruin in 1984 had Jack Tramiel not walked out of Commodore after a vocal fracas with financier Irvin Gould. It is even slightly possible that Commodore would be around today had Jack stayed around, possible but unlikely.

One company had an advantage and that would be Commodore as they designed and manufactured the CPUs that were used in the Apple I & II and Atari computers as well as all Commodore computers.

Estimated company value in 1980:	
Atari	$415 million
Commodore	$125 million
Sinclair	£131K
Apple	$118 million
Amstrad	£8.8 million

It was only a few decades ago that Commodore was making mechanical typewriters and adding machines, Sinclair was making amplifiers and radios.

Atari's Nolan Bushnell and Ted Dabney founded a company called Syzygy Engineering, this in turn became Atari and made an arcade game or two before embarking on what would be a rather popular home console. This was the beginning of a consumer battle between the U.S, Europe, and Japan. The UK would primarily use British and American computers. While the far East, U.S.S.R and some Eastern European countries would develop numerous copies of hardware like the Apple II and the Sinclair Spectrum, although as far as I know – no copy of a Commodore or Atari home computer was ever made during the 1980s.

We live in a different world now, where instant news is required and every device must stream Netflix, it wasn't always so. Today our smart watches and phones inform us of breaking news, emails, and text messages, remind when it's time to sleep and when to stand up. The humble TV set which was invented in 1927 by American Philo Farnsworth has been upgraded to 'Smart status 'of late and it delightfully informs us what to watch and what news is breaking. It seems that we are no longer capable of making such import decisions, fortunately in the 70s and 80s we had to make our own decisions – right or wrong. Imagine, buying a high value item at a store with no knowledge of the item, not only that but no clear idea of what that item does or what it is for? You have no internet, no Twitter and no Metaverse to search and no Discord to ask.

The sight of a computer beeping away is a wondrous thing to me, steeped in mystery and wonder. Show me a computer from the 1970s and 80s and I'll be fascinated, conjuring up images of Sci-fi films and flaky tv shows but show me a modern PC and I'm instantly bored rigid. You see I was a child of the 1970s and I can just about remember a world without computers in every home and that really wasn't very long ago.

My first introduction to video games happened at a camping site in southern France, on our summer holidays in late 1982. Lunar lander and Asteroids by Atari in tabletop configuration were there in a large, wooded hall, sunlit by the warm evening sun. I was transported to another world for the price of ten pence, a bargain in anyone's currency. Admittedly the game would only last about sixty seconds or so depending on your skill and reflexes.

I am fairly sure that the first computer that I ever saw was in the film, Colossus: The Forbin Project from 1970, it must have been on UK TV in mid 1970s and I was fascinated by that film, the premise is this. Dr Charles Forbin creates a massive supercomputer, designed to oversee the defence of the United States-called Colossus. This computer is intended to stop nuclear war, but Soviets have their own supercomputer called Guardian and a battle of computers commences. It was great! Or so it seemed all those years ago, but I was child then and it is most probably rubbish. I refuse to re-watch on the off chance that its dreadful!

It would be the TV advertisements in the early 1980s that really got my attention, WHSmith's famously asked "what would you do with a computer?" who knew? We didn't know and neither did the manufacturers but that didn't matter just yet. It was 1981 and this was an early advert for the new £69.99 Sinclair ZX81 home computer. Advertisers were new to all this computer stuff, and they didn't really know what to do with them. There was always the mortgage calculator to promote, tax returns and letter editor but these didn't capture the imagination at all. Recipe writing was another as was cheque book balancing and phone number recording. Pretty exciting I'm sure you will agree.

A more useful use of one's time would probably be a phonebook and a pen. This was the failing of the first computers. What on earth were they for? What is the point of them?

With the launch of the ZX80 in 1980, the UK home computer scene became one of the most frenzied in the world, with new computers launching and failing every few months or so. For some reason, the UK loved home computers to such a degree that they were almost disposable by the latter half of the 1980s.

We didn't have the American computer games sales crash in 1983 and so we didn't suffer the fire sales when everything seemed to be sold at bargain prices in an effort to clear dead stock. No, we had cheap software supplied on cassette tape and we loved it. What's not to like about software priced below £5? We loved computers and we wanted to buy games not balance a cheque book and to keep data base, well most of us did anyway.

ACORN ATOM

You may think that the 1980s home computer boom is a long, forgotten piece of history but the effects of it are still impacting the video game and entertainment market today. Where do you think all those bedroom coders and hardware engineers went to work? They went to Sony, Microsoft, Apple and so on…

My turn.

As the bell rang out, I knew I had just one hour to make it home and maybe just maybe, I could save the day and save the six-scientist trapped in an eradiated underground chamber. I knew it was down to me and me alone! Looking left and then right I raced across the main road and on to the pavement, over the over-grown bushes and I was on my way home. A short cut over the abandoned road passed the houses on the right and along the farmer's fields. I had allocated nine minutes to run the mile or so home! I could do it; after all I had done it before. Deep gasping lungs of air raced into my lungs as I climb the hill, passing the courtyard and old folk's homes at the top of the hill. Now it was easy, few hundred yards on the flat and then a steady decent down the hill on the other side and into my little village and home.

Running along the lane and down the road to my house, my parents bright red 1980 Ford Granada shined in the mid-day sun – I was almost home and then I had done it! Nine minutes and thirty seconds from school to the front door – a personal best according to my Casio watch.

I ran into the house with the moaning of my mum echoing in my ear, "Slow down she bellowed" but she wasn't to know that lives depended on me! It was now or never. I turned the wood grain 20-inch living room TV on, switched the channel to number 5 and waited for the yellow screen to appear. My computer had been powered up for 24 hours since lunchtime yesterday when I started loading a cassette.

It had taken a relatively quick three minutes or, so to load, which was okay by 1984 standards. I rarely saved all of the in-game scientists, but I tried most days when I was allowed access the living room TV (we only had one tv in those days).

This was a game of course and the game was Nuclear Disaster by PJ Finkell on the Texas ti99/4a computer, and this was 1984. This was the start of an obsession with computers that would last for the next forty years and beyond. In early 1984 and as a 13-year-old I didn't know any of this, all I knew was that I had a computer, and I was awesome! But that was until went to school I realised that I was the only kid with a Ti99/4a and everyone else had Sinclair or Commodores. While the cool kids talked about Jet-Pac and Choplifter, I had Parsec and Alpiner to play and no one else knew what they were. I would have to wait to play the games that everyone else talked about, but I wouldn't have to wait long as Mr Jack Tramiel from Commodore had frantically culled the computer market, cut costs, and drove companies out of business by becoming Japanese and learning the art of war or so he said. The list of casualties was impressive too.

I was lucky, incredibly lucky. My mother whether by necessity (to stop me moaning) or good luck (computers were cheap then) decided that I should be kept occupied and my response was that I needed a computer, consoles didn't interest me one jot and so I was furnished with a Texas Instruments Ti99/4a home computer and many more as the years went by.

The computer market in the 1980s is a little like the mobile phone market now. A modern late model iPhone for example can cost hundreds of pounds but a three- or four-year-old model is almost worthless and that was the same as the home computer market but magnified somewhat. A new iPhone can appear every year or so, but the home computer market was swamped with computers from dozens of manufacturers and almost none of them were software or hardware compatible and few made an impression on the public and lasted long enough to be a commercial success.

For example, the Commodore range of computers could not use Sinclair, Amstrad, Acorn or Apple hardware or software, the same followed for the MSX or Texas Instruments or indeed another! The only chance of anything possibly working from one machine to another was if you stayed with the same manufacturer, a cassette drive or joystick was the only possible exception to this rule as they could often be used on any machine but…not always… The manufacturers didn't care as it meant you had to buy their products and not a competitor's product, this they seemed to think was the key to commercial success.

It was a nightmare for mums and dads buying something for their kids, say you had a Sinclair Spectrum at home, and you wanted a joystick to play some game or another. A simple request you would think, and a Joystick was a cheap device to buy. A Quickshot 2 joystick cost about £9.99 for most of the 1980s. So armed with your new joystick, you rush home only to find that the Sinclair Spectrum didn't have a Joystick port or a connector anywhere on it. So, with the joystick in hand and no conceivable way to connect it to the Spectrum, what do you do? Well, you needed a Joystick interface, and these were sold by many companies, including Sinclair themselves.

It was a bit of a minefield in those days any it never improved very much. Standards never mattered to manufacturers very much, printers were another problem and to a lesser extent, so were cassette players or data recorders as they were often called. Commodore offered their own digital unit, which did fit all of the commodore range (almost). Sinclair used a regular domestic player that could also record the music charts every Sunday.

Amstrad bucked the trend and a cassette drive built in, on the CPC range of computers, managing to create one of the longest all-in-one keyboard style computers ever made. It was huge!

So here is my introduction to the wonderful world of computing. I did not own all of these; I did borrow some of them over the summer holidays and the bank of mum would finance the others as the years went by. Bizarrely the only 'new' computer was the Amiga in February 1988 and that cost the most amount of money.

- 1982 Pong console. (Paddles and a light gun)
- 1983 Atari VCS (Spider man and The Empire Strikes Back)
- 1984 Texas Instruments Ti99/4a
- 1984 Acorn BBC Micro model B
- 1984 Sinclair ZX81 (Swapped for a TCS slot racing system)
- 1985 Acorn electron (My friend's computer)
- 1985/6 Sinclair ZX Spectrum 48k+ (lots of copied games)
- 1985 Commodore VIC-20 (My friend's computer)
- 1986/7 Commodore 64 (vast collection of copied games)
- 1988 Commodore Plus4 (Friends computer)
- 1988 Commodore Amiga A500 512KB 1.2 (£399.99)
- 1990 Commodore C64 / 1541 disk drive*

*Primarily to play Ghosts and Goblins and the huge bag of games that I had been given – oh and Leaderboard too.

Matthew Smith with a TRS-80 which was used to program the ZX Spectrum version of Manic Miner.

While a battle raged in the 1980s for our wallets another, smaller but equally important battle was taking place and that was software. Software is nothing without a computer and the same applies to a computer without software. It would be a disaster, poor software support would always equal poor hardware sales and computer manufacturers knew this – well mostly anyway.

Magazines could praise a computer, and they often did as they were written by the same young geeky kids that were buying the computers in the first place but if the software never came, especially computer games in these early years then the computer was doomed to fail. A computer could go from concept to sale in as little as a few months, in the case of the Amstrad CPC or it could be a long painful development like the Acorn Electron or MGT Sam computers. Software could be equally as fast or slow for example.

Matthew Smith wrote the colourful Monster Muncher on the Commodore VIC-20 in about 3 hours. That is more of an exception that the rule of course. It could be a lucrative practice in the early 80s to get games written as quickly as possible as new publishing houses would pay good money for games. Matthew Smith earned £300,000 for the game STYX on the ZX Spectrum and Matthew got to keep the ZX Spectrum too. Speaking of Matthew Smith, Manic Miner was written in 9 weeks, mostly on an evening for Bug-Byte software although the rather manic schedule and Matthew's desire to form his own company ended that relationship.

(3D) Monster Maze was one of the earliest software must haves and became something of an early software hit. A survival computer game developed from an idea by J.K. Greye and programmed by Malcolm Evans for the ZX81. Released in early 1982 for the Sinclair ZX81 with a 16 KB memory expansion. This game was unique in these early years of gaming in so much that it was genuinely a little frightening, even with block graphics, and no sound it still managed to generate a 3D maze on the little ZX81 and yes it was never called 3D Monster Maze, it is just had 3D in large writing on the cassette case.

Sinclair and Commodore would become two of the fastest companies to turn hardware from concept to a product that a consumer could buy on the high-street. Commodore would often strive to have a new product or even a line of products available to show at the Consumer Electronics Show. Whereas Sinclair would try to release a new computer from 1980 and every year on... At least until the wheels feel off Sinclair business model. Sinclair would develop a computer and software for it while producing last year's machine at a budget price. A successful tactic that would make Sinclair millions of pounds.

Some software and hardware would take months or years to produce, often arriving late to market and garnering less-than-favourable reviews. Of course, some hardware would never appear, even bringing the company that was developing it to its knees. Software could suffer the same fate too.

Bandersnatch famously from imagine Software – the poster boys of quality software on the Spectrum was originally intended for release on the Spectrum in 1984, at a higher price that was usual for computer games at the time. Most games of the era retailed at budget £1.99 or mid-priced £5.95 to the premium big, boxed range of games at £10 to £12. Bandersnatch was due to cost £39.95 with a cartridge or dongle to support extra features like better graphics and sound. However, Imagine Software went bankrupt owing to massive financial mismanagement, fortunately this came to head just as the BBC arrived to film a documentary called Commercial Breaks.

The TI-99/4A, released in 1981 proved to be a popular and high selling home computer from TI. However, by 1983 the Ti99/4a was losing sales to the massive selling Commodore 64 and budget Sinclair models. TI designed and test produced the upgraded Ti99, the Ti99/8, expecting a 1984 release. The TI-99/8 was to be fitted with 64K RAM, built-in Pascal programming language, a larger keyboard, an integrated speech synthesiser and a faster CPU than the Ti99/4a.

Sadly, along with the cheaper TI99/2 (a Sinclair zx81 like machine) But it never made it to market, getting the axe in October 1983 during the hight of the computer wars. Some of the test production computers have popped up for sale on eBay from time to time along with disk drives, printers, and TI's universal serial HEX-BUS adaptors for the TI99/4a.

Toy company Mattel, best-known for its Barbie toys at the time changed direction completely in the late 1970s and entered the video game market with the Intellivision in 1979.Moving on to the Aquarius personal computer in 1983 which was developed by British electronics firm Radofin. Designed to be a budget Sinclair like machine, the Aquarius shunned many standard features of the era having little of interest when it was finally released. It shipped with a poor-quality rubber chiclet keyboard and 4KB of RAM. Of course, it didn't sell well. The new Aquarius II (1984) sought to rectify those problems by having a proper keyboard and 20KB of RAM, however by the time of its would be release, the computer market was so well established that it was cancelled.

Even the mighty Commodore International managed to cancel computers before release, adding to the mythical status of such things. Commodore was often indecisive and chose the wrong path and the Commodore 65 is probably one of those wrong paths. A successor to the now eight-year-old Commodore 64, the 65 would have enhanced features and breathed new life into the range while still offering C64 compatibility, much like the C128 did in 1985. However, Commodore had just bought Amiga for $27 Million, and money was perilously tight, the decision was taken to kill the c65 project in 1990. Again, test machines, power packs, boxes and manuals had been created before the production was cancelled and these managed to appear in sales later.

Sinclair's "Super Spectrum", codenamed Loki or LC3. Was to of been an Amiga-beater, with custom graphics and sound chips, 512x256, 256 colours and a 128K memory. With RGB, composite and TV display outputs, a serial port, joystick ports, light pen, MIDI port, stereo sound, floppy disk. All this for as little as £200. The machine appears to have got no further than the design phase and was abandoned by Amstrad as a project, probably the right thing to do as the Amiga with all its custom chips cost far more than £200. Some aspects of the computer seem to of appeared or inspired the SAM Coupe by MGT and the Flare machine that was bought by Atari, becoming the Jaguar.

Sinclair's illusive Janus project is more of a mysterious computer or console design rather than a real product. Or was it? There is almost no information other that a mock-up of it appears to have been produced and photographed in 1986.

The process of design and cancellation of productions is nothing new and it continued in the 1990s. Atari would continually research designs and concepts that would never see the light of day. Prototypes of the Falcon 68040 inside a MicroBox case, a design that strikingly resembles Sony's PlayStation 2. In fact, the Falcon "MicroBox" is mentioned as part of the PlayStation 2's patent US D450,318 which in turn looked like the Sinclair Janus from 1986.

It may have been easier for established companies to cancel almost ready products but for smaller companies it was often the death knell, companies like Atari, Commodore, Sinclair, and Amstrad all had products ready to launch at some point and then pulled the plug at the last moment. That is business and generally good sense would prevail as they may have been late to market, compete with another product or deemed to be simply pointless in the marketplace.For all the successful computers, companies and software houses that made it through the 1980s. Many didn't make it and either folded or simply failed to produce a single item before the money ran out. Of course, other reasons may exist for the cancellation of a rumoured project, for one it may have never existed in the first place or of been nothing more than a design on a piece of paper that was leaked to an eager journalist in the hopes of increasing the share price!

Chapter 5 -1980

Commodores Pet 2001	£645.00
Sorcerer S-100	£740.00
Apple II 16K ram	£750.00
Tandy TRS-80 4K	£365.00
Compucolor 2	£1058.00
Texas Instruments Ti99/4	£569.00
Sinclair ZX80	£99.99

Buying a computer in 1980 was something of a minefield. What do you want it to do? Is it a scientific research machine or an industrial CNC controller, or perhaps you need one to write office documents and complete the payroll? In reality, home computers of the 1980s were ill suited to most of these tasks. You might think that by 1980 the role of the computer had been clearly defined, but this wasn't the case at all. In fact, computers were still seen as education or business machines and that was it. No serious thought had been given to the role of a computer in the home. But Apple had released the Apple II in 1977? Commodore had the all-in-one PET and Tandy sold us the TRS-80 but it was Atari that grasped the concept of entertainment on a home computer. Especially in Europe. Apple had cornered the business market in the U.S by now and entertainment software soon followed.

Atari had the 400 and 800 computers and these used cassette, disk, and cartridge as storage options, and they would become the staple for data usage on home computers. The UK had yet to fully embrace the disk drive as costs and availability were a big problem. For example, the Commodore 1541 disk drive would not be available until 1982, and it cost a whopping $400 in the U.S.

Estimated sales figures for 1980 show that the UK had over 40,000 computers in circulation, Apple, ITT, and Commodore took about 20% with Tandy bringing up the rear with 10%. The rest were taken up the like of Acorn, Atari, Heath, and Altair. Computer manufacturers seemed to have produced rather creative sales figures, for example Apple advertisements believed that they were the biggest selling computer in the world around this time, despite Tandy selling many more units (50,000) than they did. (https://cybernews.com/editorial/from-hero-to-zero-meteoric-rise-and-fall-of-tandy-computers/)

As far as education went, schools and colleges had already begun placing microcomputers into classrooms and science laboratories. Most of them were the Oxford-based Research Machines' 380Z, a Z80A computer in a big black box with two front facing handles and was intended to be slotted into racks rather than sitting on a desktop. While this wasn't and would never be a home computer, it did play games, and it was often used to play Space Invaders or The Valley.

With the possible exception of the Atari 400/800 and the Ti99/4, none of the current computers were what, could be called home computers.

When did the home computer become the home computer?

The definition of a home computer is probably a computing device with a keyboard that connects to a domestic TV set, at least in early 1980s terminology. One that is used for entertainment as well as education and business work too perhaps. If we decide that a domestic TV is a requirement, then most if not all the early home-built kits are now void – a few exceptions could be allowed but let's not split hairs. The Apple II could not connect to a domestic TV set until the PAL modulator became available but if you were spending almost £800 on a computer then you would probably be able to afford the Apple monitor too.

The Texas Instruments TI99/4 was initially only sold with a monitor – a repurposed TV but without tuning capabilities. A TV that cannot receive TV signals is a monitor, but it provided no better picture quality than a normal domestic TV. Tandy did the same with the TRS-80. Texas Instruments decision to only supply the computer in a bundle could have been seen as a great all in one computer system and some people did buy it, but not many did.

The cost of the TI99 was prohibitive, it even made the Atari 400/800 seem like a bit of a bargain.

So that only leaves the Atari 400/800 as an option for January 1980, so we had better have a look at them and to what else is coming along.

…. Other computers were hot on the heels of the Atari 400/800, some were arguably better but perhaps more importantly – most were considerably cheaper.

Atari 400/800 (1979)

Image source – mjnurney

- CPU: 6502B Microprocessor: 0.56 microsecond cycle. 1.8MHz
- Colour: 16 colours: each with 8 intensities.
- Sound: Four independent sound synthesizers for musical tones.
- Internal speaker (in addition to audio through TV).
- Memory: Includes 16K bytes of RAM and 10K (ROM)
- ROM expansion may be expanded with a user cartridge program.
- Keyboard: 57-key alphanumeric keyboard plus 4 function keys.
- I/O: Serial input/output port, four controller ports.
- Display: 320 x 192, 24 x 40 characters. 3 text modes, 8 graphic modes.

Shortly after delivery of the Atari VCS game console, later renamed the 2600. Atari designed two microcomputers with gaming capabilities with great graphics and sound, namely the 400 and 800.

The 400 served primarily as a game console with a wipe clean plastic foil keyboard, while the 800 was more expandable and had more RAM, this was the real home computer. The Atari 400 was released by Atari, Inc. in 1979 as part of the new Atari 8-bit family. It was designed to be an entry-level computer for younger children, with a clean and uncomplicated design and a tactile membrane keyboard that prevented damage from food and small objects. The 400 had a single ROM cartridge slot to keep costs down and initially shipped with 8 KB of ram. It was powered by a MOS Technology 6502B, or MOS Technology 6502 SALLY CPU clocked at 1.79 MHZ (1.77 MHZ on PAL versions of the computers).

70

The graphics were provided by the same custom coprocessor chips as the Atari 800, which allowed for advanced graphics and sound capabilities. The Atari 400 had a resolution of 320×192 pixels with 16 colours. It also had four joystick ports, one SIO port, and one composite monitor port.

The Atari 400 was marketed as an affordable alternative to the Atari 800, which was packaged as a high-end model. Despite its limitations, the Atari 400 was popular among home computer users in the United States and Europe. It was eventually replaced by the Atari XL series.

While only having 8KB or later 16KB of ram from Atari, it was quickly discovered that 32KB or 48KB could be fitted internally which allowed all the current Atari 8-bit computer software to be used on the machine.

The Atari 800 was released in late 1979, alongside the Atari 400. It is based on the same MOS6502 microprocessor as the Atari 400. It was available with either 8KB or 16KB of RAM initially, which was expandable to the maximum of 48KB. Later the 800 came with 48KB as standard from Atari. The 800 came with a full-size keyboard and two hidden cartridge slots, which allowed you to plug in software cartridges. However, it was also quite expensive with an initial price tag of $999.85 in the USA.

Atari's 8-bit computers were the first home computers with architecture that used coprocessors, enabling more advanced graphics and sound than most of the competition at that time. Designed by the legendary team headed by Jay Miner, who also designed the Atari 2600 VCS. Video games are key to its software library, and the 1980 first-person space combat simulator Star Raiders is considered the platform's killer game. The resulting system was far in advance of anything then available on the market.

Sinclair ZX80

Image source: mjnurney

- Built-in language Integer Basic
- Keyboard: Membrane keyboard, 40 keys
- CPU: NEC 780C-1 or Zilog Z80A, 3,25 MHz
- RAM: 1 kB, max. 901 bytes available for user.
- ROM: 4 kB, could be upgraded with the 8 kB ZX81 Rom
- Text modes:24 x 32 characters, 64 non-ascii / uppercase letters only.
- Graphic modes: 10 block graphics characters for 64x44 'pixel' graphics
- Colours: None / Monochrome
- Sound: None
- Size, weight:21.9 x 17.5 x 4 cm
- I/O ports: TV out, tape in/out (~300 bps), Z80 extension bus
- Price Kit: £69.95 (1980, UK) or Assembled: £99.95 (1980, UK)

The Sinclair ZX80 was a home computer brought to the market in 1980 by Sinclair Research of Cambridge, England. It was notable for being the first computer available in the UK for under £100. It was available in kit form for only £69.99, where purchasers had to hand assemble and solder it together. Sinclair included an instruction sheet showing part locations.

The ZX80 was immensely popular straight away despite a delay in manufacturing and delivery. Launched on 29 January 1980 by Science of Cambridge Ltd. (later to be better known as Sinclair Research). The ZX80 was advertised as the first personal computer for under £100 and received praise for its value and included documentation. It was designed around a Zilog Z80 central processing unit with a clock speed of 3.25 MHZ and was equipped with 1 KB of static RAM and 4 KB of read-only memory (ROM) which contained Sinclair's BASIC. The machine was mounted in a small white and very fragile – vacuum formed plastic case, with a one-piece blue membrane keyboard fixed to it.

The ZX80 had no sound output or colour, and its display was over an RF connection to a household television. It had a straightforward way of storing programmes using a cassette recorder. The ZX80 was designed to be a low-cost introduction to home computing for the public. However, it faced criticism for screen blanking (no display) during program execution, its small RAM size, and the unresponsive keyboard. Despite these limitations, it was immensely popular and for some time there was a waiting list of over several months.

Its curious name comes from the computer's Z80 microprocessor which runs at 3.25mhz (PAL). The computer featured 1K of RAM and 4K of internal ROM. It is housed in a small plastic case and at the rear had a 44-pin edge connector and four sockets - mic, ear and power, and phono socket for a coaxial lead to connect your computer to a TV. The first computer from Sinclair to use Sinclair's own version of BASIC. Developed for the ZX80 by John Grant and Steve Vickers from Nine Tiles and then used in the ZX81 and ZX Spectrum. An unusual feature was that instruction commands were not fully typed but shortened to just pressing one of the keyboard keys, each key had a command associated with it. For example, pressing the key "J" resulted in "LOAD" being entered.

Texas Instruments TI99/4

- Released: November 1979 (USA), (1980 UK)
- Price:US$1150 (with monitor)
- CPU: TI TMS9900, 3MHz
- Memory:16K RAM, 26K ROM
- Display: Video via an RF modulator / Monitor out
- 32 characters by 24 lines text
- 192 X 256, 16 colour graphics
- Ports: ROM cartridge, Audio/Video output, Joystick input
- CPU bus expansion
- Peripherals: Speech, PEB, Disk drive, RAM, Modem, cassette
- OS: TI ROM BASIC

Based around the Texas Instruments TMS 9900 16-bit CPU running at 3 MHZ, the TI 99/4 had one of the fastest CPUs available in a home computer but was restricted by a dreadfully slow implementation of BASIC. The TI99/4 had a wide variety of expansions and an expansion box (rather like a PC), with an especially popular speech synthesis system. The TI 99/4 was expensive and a slow seller, causing TI to redesign the computer soon after its release.

When the 99/4 finally emerged in 1979, it received mostly disparaging reviews. Benjamin M. Rosen of Morgan Stanley, who was then the leading semiconductor analyst and fast becoming the leading personal computer analyst as well, wrote a humorous article about the disappointment of what was expected to be a major contender in the personal computer business.

TI had intended to create both a video game console and a low-cost personal computer, but while in development those products merged together into what became the TI-99/4. Due to strict FCC emissions regulations, the Ti99 shipped with its own 13" custom made colour TV set which was used as a monitor. From the beginning, TI wanted to maintain tight control over who developed software for its 99/4 platform, they didn't publish any technical specifications or initially release an editor/assembler package that would allow for advanced programming on the system. This locked out third-party developers like Atari and others who made the big arcade games of the day.

Due to its poor chiclet-style keyboard, limited application support and high price due to required colour monitor, the TI-99/4 received generally poor reviews and flopped in the marketplace. Varying reports say that it sold somewhere between 20,000 and 100,000 units in total it was not the success that TI had hoped for.

That concludes the home computer line-up of January 1980, little choice, and expensive options but home computing had begun. While payroll, cheque book balancing and cross word solvers were all available it was the opportunity to play games and to provide entertainment that really drove the home computer forward. You don't need fancy graphics to draw a chart or to display columns on a spreadsheet but to play a cracking game of Space Invaders or Pac-Man you most definitely do. So, let's move on and look at what else was happening in 1980, who was making the decisions that would carve the future of the industry and who was going to get rich quick or fail fastest. Something special happened in the UK at the start of the 1980s and it altered the face of computing as we know it. You may believe all that ever happened in the past was Apple and IBM, but not so. In the UK there was an explosion of machines unlike any other before or since. To mark the 40th anniversary of the ZX81 we look again at these remarkable micros.

To put things into a modern perspective, the original retail price of the Apple II was US$1,298 (with 4 KB of RAM) and US$2,638 (with the maximum 48 KB of RAM). The price of a Commodore PET in the UK was around £600, and the Tandy TRS-80 £500 but the UK market was really looking for something that cost at most £200/$300 and preferably less than £100/$150 for an entry level machine.

This resulted in the single board "naked" PC style of machine, such as the NASCOM, being popular. This was fine if you were interested in electronics, or at least not frightened by it, but there was no real prospect of this sort of machine being acceptable to the mass market or casual consumer.

Acorn Atom (1979)[xl]

- CPU: 1 MHz MOS 6502 CPU
- RAM: 2K RAM and 8K ROM.
- VIDEO: Motorola MC6847 (32X16 characters) or 2 colour graphics
- 6522 VIA controls the serial and parallel ports.
- INS8255 PPI drives the cassette interface and keyboard.

At about the same time as the Sinclair ZX80, Acorn, who also already had a simple 6502 module system, announced the Acorn Atom. This was to be a complete computer but nowhere near as primitive as the Sinclair ZX80. The Atom used a 6502 processor and, like the ZX80, only used integer BASIC but it was expandable, unlike the ZX80.

It may have been more like a traditional machine, but it cost £120 as a kit and £150 built, which made a lot of people think twice about it and why it never sold in huge numbers. Of course, its design then leads on to the later and more popular BBC Micro. The Atom was a progression of the MOS 6502 CPU-based machines that the Acorn had been making from 1979. The Atom was a cut-down Acorn System 3 without a disk drive but with a good quality integral keyboard and cassette tape interface, sold in either kit or complete form. In 1980 it was priced between £120 in kit form or £170 for a factory assembled unit. Options took it over £200 for the fully expanded version with 12 KB of RAM and the floating-point extension ROM. At minimum spec the Atom had 2KB of RAM and 8KB of ROM, with the maximum specification machine having 12 KB of each. An additional floating-point ROM was also available from Acorn. The 2 KB of

RAM was divided between 1 KB of Block Zero RAM and 512 bytes for the screen display (text mode). This left a meagre 512 bytes for programs in BASIC. 8:13 pm. The ATOM had an MC6847 Video Display Generator chip, allowing for both text and graphics modes. It could be connected to a TV or modified to output to a video monitor. Basic video memory was 1 KB but could be later expanded to 6 KB. Since the video display could only output at 60 Hz it meant that the video could not be displayed on a large proportion of UK TV sets, a 50 Hz PAL colour card was later made available to address this problem. Six video modes were available, with resolutions from 64×64 in 4 colours, up to 256×192 in monochrome. At the time (1980) a 256×192 video output was considered high resolution.

While the ATOM was a well-built computer that looked far superior to anything that Sinclair made, the high cost prevented its market penetration from being anything like the ZX80. In late 1982, Acorn released an upgrade board for the Atom which allowed users to switch between Atom BASIC and the more advanced "BBC BASIC" as used by the new BBC Micro. The upgraded ROM was purely to the programming language. All of the Atom's hardware capabilities remained unchanged, and hence, contrary to some pre-release beliefs, the BBC BASIC ROM did not allow Atom users to run commercial BBC Micro software, since nearly all of it took advantage of the BBC machine's much more advanced graphics and sound hardware and greater RAM capacity. Commercial BBC Micro cassettes could not have been loaded anyway, as they ran at a transfer rate of 1200 baud and the Atom's cassette interface only supported 300 baud.

It would take Clive Sinclair to really grasp the UK market in 1980 and he created a computer for everyday use that was cheap and almost disposable with its bargain price, no one could compete with Sinclair, initially at least. But Sinclair was always held to ransom by poor finances, and this didn't change until the ZX Spectrum became popular.

Chapter 6 - 1981

Sinclair ZX81

- Production: March 1981 (UK) - 1983
- language: Sinclair Basic
- Keyboard: Membrane keyboard, 40 keys
- CPU: Zilog Z80A or NEC D780C-1, 3.25 MHz
- RAM:1 kB, up to 901 bytes available (upgradable to 56 kB)
- ROM: 8 kB
- Video: Text modes 32 x 24 lines, 64 non-ascii characters
- Graphic modes: 64 x 48 rows using 10 block graphics characters
- Colours: Monochrome
- Sound: None
- I/O ports: TV RF, Z80 bus, tape ear / mic (approx. 300 bps),
- Price: Kit: £49.95 (1981, UK) Assembled: £69.95 (1981, UK)

The ZX81 computer was produced by Sinclair Research and later manufactured in Dundee, Scotland, by Timex Corporation. Launched in March 1981 as the successor to the successful Sinclair ZX80 and designed using the tried and tested method of being both cheap to produce and cheap to sell. The low-cost introduction to home computing for the public was another successful move for Sinclair, with more than 1.5 million units were sold domestically. As a cheap entry-level machine, it was never meant to be anything more than a low-cost computer to further the acceptance of computing in the UK. In the United States it was initially sold as the ZX-81 under licence by Timex.

Timex later produced its own revision of the ZX81, namely the Timex Sinclair 1000 and Timex Sinclair 1500. Unauthorised ZX81 clones were produced in several countries like Russia and became extremely popular. With no moving parts – the ZX81 featured a touch style membrane keyboard, an exposed edge connector, TV out and MIC/EAR 3.5mm jack connectors. With no power switch, it was switched on and off by attaching or removing the power supply connector at the rear. The ZX81 was able to successfully appeal to not only hobbyist users but also much of the UK's public. It was the ZX81's introduction that sparked the massive adoption of computing here in the UK and in turn, kick-starting the home computing boom.

The ZX81 came with 1KB of internal memory which it shared with its graphic display – this made programming the ZX81 tricky because any sort of complex program required more than the standard 1KB of memory to run. Fortunately, the Sinclair 16KB ram expansion became essential to almost all ZX81 users in the same way that it had on the ZX80. The ZX81 could be bought via mail order preassembled, or for a lower price, in DIY kit form.

It was the first inexpensive mass-market home computer to be sold by high street stores, led by W. H. Smiths – the popular UK stationary retailer and soon many other retailers followed (such as John Menzies and even Boots the chemist). The ZX81 marked the point when computing in Britain became an activity for the public rather than the preserve of business and electronics hobbyists. It helped produce a huge community of enthusiasts, some of whom founded their own businesses producing software and hardware for the little ZX81.

ZX80/81 designer Rick Dickinson joined Sir Clive Sinclair's Sinclair Research Ltd in December 1979 and became the in-house industrial designer at Sinclair Research Ltd. He designed both the ZX80 (initial design was by John Pemberton) and ZX81 home computers, including the cost saving touch-sensitive keyboard.

The ZX81 won a British Design Council award in 1981.

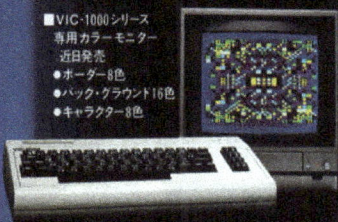

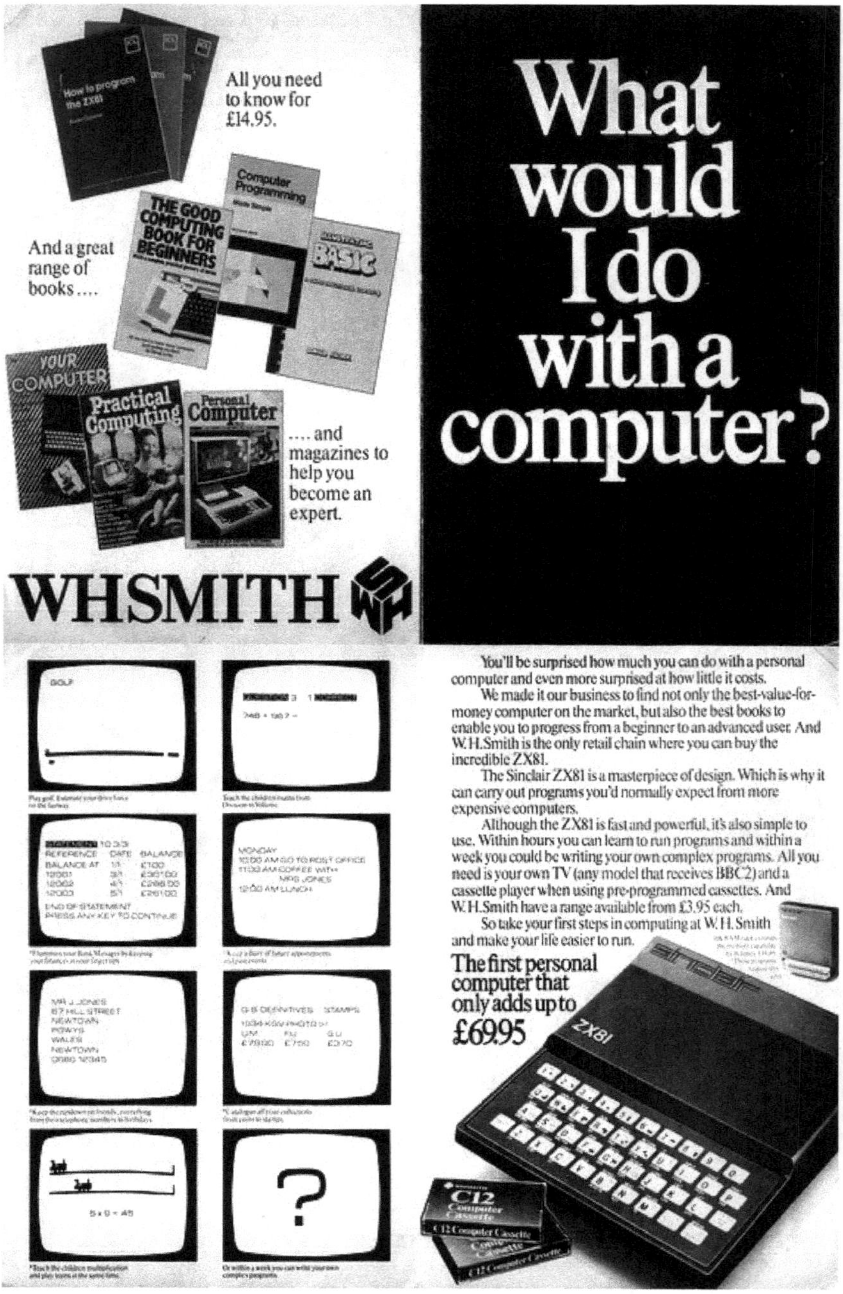

Source: https://www.pinterest.co.uk/pin/8866530494226873/

The BBC. Problem.[xli]

The BBC Corporation's plans for a television series on personal computing, to be broadcast in 1982, offered a great opportunity to demonstrate and educate the public about the possibilities of computing but there was a small problem, the BBC Corporation didn't have a computer to use and had enlisted ranks of academics to help them find a suitable computer to base its new show upon. The BBC insisted it would examine and carefully choose an established computer, should a suitable one be available. But why did the BBC feel the need to champion the computer? It all started with a landmark TV event: The Chips are down.

During March 1979, a documentary called the *Chips are Down* by Edward Goldwyn, was shown on British television. It was part of the Horizon TV series and aroused great public interest by showing some of the extraordinary new technological changes that were coming. The BBC Continuing Education Television Department held a series of discussions on which an educational series in this field might be done. This led to proposals for a series of three major documentaries to be filmed.

1.**So, What's It All about?** First broadcast: 19th March 1980

The silicon chip, unnoticed by most of us a few years ago, is now something everybody has heard about, few understand, and many are beginning to fear. Is it really the basis for a revolution as profound as the industrial revolution? Bernard Falk takes a layman's view of what the silicon chip is, how it's made and works. From a Chicago millionaire's home to a Birmingham car-test track, and from a psychiatric hospital in Scotland to a Swedish factory, we look at how the new technology is being used and what it could do in the future.

2. **Sink or Swim?** First broadcast: 26th March 1980

Is British industry falling behind in its use of silicon chip technology? By using microelectronics in its products or in production, a company can improve its competitiveness enormously. But to ignore the opportunities offered by the chip could lead to disaster when other - largely foreign - competitors are forging ahead. And what of the effects on the workforce if a company 'goes micro '? Are our fragile industrial relations capable of adjusting to the changes the new technology will force on us? Bernard Falk reports from Holland, Sweden, and Norway to put the British position into perspective.

3. **And What of the Future?** First broadcast: 2nd April 1980

How will the silicon chip affect the quality of our lives and our attitudes to work? Starting in America, Bernard Falk visits places already using the new technology to find out what could be in store for white collar, blue collar, and professional workers in the next decade. What kinds of jobs will change or disappear? Are there areas where employment will increase? What will be the effects on the professions? How must our attitudes change if we are to enjoy the benefits of this new revolution and not suffer its worst effects?

People had been asking 'How will this affect my job, or my company, or my industry?' However, the questions were now changing to 'What is a microcomputer? What is a computer language? What is computer memory? How can a computer control a machine, or draw pictures, or play games?' Perhaps most importantly — 'How can I control a computer?' These were now very real questions for a great many people and now that microcomputers were becoming cheap enough for the home computer to become a reality, these types of questions became the basis of what was to become the BBC Computer Literacy Project and that would include a British Government contract to supply education.

An endorsement by the BBC would enable a computer manufacturer to sell into the large UK education market and possibly the UK government too. With companies including Acorn Computers, Sinclair Research, Tangerine Computer Systems, NewBury Laboratories and Dragon Data showing interest in the project. A prototype ZX81 was demonstrated to BBC representatives in January 1981, while Sinclair's local rival Acorn Computers put forward their proposed Proton computer, a design – of which a prototype did not yet exist – based on the Acorn Atom. To Sinclair's dismay, the contract to produce the BBC Micro was awarded to Acorn.

Later, Paul Kriwaczek, the producer of The BBC Computer Programme, explained his reservations in a March 1982 interview with Your Computer: "I would have been very reluctant for the BBC to sell something like the Sinclair ZX81 because it is so limited". When Clive Sinclair heard of the BBC's project in December 1980, he wrote to the BBC informing them that he would be announcing an updated version of the ZX80, to be called the ZX81, in early 1981. It would remedy some of the ZX80's deficiencies and would be both cheaper and more advanced. Sinclair wanted the ZX81 to be a candidate for the BBC contract and lobbied for it. He pointed out that there were already 40,000 users of the ZX80 and that by the time the series was broadcast there were likely to be upwards of 100,000 ZX81 users in fact it would be more like 400,000 users.

In February 1981 it was decided that the bid from Acorn Computers, of Cambridge, was the most attractive, since their machine, of which they had been able to demonstrate a prototype, seemed to offer the best combination of hardware and software. The company were also committed to a design philosophy of high expandability, and they had a particularly strong in—house research and development team. Acorn was contracted by BBC Enterprises Merchandising Department, headed by Roy Williams, to produce the British Broadcasting Corporation Microcomputer System.

In deciding to run a television series on computing which required viewers to buy a BBC computer, the BBC was setting a strange precedent. The most famous director general of the BBC, Lord Reith, said that the role of the public broadcasting corporation was "to inform, educate and entertain". He never added "and manufacture".

In doing so, it could appear that the BBC was inadvertently using its great influence to upset the delicate balance of competition in the personal-computer industry — competition which had, in the space of three to four years, created an industry currently worth about £45million and likely to double in the next 12 months.

It was still possible that the BBC would be forced to change its plans. The cost of developing special software for the BBC computer may have proven prohibitive. It may have had to revert to using computer programs written in a standard form of the popular language BASIC.

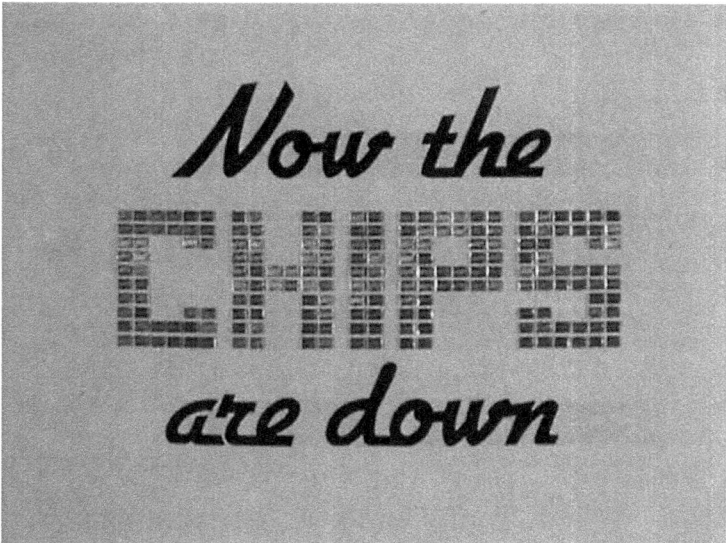

Now the Chips are Down (1978) Horizon BBC TV

Clive Sinclair was critical of the BBC's lack of interest in the ZX81, accusing it of incompetence and arrogance. Shortly after Acorn won the BBC contract the UK Government issued a recommended list of computers, including the BBC Micro and Research Machines 380Z, that schools could purchase, with the aid of a grant, for half price. Sinclair's computers were not on the UK Governments list.

Sinclair responded by launching his own half-price deal, offering schools the chance to buy a ZX81 and 16 KB RAM pack for £60, plus a ZX Printer at half price, for a total cost of £90. As the cheapest Government-approved system was £130, this was an attractive offer for some schools and about 2,300 bought Sinclair's package, although 85% adopted the BBC Microcomputer.

ZX81 hardware options

ZX 16K RAM pack

Some of the more elaborate software programs can be run only on a ZX81 augmented by the add-on RAM pack. (The description of each cassette makes it clear what hardware is required.)

The ZX 16K RAM pack provides 16-times more memory in one complete module. It can be used for program storage or as a database.

The RAM pack simply plugs into the existing expansion port on the rear of a ZX81 Personal Computer.

ZX Printer

Designed exclusively for use with the Sinclair ZX range of computers, the printer offers full alphanumerics and highly sophisticated graphics.

A special feature is COPY which prints out exactly what is on the whole TV screen without the need for further instructions. So now you can print out your results for a permanent record – and you may well find a hard-copy listing of interest when examining how some of the software works.

The ZX Printer connects to the rear of your computer – using a stackable connector so you can plug in a RAM pack as well.

Acorn BBC Micro.

Image source mjnurney

- Released: December 1, 1981
- Price: £299 Model A, £399 Model B
- Produced: 1.5+ million
- CPU: MOS 6502 @ 2MHz
- Memory: 16K Model A, 32K Model B
- Display: (PAL) 640x256 graphics, 80x32 text
- Ports: Serial, printer, video, system bus
- Storage: Cassette tape, optional floppy drive
- OS: BBC BASIC

The BBC-A has a full 73 key full stroke keyboard with function keys, arrow keys and auto repeat and had what was considered an extremely good keyboard. Various graphic modes come as standard from mode0 – high resolution 640x256 with two colours, to mode7 which is standard teletext display. Mode2 would prove to be popular as it allows 160x256 with the full 16 colours on screen at once. The secret "up the sleeve" of the BBC Micro was the huge expansion that it offered. Numerous I/O ports were placed around the rear of the computer and under the base of the unit. Acorn expected ROM and CPU expansions to be available soon after launch. CPM and 128KB as well as 3MHZ 6502 co-processor and 16-bit processors would also become available during its life.

Acorns BBC Micro was initially released in two models: Model A and Model B. The Model A had 16 KB of RAM and no disk drive. The Model B had 32 KB of RAM, an additional sound chip, and a disk drive option. The BBC Micro was powered by a 2 MHZ MOS Technology 6502/6512 CPU and had a display resolution of 640×256 with 8 colours. It also had a Texas Instruments SN76489 sound chip with 4 channels, mono TMS5220 speech synthesizer with phrase ROM (optional), and twin analogue joysticks with fire buttons as input devices and Econet networking available.

The BBC Micro used the BBC BASIC programming language, its own version of the popular BASIC programming language. It was created in house, mainly by Sophie Wilson. The computer is housed in a large keyboard style case which includes an internal power supply and a 64-key keyboard with 10 additional user-definable keys. On the back of the case there are ports for UHF video out, RGB video, RS-423, cassette, analogue in and Econet.

Acorn was disappointed by the sales of the capable but expensive and low selling ATOM. When Acorn released the BBC Microcomputer (model A), they predicted an estimated sales figure of around 12,000 units. The company expected the Micro to be a best seller. Priced at £225 it was considered a joy to use and even the pre-production model was praised by the press for its full keyboard and quality of design and build. Reviewers of the day ran BASIC language loops tests as speed tests and here are those results.

A count test loop, counting 1 to 1,000 in BASIC.

- Atom   1 min 23 seconds
- MZ80K   50 seconds
- BBC Micro A   14 seconds.

The BBC A and B models would go on to conquer the UK school market, it was so popular in schools that almost all children that were schooled in the 1980s and 1990s would have used one at some point.

Unfortunately, the hard-core gamer had nothing to envy with the computer as its colour resolutions and sound capability while good were nothing new or exciting. The business world, education and hobbyist would be the market for this computer going forward. That isn't to say that gaming wasn't a thing on the micro, it was and for a period in the mid-80s many popular titles were published for the computer, but it was never able to compete with the Commodore 64 or Sinclair Spectrum as an entertainment device.

One highlight of the BBC Micro was the creation of the game, Elite. Elite was written on the BBC Micro and for several years it was a bestselling title. It was later ported to almost every other popular computer and console systems. It's not a game that I ever liked or enjoyed but many did.

While nine models were eventually produced with the BBC brand, the phrase "BBC Micro" is usually used colloquially to refer to the first six (Model A, B, B+64, B+128, Master 128, and Master Compact); subsequent BBC models are considered part of Acorn's Archimedes series.

BBC MICROCOMPUTER

Texas Instruments Ti99/4A[xlii]

Image source: mjnurney

- 16 Colours graphics
- 16K RAM. Expandable to 32K via RAM expansion card.
- 26K ROM including U.S BASIC
- Command modules add up to 36K ROM.
- 13-digit floating point math.
- TI BASIC in ROM

The Ti99/4a arrived in late 1981 and it was on general sale from 1982, this is what 'Your Computer magazine' had to say about it…

"Even if you're new to computers, you'll be using the TI-99/4A within minutes of plugging it into any standard TV set. Because the TI-99/4A is a true computer for the home it is immediately accessible to the whole family. All for around £299- Just snap in one of the wide selections of Solid-State Software Command Modules, touch a few keys, and you're ready to go. The 40 modules from Texas Instruments can sharpen your children's maths, teach you to win at chess or even help you with household financial decisions. And much more besides. In all, over 400 programs are available."

The Texas Instrument Ti99/4a was an upgrade of the earlier Ti99/4 computer that had sold poorly from 1979, TI had upgraded it slightly and put it on sale in 1981, hoping to succeed where the Ti99/4 had failed and why wouldn't it?

TI were not new to computers; they were a trusted and respected brand with huge resources. The computer press expected the Ti99/4a to do very well indeed and so did their competitors. With 16-colour graphics, audio, and a half-sized keyboard, the Ti99/4a was well made and a pleasure to use. With options like the Solid-State Speech Synthesiser unit which can reproduce the human voice, the computer is perfect for the family to use and when used with the new Emulator Command Module, the speech synthesisers vocabulary is unlimited.

Other languages like the child friendly logo or UCSD pascal, TMS Assembler and hardware options like the Speech Synthesiser, Thermal Printer, RS-232 Peripheral Adaptor, 5.25 Inch Disk Drive System. And not forgetting the rather hideous Texas Instruments Joysticks...

Languages like the UCSD Pascal needed a disk system and a plug-in card for the PEB expansion unit and not a plug-in cartridge like TI's own Extended Basic.

Texas Instruments used their own version of the BASIC language in the Ti99/4a, and it contained many odd commands that were unique to the system some of them are seared into my memory. TI BASIC is based on Dartmouth BASIC, the original version of the BASIC computer programming language. It was designed by two professors at Dartmouth College, John G. Kemény and Thomas E. Kurtzand. The first version ran on 1 May 1964. Its final release was in 1979.

Examples of Texas Instruments Basic commands.

- OLD CS1 & SAVE CS1 for loading and saving from cassette, it featured two sets of jack plugs for using two cassette recorders.
- BYE will quit the BASIC command line and reset the computer (obviously losing all stored programs too).
- TRACE will track a BASIC program as it runs in memory and stop when an error occurs, useful for editing and writing programs but the error "Incorrect Statement in line xxxx" did a similar job.
- DISPLAY prints a statement to screen very much like print would do.
- CALL SOUND instructed the computer to make sound.

There were a host of other strange commands too, even the keyboard was odd. With two key presses, the computer would reset and anything you were programming was lost forever. The first computer game listing that I ever typed in was on a TI99/4a and I can even tell you when and where, the listing was in C&VG issue 30 from April 1984. This was in the pages of a dog-eared magazine that I borrowed from School to type in at home. The game was Hunchback, and it was 300 or so lines of pure BASIC code, it took about 3 hours to type it in and it never worked. I even saved it to cassette and that never loaded back into the computer either, such was the joy of having a cassette-based system.

However, my TI99/4a performed well and never missed a beat otherwise. Reviewers of the day said of the Ti99/4a, it was well made and a capable computer.

The TI-99/4A is a small machine, measuring only 15" by 10". It has a half-sized standard layout keyboard, which does feel a little cramped in use. The case is made from a stainless-steel cover over a plastic case. A major feature of the TI-99/4 is the use of its plug-in software modules (cartridges). If you want to use a particular program all you do is push the appropriate program module into the slot at the front of the machine and switch the computer on. The first thing that you see on the screen is the announcement 'Texas Instruments Home Computer' and some very pretty colour bars on a blue background.

If you press any key, you immediately jump to a menu asking you to select what you want to do - Press 1 for TI BASIC or press 2 for the inserted software module.

The TV display is 32 characters by 24 lines of very clear characters. The colour graphics that so many of the software modules produce are generated by defined characters sets. As each character is made from 8 by 8 this gives you an effective resolution of 256 by 192. With 16 colours that are used by most of the software modules to very good effect. Coupled with the good colour graphics is an excellent sound generator by TI. It is capable of three simultaneous tones over three octaves plus a noise generator for the pops and bangs that are an essential part of computer games. All the sound (including that from the optional speech synthesiser) is produced through the TV set speaker.

The TI-99/4A is excellent value for money and makes an excellent home computer. The features of this machine are tailor made for good, animated graphics, speech synthesis and game playing. Once you've acquired the machine you can hang on the peripherals to build it into one which has the capacity, though unfortunately not the speed, of lots of systems that come in much bigger cases. The TI-99/4A is as a computer that the whole family can have fun with. It will appeal to every generation and is a particularly suitable choice for introducing children to computers.

(Electronics & computing monthly 1982)

Texas Instruments was a huge company in the 1970s and such was the power of Texas Instruments that most computer companies panicked when TI said they were entering the home computer market. TI controlled much of its own stock, assemblies, and production but they some had some issues, and we should look at them before we continue...

So where did the 4A version come from? The TI99/4 was not received well by the buying public in late 1979. Few software developers were interested in it, and sales were low, it was an expensive computer to manufacture, and it wasn't selling at all well. Worse still the feedback from customers was not good, they disliked the tiny plastic keyboard, the games were of mediocre quality, there were few peripherals to buy, and the retail price was too high!

TI then decided that it would licence all of its software and that no unlicensed software would be allowed to be published, very much like what Nintendo and Sega would do years later, this restricted software even more. Few companies were interested in creating software for it and having to pay TI for the privilege and it's not as though it was popular anyway. The result was extraordinarily little software on modules (cartridges) other than TI's own was written for the machine initially. Cassette software, which was limited to 16k was appearing on sale, but this was generally of extremely poor quality and very slow, but it was license free. TI's own software was often sold on command modules and offered such delights as like statistics, early reading, mortgages, and tax investments. The computer was quickly reduced to $999.95 in an effort to boost sales. Texas Instruments focused on the home market with its new TI99/4a, believing it to be the next step in computing. TI stated that they had increased software from 100 titles to over 1000 by 1982 and to convince customers of the quality of the Ti99/4a they then hired actor and comedian Bill Cosby to become spokesman for the Texas Instruments home computer range.

ARE YOU KEEPING UP WITH THE COMMODORE?

'CAUSE THE COMMODORE IS KEEPING UP WITH YOU!

We have a surprise for all those people who think that in order to get more you have to pay more.

The Commodore 64™.

We also have a surprise for all those people who think they have to settle for less just because they're paying less.

The Commodore 64.

The Commodore 64 has a full 64K memory, high fidelity sound and high resolution, 16-color graphics.

It's fully capable of running thousands of programs for school, business or funny business.

But the Commodore 64 is about one third the price of the 64K IBM PCjr™ or the Apple IIe™. In fact, for about the price of those computers alone you can get the Commodore 64, a disk drive, a printer and a modem — a powerful system.

We don't do it with mirrors, we do it with chips. We make our own.

So we can make them for less, more efficiently and more economically than people who don't. (Which is just about everybody else.)

And so because it's a 64, it's powerful. Because it's a Commodore, it's affordable. And because it's a Commodore 64, it's the world's best selling computer.

COMMODORE 64

Commodore VIC-20

- CPU: MOS 6502, 1MHz
- RAM:5K (3.5K for the user)
- Display: 22 X 23 text
- 176 X 184, 16 colours max
- Ports: composite video, joystick, cartridge, user port, serial port
- Peripherals: cassette recorder, printer, modem, external floppy drive
- OS:ROM BASIC

The VIC-20 debuted in June of 1980 at the Computer Electronics Show in Chicago, but its development started some two years earlier. Commodore had designed and manufactured the "Video Interface Chip - 6560" or VIC-1 as it became more commonly called for the video game market, but they failed to sell the video chip to any companies for use in their video game consoles, so what do you do with a video chip that no one wants to buy? Design and manufacture your own game console or computer! Commodore began to develop the VIC-20 as an inexpensive home computer with colour and sound but at a cheap price point than the competition. This was a key element for Jack Tramiel.

MOS Technology engineers Robert Yannes, Al Charpentier and Charles Winterble started with a design project called the TOI (The Other Intellect) from the legendary designers Chuck Peddle and Bill Seiler. This was to be the Apple 2 killer that Jack Tramiel demanded, but the TOI project had a few problems. It became apparent to the team, that the TOI was not going to get to market anytime soon. It required expensive static RAM chips and an 80-column display which was just not financially practical to achieve the cost widow that Jack required. However, Robert Yannes had a secret project that he was designing at home and with additional work from Charpentier and Winterble, they showed their cost reduced version of the TOI to CEO Jack Tramiel in late 1979.

Jack Tramiel knew that the Apple II was starting to sell in reasonable numbers – enough for Commodore to notice. In fact, Apples Steve Jobs and Steve Wozniak had tried to sell Apple to Commodore only a couple of years earlier but by then Commodore was about to release the PET.

Jack insisted the new low-cost home computer be ready to demonstrate at the Consumer Electronics Show in January 1980. The pressure was on the three MOS engineers, and they worked seven days a week on "Project Vixen" to make it happen.

But what they had been shown to Jack was not a fully operational computer. The "Vixen" computer was a little more than a concept computer thrown together as quickly as possible to show Jack. Everything had to be reworked and massively cost reduced to meet Jack's expectations. Worse still, resources at the company were limited and Commodore engineers wanted a business computer and not a toy to sell at Christmas. We couldn't get any cooperation from the rest of the company who thought we were jokers because we were working late, about an hour after everyone else had left the building. We'd swipe whatever equipment we needed to get our jobs done. There was no other way to get the work done! – Neil Harris (VIC-20 developer)

Jack Tramiel instructed his engineers to use 1Kb RAM chips in the new machine because Commodore had huge inventory that they were unable to use in any other product. After much internal debate the VIC-20 was given the relatively tiny amount of 5.5kb of RAM, 2Kb of which was used by the Basic Operating System. This left only 3.5kb of free ram for the computer to use.

The Commodore VIC-20's competitors were the Apple II, Atari 400 and TI99/a but it did have some interesting features apart from cost. It came equipped with a nice keyboard, a joystick port and a digital cassette player (a carry-over from the PET) The VIC-20 would also appear to have sharper images on the screen that its competitors because it used a composite connection to a computer monitor. The VIC would ship with a free RF modulator that produced a lower quality image, but Commodore usually demonstrated the VIC-20 with higher quality monitors rather that domestic TV sets which gave the impression of a superior picture quality.

Commodore also included Micro-soft BASIC with the VIC-20, which given the low price of the computer is quite impressive. It is only when we realise that Jack made a deal with Bill Gates for a perpetual licence. Bill Gates originally asked for $3 per use of BASIC when sold with a Commodore machine. However, Jack Tramiel turned down Bill Gates's offer, furiously saying *"I'm already married!"*. Jack Tramiel was adamant he would pay no more than $25,000 for a perpetual license from Microsoft on a "pay once, no royalties" basis.

Chuck Peddle recalls the 1976 trip to Microsoft's office in Albuquerque. Bill Gates had by now instructed Marc Weiland to "just get rid of it as he thought it was a waste of time". Consequently, Chuck Peddle achieved a deal that provided, as Jack Tramiel intended, a perpetual licence for a ROM-based version of Microsoft BASIC on any Commodore device with a 6502 CPU. As part of the deal, Commodore was allowed to enhance Microsoft's BASIC, but they were to provide any updates they make back to Microsoft. There was no requirement to have the word Microsoft shown anywhere in the product. A great deal for Commodore in 1977.

The question then arose of what version of Commodore Basic to install in the VIC-20. Would the new PET BASIC be used or the older and smaller version, It was decided that the older Commodore Basic version 2.0 from the original PET 2001 days would be best because it had fewer features, time was very tight and it fitted on to a smaller (cheaper) ROM. Jack also liked the idea that Commodore could sell upgraded ROMS or cartridges that enhanced the machine at an extra cost.

It became a best seller for Commodore and the first computer to sell 1 million units. At one point Commodore were producing 9000 computers a day.

Chapter 7 - 1982

1981 was an extremely optimistic year with more magazines and adverts in newspapers and on television than ever before, the home computer was everywhere but in 1982 it would be increased dramatically. Hollywood got in on the act too with a slew of films featuring computers. The Disney classic TRON appeared, released on July 9, 1982. The film was a success at the box office receiving positive reviews from critics who praised the ground-breaking visuals, which looked like real computer graphics. However, the storyline was criticised at the time for being confusing but then this was 1982.... Tron received nominations for Best Costume Design and Best Sound at the 55th Academy Awards Tron but was not nominated in the "Best Visual Effects category". Unbelievable but true.

Star Trek II: The Wrath of Khan continued Kirk's voyage across the stars. For Star-Trek II, computer graphics company Evans & Sutherland[xliii] used the computer graphics-based Digi star planetarium system to generate the fields of stars. Based on a database of real stars, and with the novel ability to navigate around and fly into the stars at greater than light speed. A two hundred and twenty second fully computer-generated star field sequence was used before and during the opening credits.

The Evans & Sutherland team also produced the vector graphics tactical displays seen on the Enterprise and bridge. But it is the second, more famous and fully computer-generated sequence of the film that is more well known. Created by Industrial Light and Magic, the animation of the Genesis Device on a barren planet, wowed studio executives. Paramount studios wanted the simulation to be even more impressive.

Having seen research done by Lucasfilm's Computer Graphics group, effects supervisor Jim Veilleux offered them the task. Introducing the novel technique of particle systems for the sixty-second sequence. The graphics team paid attention to details such as ensuring that the stars visible in the background matched those visible from real star light-years from Earth. The animators hoped it would serve as a case study for the studio's talents. The studio would later branch off from Lucasfilm to form Pixar. The sequence would be reused in Star Trek III and Star Trek IV as well as in the Laserdisc video arcade game Astron Belt by Bally Midway.

By far the most influential film of the decade is 'probably' Blade Runner, directed by Ridley Scott and starring Harrison Ford. It is an adaptation of Philip K. Dick's novel "Do Androids Dream of Electric Sheep". The film is set in the future, in a dystopian run-down Los Angeles of 2019, where the rich live in high rise towers and the rest of us live in squaller beneath them. But a better life is promised off-planet. Synthetic humans known as replicants are engineered by Tyrell Corporation to work on space colonies as slaves. When a rebellious group of advanced replicants led by Roy Batty – a Nexus 6 android, escapes back to Earth. Worn out cop Rick Deckard (Harrison Ford) agrees to hunt them down in true film-noir Hollywood style. Author Phillip K Dick lived just long enough to see the raw cut of the film as ask how they saw his vision?

The film has influenced many science fiction films, video games and television series, along with Star Wars and Star Trek it provided a vast amount of inspiration for the following decade. The 1980s would become the Sci-Fi and fantasy decade of choice in many ways.

Back on Earth, 1982 greeted us with the news that the BPI (British Phonographic Institute) were trying to impose a price increase to the humble cassette tape. Lobbying of the British government is starting to show interest from some MPs. It is feared that a rush on C15 cassette tapes could affect shares in WHSmith's. The BPI believes it is powerful and influential enough to persuade the British Government to include the levy proposal in the forthcoming revision of the law of copyright.

Otherwise, 1982 gets off to a great start, numerous new computers are arriving this year, and the old ones will be quickly cast aside as the march of technology continues or, so we are led to believe. The Acorn Atom can be had for only £170 and 2114 Ram is down to only £2 each which will affect the retail price of some computers.

The Atari VCS console is retailing at £95.45p and electronic games including my favourite, Galaxy Invaders is down to £19.95. Software is starting to appear for last year's best-selling computers, it takes anything from a few weeks to a year to write a program of varying quality. For the ZX80 owners a new course on BASIC is available to help you navigate the pitfalls and hopefully to create a masterpiece before the small market that the ZX80 has, disappears for good now that the ZX81 is selling well.

Atari reduce the 400 to only £345 with 16K of RAM and the 800 with 16K of ram is a colossal £645 (the 800 model is expandable to 48K maximum). Sinclair release a bundle of dubious software for the ZX80 for only £3.95, classics such as SNIPER and WOLFPAC are available. Meanwhile they continue to push the ZX81 for £69.95 and a thermal printer for only £49.95. I must confess I have this very setup, and it does still work just as well or as poorly as it did in 1981 but for the low price, it was unbeatable in the market.

Since its introduction the Sharp MZ-80K has proved to be a successful and versatile microcomputer system. Sharp now have a comprehensive range of products ready to make the powerful MZ-80K with its printer and disc drives even more adaptable. Products include Universal Interface Card, machine language and Z-80 Assembler packages. With CP/M plus a comprehensive range of software. Time will tell if the Sharpe can take on the might of giants in the marketplace. Apple release the EURO plus machine for £599+vat, as a comparison the TRS-80 III is £619+vat and has a monitor built in! A video genie is £279 and the comukit UK101 is £99.99.

The Phillips G7000[xliv] which retails at £95 now has acquired an assembler cartridge so you can at last, write and assemble your own software on a console. However, it is slightly limited in its scope at there is no way to save the data that you have created.

Clive Sinclair has good reason to look pleased with himself. Mitsui, the giant Japanese trading company [xlv] are about to begin marketing the Sinclair ZX-81 microcomputer in Japan. "We will retain the English- language keyboard — the difference in languages will not be important in the market where we are selling. We regard the ZX-81 as an educational toy" say the Mitsui executives. The announcement was made simultaneously in London and Tokyo and is of a great deal of importance as Mitsui ^{xlvi}is responsible for 10 percent of all imports to Japan — everything from British Leyland cars to Scotch whisky. Clive Sinclair said that he originally believed that the Japanese market was too difficult to enter. However, with the expertise and resources of one of the world's largest trading companies behind him, he said he was confident. Sinclair is also in the news as more than 2,300 secondary schools have opted for the Sinclair ZX-81. The machines were sold to the schools under a special low-price scheme which was run earlier this year by Sinclair in conjunction with educational distributors Griffin and George.

The scheme was Clive Sinclair's personal bid to widen the choice of microcomputer equipment available to schools.

Computer shows were becoming a thing too, the first ZX Micro fair was such an overwhelming success that people queued all the way around London's Central Hall, Westminster, for hours in the pouring rain. Considerably more than 5,000 ZX enthusiasts attended, and the opening hours had to be extended so that everyone could have a chance to see the exhibits. The 50 stands in the packed hall had reported extremely brisk business, with some stands recording sales well into four figures. Because of the response, organiser Mike Johnston is planning a second fair to be held at Central Hall, Westminster, on Saturday January 30. This time, to cope with the rush, the doors will be open from 10.30am. Speculation, rumour, and a sense of excitement hangs over the computer press in early 1982, as Sinclair announce the ZX Spectrum colour computer for the yet unknown but cheap price that we have become accustomed to from Sinclair.

Commodore and Acorn seem to be waiting for something, but no one seems to know what for, Commodore have issued statements about price cuts and then retracted them as everyone waits for Clive Sinclair to shake up the computer industry once again.

The Spectrum sounds like a good machine but is it as good as Clive lets us believe, Sinclair is known for overestimating both the usefulness and the popularity of his machines. Even if the release goes well, everyone expects production delays but what if Sinclair gets it right and creates a computer that outperforms and undercuts the opposition? Commodore clearly takes it seriously issuing statements daily and then having to retract them. Acorn have yet to issue a statement.

Image source: mjnurney

1982 price: £125 (16KB) or £175 (48KB)

- RAM: 16K or 48K
- ROM: 16K
- CPU: Z80A @ 3.5MHZ
- Video Output: RF Modulator
- Display Resolution Text: 24 lines x 32 characters
- Display Resolution 256 x 192.
- Colours: 8
- OS Language: Sinclair BASIC in ROM
- IO Ports: 1x Expansion port and cassette I/O at 1200 baud
- Keyboard: QWERTY rubber keyboard with 40 keys
- Internal audio beeper

The ZX82 from Sinclair was fortunately renamed to the Sinclair Spectrum due to its colour capabilities and ZX82 being a very dull name, it becomes a first for Sinclair as the ZX80 and ZX81 had no colour at all. The Sinclair Spectrum also features sound – well a sort of sound, a beeper which beeps and hisses. It beeps a rather horrible and harsh electronic buzz but with skilled programming it can create music but at the expense of CPU cycles.

Sinclair designer Rick Dickinson said at the time, "I like the Spectrum much more than the ZX-81. It was much quicker to design but much more complicated. It is a step upmarket, and I was really trying hard for a super-smart machine. It is not for quite the same amateur market as the ZX81".

The ZX Spectrum featured 16k of RAM as standard or for the upgraded model, 48K of RAM. Bizarrely it actually contained 64K of RAM, but Sinclair used faulty RAM chips and by-passed the faulty area by only accessing the working 48K. What Sinclair managed to do was launch not only a home computer but a sales sensation, it was cheap and available to buy almost immediately but manufacturing proved troublesome at first and a waiting list formed in what would become a common Sinclair characteristic.

Sinclair launched the Spectrum on the 23rd of April 1982, one year after the ZX81. It ushered in the birth of the British gaming industry. It was more affordable than the competition of the era, like the BBC Micro, Commodore VIC-20 and much better than the earlier ZX81. The troublesome launch was quickly forgotten as the run up to Christmas 1982 came and the Sinclair Spectrum was found under most British Christmas trees that year.

The 16KB model was quickly dropped and the 48KB became the standard machine to buy and use, most software by 1984 had forgotten the 16KB model and supported the 48KB model completely. All was not lost as early 16KB models could be upgraded by Sinclair for a few pounds, to the maximum of 48KB. Sinclair's Spectrum carried the mantle of the ZX80 and ZX81 before it, in some ways it was partially compatible and used much of the same BASIC, although it was expanded with extra commands for graphics and sound. Sinclair's computers were always beautifully packaged, and the Spectrum was no different, packed in a polystyrene case, inside a black card sleeve with bold graphics and very 1980s styling. The single key command entry was kept for the keyboard, allowing fast typing if you could decipher the multiple key presses that were needed.

Sinclair knew the problem of having no software titles at launch and with this in mind a cassette was included in the packaging called horizons

Source: Horizons by Psion 1982 – images captured by mjnurney 2022

Horizons is the introductory software cassette by Sinclair, It has been designed to introduce you to the Sinclair Spectrum. Its aim is to describe some of the hardware and systems features of the Spectrum, to teach you how to use keyboard of the Spectrum and to entertain, amuse and enlighten you to the possibilities of the use of your personal microcomputer. Side A includes a sample interactive description of the Spectrum and an interesting sequence of lessons to enable you to get used to the complex features of the Spectrum's keyboard. Side 'B' contains a range of interactive programs including games, numerical experiments, the use of the Spectrum for draughtsmanship, programs to illustrate sorting and filing and utility routines which you may find useful later in writing your own programs.

The Sinclair Spectrum is famous for many things, like being cheap to buy, starting a coding revolution and perhaps the unique way of storing sprites (moving graphics) to be more memory efficient and limit the use of the 48KB of RAM. The chosen solution meant that colours would often leak between objects on screen – a phenomenon known as attribute clash.

This rather hideous effect would bleed colours from one sprite to another, giving a kind of coloured glow around graphics if the colour used on the sprite was a different colour to the next graphic to it. The Spectrum can generate 16 colours, 8 low intensity colours and 8 matching bright variants. Richard Altwasser, the engineer employed by Sinclair to develop the Spectrum's graphic systems was setting the standard at a high level in 1981 when the computer was designed, 16 colours was seen as a high benchmark standard then, but compromises had to be made to keep costs low.

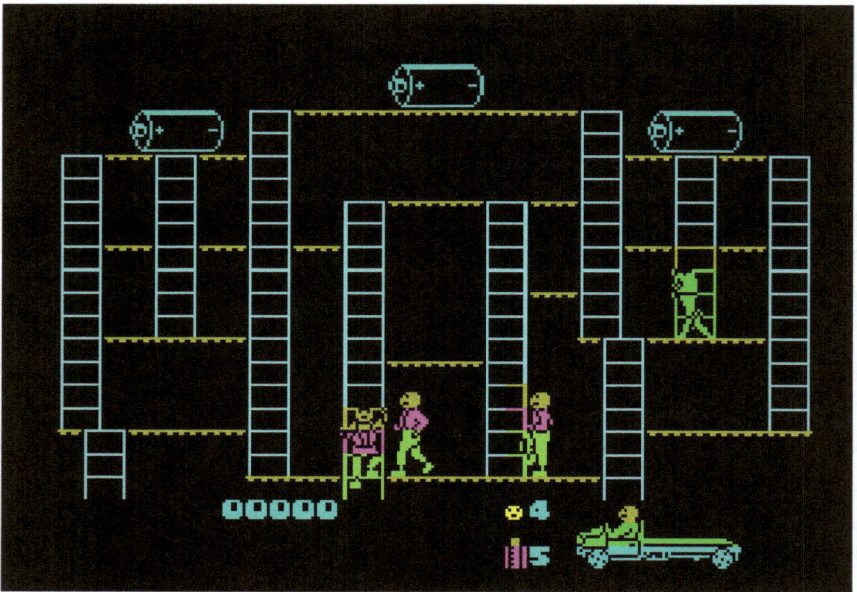

Bear Bovver 1983 Artic Computing.

Sinclair Spectrum Colour Palette.

It was Sinclair's pricing limit that caused so many of the computer's limitations. The ZX Spectrum had no dedicated graphical sprite generation chip, The Z80 CPU and ULA (a combined chip that reduced the chip count inside the computer) would do all the graphical computational calculations, memory, sound, and I/O work. The Spectrum CPU did everything and that meant it was working extremely hard to carry out all the required tasks at the same time. Fortunately, the Zilog Z80 CPU ran at 3.4MHZ and in some ways that masked the problem. The Spectrums limited design called for innovation, and they got it. The computer held 6912 Bytes of RAM to be used for a display file and an attribute array. The display file holds 256×192-pixel data in 32×24 characters blocks, taking 6144 bytes of RAM, leaving a total of 768 bytes for the attribute array. 6144 bytes of bitmap data at memory address &4000 and 768 bytes of colour attribute data at address &5800. The bitmap data consists of 192 lines of 32 bytes. Pixels are encoded as bits; 32 x 8 gives the horizontal resolution of 256 pixels. This limited but clever design allowed the computer to have a relatively high graphic resolution while conserving the valuable 48KB of memory.

Strange as this may seem, colour clash almost became a feature of the computer later in its life and could be used to profound effect. However, earlier on in the computers life cycle it was seen as a hinderance and a failing, showing the general cheapness of the computers design. Heroic effort was needed to combat this, and some clever programming could be employed to hide this failing. This phenomenon would be the cause of huge ridicule by other computer users at the time and it would be used in a constant battle in the school playground about which computer had the best graphics.

Manufacturing of the ZX Spectrum started at 20,000 a month, with 3 to 4 thousand machines expected to be sold in the first year. Sinclair didn't get his figures right, demand was enormous, far outstripping supply and the first machines did not reach the shops until June 1982.

By July, Sinclair already had a backlog of 30,000 orders in the UK alone, but the situation worsened. By summer, the delivery delays were up to three months and in October the company was severely rebuked by the Advertising Standards Authority for failing to meet its promise of a "28-day delivery".

The Spectrum probably became the most cloned computer of the 1980s, with cheap and simple hardware it was not uncommon to see machines in Eastern Europe and Russia. Some of these clones remained in production long after Sinclair stopped making computers. Two authorised clones of the Spectrum were produced by Timex Inc. of the United States, although these met with little success due to compatibility problems with Spectrum software and by being considered low quality by American standards.

Sinclair eventually responded to the surge in demand by ramping up the production of the Spectrum and by March 1983 more than 200,000 Spectrums had been sold by mail order. This earnt Sinclair Research nearly £55 million. Sales continued to increase as major high street stores such as W.H. Smith, Boots, Curry's all started selling the Spectrum and various peripherals.

Soon up to 15,000 Spectrums were being sold every week in the UK, driven by Sinclair's latest price cut to £129.95.

Commodore 64. (CBM64, C64)[xlviii]

- How many:17 - 30 million
- Price: US $595. (1982 USA) £695 (1982 UK)
- CPU: MOS 6510, 1MHz
- Sound: SID 6581, 3 channels of sound
- RAM:64K
- Display: 25 X 40 text
- 320 X 200, 16 colours
- Ports:TV, RGB & comp video, joysticks, cartridge, serial peripheral.
- Peripherals: cassette recorder, printer, modem, 170Kb floppy drive
- OS:ROM BASIC

The commodore 64 had no right to be so good, in fact the rushed development and tight schedule should have meant it was a disaster from the start, but thankfully it wasn't. The C64 is a testament to the over ambitious engineers that didn't know any better, ridiculous work ethics and a tyrannical president in Jack Tramiel. All of which somehow worked.

1982 would see the unstoppable rise of Commodore, the earlier VIC-20 had been a worldwide smash, the first computer to sell over a million units globally. The next computer, the Commodore 64 would set the bar even higher for a home computer and in many ways, it easily beat business computers of the era like the 64k IBM PC, Commodores own PET and the Apple II. The commodore 64 would arrive in the UK in late 1982, becoming a sensational machine that everyone wanted but few could afford - the price was a little high for UK buyers at the initial launch. It was seen as the peak of home computing in 1982 with bright colourful graphics, a full audio synthesiser chip, a proper keyboard and accessories like disk drives, printers and monitors available at launch in stark contrast to Sinclair who didn't even provide a joystick port on the ZX Spectrum.

In terms of popularity, performance and software availability, the Commodore 64 was top of the 8-bit home computer sales during the mid to late 1980s, dominating the home computer market for most of the decade.

Initially a slow seller due to its price of £599.99 this quickly fell to a more palatable £399.99 within a few months. Jack Tramiel wanted the C64 to crush the Apple II and within that remit, crush all the competition leaving Commodore as the sole computer manufacturer for the home consumer. He almost did it too.

Born out of the desire to crush the Apple II, the VIC-20 replacement was a rushed and, in many ways, flawed computer but the things it got right far outweighed the things they got wrong. From announcement to delivery, Commodore pushed the C64 relentlessly, creating a phenomenon.

"All we saw at our booth were Atari people with their mouths dropping open, saying, 'How can you do that for $595?'" -- David A. Ziembicki, co-designer of the Commodore 64.

Perhaps the best explanation for the C64's unparalleled success was the combination of talented engineering and total management control by Jack Tramiel. The C64 was designed by Robert Russell, Robert Yannes, and David Ziembicki. Commodore had been working towards vertical integration since the mid-1970s, when they purchased MOS Technology, who had previously produced Commodore's microchips. This vertical integration meant that Commodore could acquire components at cost, driving prices much lower than the prices paid by Commodore's competition.

Each Commodore 64 had an estimated production cost of around $135 in 1983, this was usually doubled and used as the dealer price. As time marched on the price was steadily reduced, often as a tool to drive competition out of the market. Within a year Commodore offered customers a $100 rebate if they traded in their old videogame console or any computer. The halls of

Commodore quickly filled with ZX80/81, TI99s and other assorted computers. It got so bad that trailers had to be hired and stored in the car park at Commodore, just to hold the relentless onslaught of second-hand computers that were traded in. Commodore staff often used the ZX81 as door wedges.

The C64 was particularly dominant between 1983 and 1987 as a home computer, sales only started to falter as the new Atari ST and Commodore Amiga computers appeared. Consoles from Japan also found a place in the market during the mid to late 1980s impacting sales in the UK but for a while the C64, outsold its rivals like the Apple II, Atari 400/800, Ti99/4a and MSX and so on by a huge amount.

The C64 faced stiff competition from British built computers such as the Sinclair ZX Spectrum, Acorn's BBC Micro and the later Amstrad CPC range. Indeed, the Sinclair Spectrum was the market leader for several years, although the C64 eventually overtook it by the late 1980s. Commodores continual rebranding and repackaging of the C64 extended the life of the machine while offering no real improvement for the user, in fact some models offered a more restricted experience but the power of advertising being what it is, the C64 still sold well. Unbelievably, the Commodore C64 was still on sale in 1994.

First released in August 1982 and discontinued in mid-April 1994 as the parent company collapsed, the C64 sold an estimated 30 million units, making it the biggest selling single model home computer of all time until the Raspberry PI came along. The C64 was considered a great computer and excellent value, especially as the price continued to fall. Atari may have had a very comparable machine but the 800 and 400 was expensive and limited to 48K. The C64 had no real problems at launch even though the computer was designed, built, and sold in under a year, other that some colour issues with the early model VIC2 video chip, which was addressed very quickly, the launch and subsequent sales went very smoothly.

Commodore decision to reduce price to around £300 was a masterstroke for sales and the C64 sold in considerable numbers in 1983 quickly becoming number two in the sales charts, behind the spectrum 48k. One common complaint of the C64 was that of the colour pallet chosen by Commodore engineers. Brown, orange, and off brown seem to feature highly in its colour range of 16 colours and none of the colours were particularly vivid.

The commodore 64 had a something of a reputation for blocky graphics and brown colour palette from early on in its life but these are very dependent on the software programmer and resolution used. One common comparison was that of the Sinclair Spectrum and the Commodore 64. While the ZX Spectrum could have extremely detailed graphics, developers would often use single colour tricks to prevent colour clash. The Commodore 64 could match that, but developers often chose medium resolution to use the full palette of colour, but medium resolution was not always pretty to look at as the sprites often looked too wide.

Let us compare some popular games on various systems.

Commodore 64   ZX Spectrum 48K

ORIC   BBC MICRO

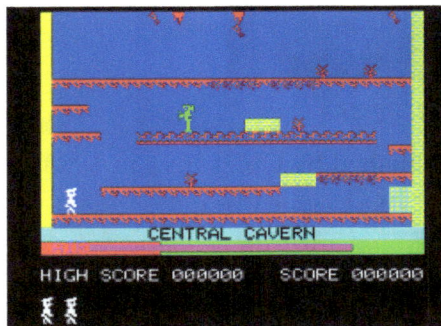 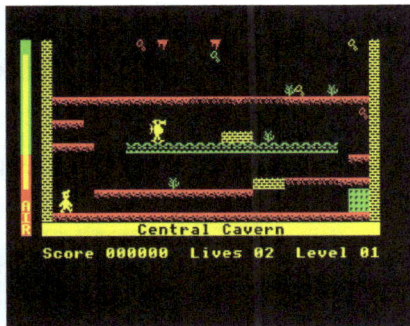

Image source mjnurney: Fuse & Vice emulator. Manic Miner originally written by Matthew Smith and released by Bug-Byte in 1983.

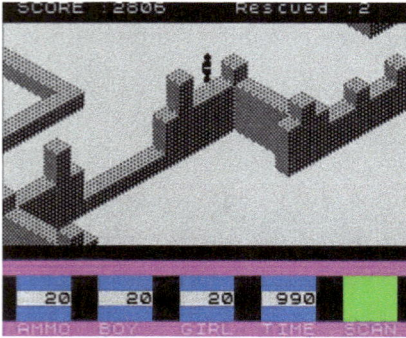

ZX Spectrum 48K   Commodore 64.

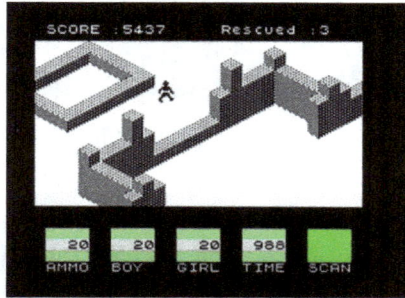

Amstrad CPC464

Ant Attack by Sandy White, published by Quicksilva in 1983.

Image source: **Computer & Video-Games-Dec 1983**

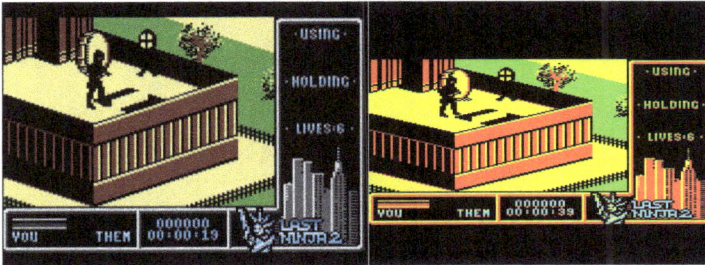

ZX Spectrum   Commodore 64

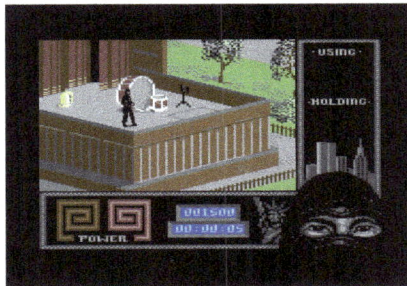

Atari 800   BBC Micro

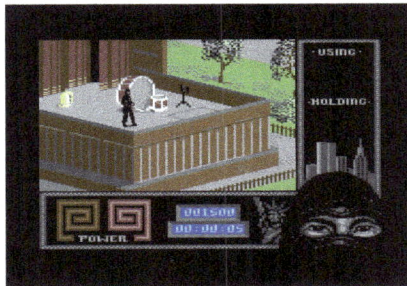

MSX

Following on the story from where the critically acclaimed Last Ninja left off. Last Ninja 2 from System 3 provides yet more action-packed ninja stuff. The game was available on cassette for almost every popular computer and console at the time.

The graphics vary hugely depending on which computer you owned. Although much is made of the C64's relatively impressive graphical capabilities, we cannot forget the absolutely stunning audio chip - SID, the system's powerful Sound Interface Device created by Bob Yannes at Commodore.

The Commodore 64' computer single handily created the chiptune music genre, and its musical quality is so good that it is still used and sampled today. Indeed, the C64 was where "chiptune" maestros like Rob Hubbard, Jeroen Tel, Martin Galway, David Whittaker and Ben Dalglish found fame.

Allister Brimble recalls:

"I was about 19 when I first started writing music for games.

To begin with it was just demo music for public domain software company 17-bit software, which progressed in to writing music for my first game – Thunderbirds by Grandslam Entertainment. Later I wrote music for Codemasters and Team17. My inspiration came from 8-bit games. Composers like David Whittaker but then I also liked Jean Michel Jarre!"

But it wasn't all arcade games and music, some of the best business software outside of the Apple II was available on the C64. Primarily driven by disk drive sales, businesses snapped up the powerful little computer perhaps not noticing the lethargic performance of the 1541 disk drives.

Within a few short years the Commodore 64 would be accompanied by the C128 and the portable SX64 soon after. The mains-powered portable unit called the SX-64 was first, it looked like the Osbourne and Kaypro CP/M computers and was released in 84, with the C128 following close behind.

Meanwhile the Atari 800 which was released in late 1979 as part of the Atari 8-bit home computers series, alongside the Atari 400 is becoming hard to sell as it is simply too expensive. A shake-up of the computer marketplace in 1982 is just starting and the capable but costly computers would take the brunt of this. Manufacturers would have to reduce costs to compete or leave the marketplace for good. Some computers are just too expensive to manufacture, this was often a result of the extremely tight FCC interference laws in the U.S. The internals of the Atari 800 for example, were enclosed in an earthed aluminium chassis that screened the internal electronics and reduced the radiated electro-magnetic interference (EMI) that the computer produced. While Texas Instruments used a full-sized steel shell. Commodore managed to avoid this costly endeavour by using silver backed cardboard on the VIC-20 and C64 computers which were enclosed in a plastic shell.

December.

Christmas time! and the fairy lights are going out all over Britain this Christmas as excitable computer users find that such seasonal nonsense as Christmas tree lights take up too many valuable power sockets in the home or so say the newspapers As new micro users are unplugging the seasonal decorations to plug in their new ZX Spectrums and Commodore 64s. Portable TVs are being wrestled into kitchens and bedrooms across the land as screeching tape loading noises can be heard throughout Christmas day.

The Christmas of old is gone forever. Families will no longer cluster around roaring fireplaces, opening presents, and arguing about which of the four channels to watch. TVs will be tuned to some obscure channel that mum and dad have never used. For the first time this Christmas, people have a real choice of usable home computers for less than £300 and an even wider selection if they can go a little higher in price but this is just the beginning of a great cull in both price and the range of computers available as 1983 will become a pivotal year in deciding the winner of the computer wars.

The close of 1982 saw the preview of the new budget BBC Micro, the Acorn Electron with 32K and an estimated price of £150. A ZX Spectrum beater! Or so said Acorn. ULA problems have thus far caused production problems, but Acorn expects an early 1983 launch.

Sinclair have announced, the ZX Microdrive and the end of ZX Spectrum delays but despite previous announcements the RS232 board for the spectrum will be delayed again, unlikely to be launched until February 1983.

Lynx announces that their computer should be on sale soon, the Lynx from Camputers should be on sale at £225 but no stock has been delivered to dealers in the UK or anywhere else for that matter. Camputers say the Lynx will be on sale sometime in the spring of 1983.

SORD M-5[xlix]

- Released in Japan 1982 and Europe in late 1982.
- Language: Basic-G, Basic-I and Basic-F on expansion cartridges
- Keyboard: membrane 55 keys. Upper/lower case, 64 graphic symbols
- RAM:4 KB (up to 36 KB)
- VRAM:16 KB
- ROM:8 KB (up to 28 KB)
- Price: £149 (UK)

SORD was founded by Takayohi Shiina in 1970 when he was 26 years old. Initially the company wrote software for the Digital PDP series of microcomputers, but later on in the 1970's branched out into hardware production. The name SORD is a portmanteau of SOftware/haRDware, reflecting the dual areas of the business.

In 1977 SORD released the M200, one of the first microcomputers in Japan. This was followed by the M100 and various other versions of the M100/M200 series, plus the multi-user M223 and M243 computers. The SORD M23 followed in 1981 and become one of the most popular SORD computers. It was one of the first to see significant use outside Japan. SORD of Japan released the SORD M-5 computer with a Z80 CPU with 4K of RAM and with 32 colours on screen. With a variety of resolutions from 32x24 to 256x196 the Sord if it sells for the estimated £100 could be a sensation and upset the whole low end home computer ecosystem.

However, on closer inspection the following modes are available. Text only 40x24, mode1 32x24 32 colour, 64x46 with 16 colours and 256x192 with 2 colours. The sord seems a good machine with DIN sockets for joysticks and audio which is much better than a spectrum. SORD is one of Japan's biggest computer manufacturers and describe the £100 M5 as a "variety computer" capable of using cassette and cartridge software with both educational and entertainment content. The machine will have 4K user RAM plus 16K video RAM, and 8K ROM with built-in monitor, with full colour graphics including 32 types of sprites.

Meanwhile DK'tronics [1]show off the new keyboard and case kit for the ZX81, turning Clive Sinclair's little plastic box into an almost usable computer. Ram expansion can be accommodated inside the case and all types are accepted 16,32 and 64KB. The whole kit can be fitted to the ZX81 in as little as 2 minutes and costs £45 with a numeric keypad or just as a case for £15.

The ZX80 and 81 created a small cottage industry of hobbyists creating add on modification for the tiny computer, so basic were they that they really did need expansions to be of much use at all. Although some of the things for sale were utter rubbish. Such as plastic vacuum formed bases that were passed off as workstations to keyboards and sound cards and even colour expansion cards that hang on for dear life, at the rear of the ZX81.

Jupiter ACE[li]

- CPU: Z80A running at 3.25 MHz
- Language: O/S: Ace Forth [not a standard fig-Forth or Forth-79].
- ROM: 2 x 4kB EPROMs containing the FORTH compiler and editor.
- RAM: 3 kB [expandable to 51kB].
- Program Storage: 1500 baud cassette tape.
- Video Display: 32 x 24 Monochrome Graphics, High Res: 64 x 48
- Keyboard: 40 key membrane and two shift keys to allow ASCII.
- Sound: Single channel buzzer.
- Interfaces: TV UHF, Cassette port, Ear & Mic, two edge connectors

In November yet another computer appears on the scene, this time it's a little unusual to say the least. The Jupiter Ace from Cantab is a personal computer that uses FORTH and not usual BASIC. Forth programs are typically four times as compact and ten times as fast as standard BASIC. Before the Ace, all personal computers used BASIC and FORTH was only available to a privileged few but now it is available to everyone for £89.95. If you already know FORTH, the Jupiter Ace closely follows the FORTH 79 standard with extensions for floating point, sound, and cassette. It has a unique and remarkable editor that allows you to list and alter words that have been previously compiled into the dictionary. This avoids the need to store source code, allowing the dictionary itself to be saved on cassette. Comprehensive error checking removes the worry of accidentally crashing your programs.

Computer Designers Steven Vickers and Richard Altwasser

formally were part of the design team creating the Sinclair ZX Spectrum and then they formed Jupiter Cantab to develop further advanced ideas in personal computing. The Ace is the result. Will the Ace be a success? it's difficult to say. Yes, it's cheap but it has no software.

Steve Vickers is a software writer with a mathematics PhD. In the early 1980s, he was employed by Nine Tiles Information Handling, a company contracted by Sinclair to develop Sinclair's ZX80's Basic and then the ZX81 and then in due course, the Spectrum. However, he was frustrated by the tight development schedule that Clive Sinclair had imposed on the project, and he wanted out. Fortunately, Vickers' work at Sinclair brought him into close contact with Richard Altwasser, he was the hardware engineer designing the Spectrum's motherboard. Altwasser had joined Sinclair in September 1980. He said later, "We felt there was an opportunity, a gap in the market for a more programmer-oriented kind of product – something more technical, a niche product, we thought we could differentiate ourselves this way." recalls Altwasser. Altwasser and Vickers worked quickly, Altwasser drew the motherboard layout by hand, Vickers coding the machine's firmware, and Forth editor and compiler in Z80 assembly language. Other CPUs were very briefly considered but rapidly rejected in favour of the Zilog Z80.

The computer press unsurprisingly focused on the new computer's strange programming language. In response, Altwasser told them: "Forth runs ten times faster than basic on the Spectrum".

The Ace had just 3KB of Ram - more than the ZX81 but a lot less than the Spectrum. But then it didn't need so much. Forth is a language that makes for compact code - functions are compiled at runtime - and can happily operate in a lot less space than BASIC can.

Christmas 1982 UK Price lists.

Computer	MRP	Release date.
BBC A	£283.00	1981
BBC B	£347.00	1982
Atari 800 16K	£449.00	1979
Commodore 64	£399.99	1982
Atari 400 16K	£319.00	1979
Commodore VIC-20	£169.99	1980
Dragon32	£194.99	1982
Sinclair Spectrum 48K	£169.99	1982
Texas Ti99/4A	£199.00	1981
Sinclair Spectrum 16K	£99.99	1982
Sinclair ZX81	£44.99	1981

Your computer magazine top 10 games 1982.		
1.	Flight Simulator	ZX81
2.	3D Defender	ZX81
3.	Gulp2	ZX81
4.	Orbiter	Spectrum
5.	Meteor Storm	Spectrum
6.	VIC Panic	VIC-20
7.	Amok	VIC-20
8.	Planetoids	BBC
9.	Defender	Atari
10.	Ghost Attack	Dragon

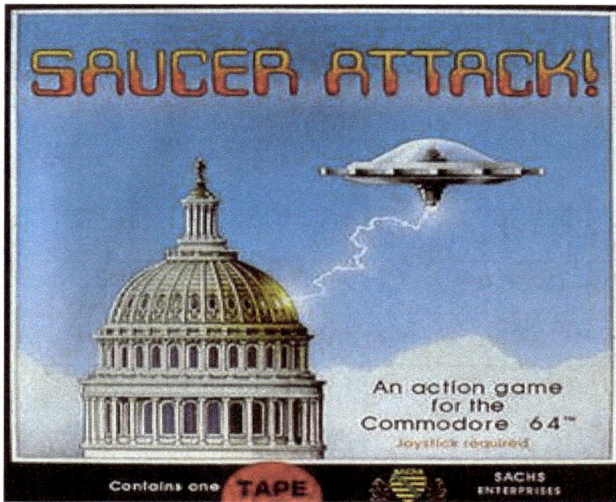

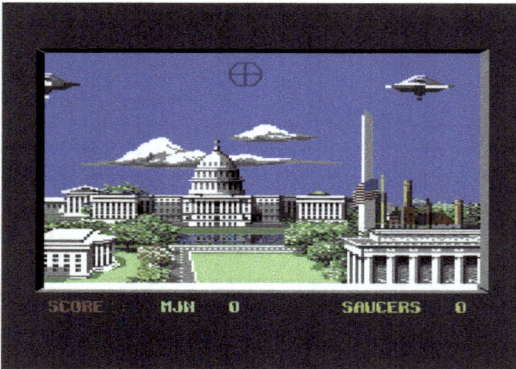

James D Sachs recalls,

"I first got into computing on the Commodore 64 but I didn't really see the potential at first. I would hear kids talking about bits and bytes and I thought that I needed to know this stuff. I bought a C64 in 1982, learned BASIC and then 6502 machine language. Although I quickly moved to using a HES-Mon cartridge and I used to code in assembly. I started coding games, but piracy made me move to the amiga later."

126

Chapter 8 - 1983

The ever-changing world of computers continues to expand with new hardware and software arriving for each of the microcomputers on sale. Some are more successful than others and some are much more capable than others. Tasks that were impossible just a few years ago, like record keeping or printing a letter can now be done at home. Most computers now offer sound and colour as standard and are beginning to look like a viable option for business too. After all, why spend thousands of pounds on an office computer when the BBC Micro can do the same tasks for a few hundred pounds. Printing, disk drives and even networking are being mentioned on the humble microcomputer, these are exciting times.

Cascade software offers an unbelievable cassette full of software for all the popular microcomputers of the day. Cassette 50[lii] - Games for your micro for only £9.95, available now for Spectrum, ZX81, Lynx, Dragon, Atari, Apple, ORIC, Sharp and Newbrain computers among others. Great games such as Space Mission, OXO, Spaceship and Ghosts are included – or said the classic advertisement.

In truth the games were simple hand typed games that featured in magazines of the day and were of an extremely poor quality, the type of thing that would be loaded in the computer and instantly switch off again in disgust.

The advertisement would last almost as long as the 8-bit era of computing, but the offer would be sweetened a couple of years later with a free calculator watch included with every Cascade cassette 50 sold. Sadly, the quality of games never improved – it was awful.

By mid-1983 the full force of advertising home computers had hit the UK, full page newspaper advertisements magazines, tv commercials and radio ads all beamed through the airwaves. In April 1983, most manufacturers had entered the marketplace, one or two were still undecided but generally the full complement of battle-ready companies had line up and were ready to fight.

BBC model B	£399.99
Atari 800 48k	£399.99
Commodore 64	£350.00
Dragon 32k	£199.99
Colour Genie	£224.48
Lynx	£225.00
ORIC 1	£169.95
Jupiter ACE	£89.95
Commodore VIC20	£129.90
Texas Ti99/4a	£154.95
ZX Spectrum 48k	£175.00
Sinclair ZX81	£49.95

Sinclair say that they are now ready to accept orders for the ZX Microdrive, exactly one year after announcing its initial release. The £40 price is a little less than expect but then a £30 interface is needed to control the drives. The drives themselves are a never-ending tape loop or stringy drive affair rather than a disk drive that most other manufacturers have chosen.

They also announce that the much-anticipated ZX83 will now probably become the ZX84 and will be released next year. It is expected to be an improved version of the ZX Spectrum will have a built-in modem for communication and networking.

Acorn has quietly said that the long-waited Electron computer will be released in April this year and may even be ready for the Midland computer fair at the end of April 1983. Dragon Data have said that they are preparing the upgraded Dragon 32K for release. Dubbed the Dragon 64, yes, you've guessed it, it contains 64K of RAM and will be available soon. The current Dragon 32k will be discounted to move stocks for when the 64K £300 machine arrives. Commodore have let slip that they are prepared to discount the Commodore 64 if the VIC-20 continues to slowdown in sales, rumour has it that the Commodore64 is currently no more expensive that the VIC-20 to produce, currently on sale for around £350.00 the Commodore 64 is selling well but it is still an expensive computer in the UK.

Car companies are finding uses for the computer chip too, everyone's favourite car company British Leyland have added voice synthesis to the Austin Maestro. The Maestro will have an MOS 6805 CPU running at 4MHZ and a 32k ROM which will include fifteen spoken commands to aid the driver. Fasten seat belt and low fuel are among the spoken commands in use, the company has chosen a female voice to issue the commands.

Another computer enters the fray, the £98 TEXET TX-8000 a computer from TEXET of Hong Kong who once competed against Sinclair in the calculator market but now seem poised to beat Sinclair at their own game. The super cheap computer has 4K of RAM, a 45 key keyboard and although it is a colour computer it seems to have strange alignment problems with the colours on screen. The computer has eight colours and a 128x64, but the audio capabilities are dreadful. Only two pages of text can be entered into the computer before the BASIC loses the whole program. Tape loading is a medium speed 600 baud, slower than the Spectrum but faster than a ZX81. In conclusion it appears to be a super low budget computer that fails to meet even basic quality requirements, although on paper the specifications seem reasonable.

In 1983, the home computer industry leader was far from decided. Globally, Commodore led the industry in sales but its position looked vulnerable. Its VIC-20 computer was underpowered, and sales were fading very quickly. The Commodore 64 was selling well, but Commodore was having trouble keeping up with demand, especially with peripherals like disk drives. The Commodore 64 was a bargain when compared to more expensive computers from Apple and Atari, but a bare computer isn't very useful. You really needed a disk drive and a printer to do anything with the system and then the Commodore 64 becomes very expensive.

Coleco saw an opening. In January 1983, Coleco announced the Coleco Adam [liii]computer.

For $525 (USA), Coleco promised a complete system. It would have 80K of RAM, a full-travel keyboard, tape-based storage, a daisywheel printer, and software including the game Buck Rogers: Planet of Zoom and a word processor. It can use an inexpensive television as a monitor, like all other home computers of the day.

The Adam was a lot like the Texas Instruments TI-99/4A, but by using a Zilog CPU, it was easier to program and cheaper to produce. It looked like what the TI-99/4A should have been.

Commodore have successfully attacked Atari by saying it made more sense to buy one of their computers rather than a games machine that could only play video games. Coleco countered this problem by introduced a version of the Adam that plugged into an existing Coleco Vision console, turning it into a full-blown computer system. It looked like a winner. It was a real computer. The software industry knew how to develop for it since it used well-known and well-understood chips like the Z80. It could play existing Coleco Vision games, so there was stuff you could do with it on day 1. The kids could do their homework on it with the included word processor, and they could then play Coleco Vision games on it. A clever strategy.

As 1983 continued, the millionth UK microcomputer was sold, a combined measure of ZX81, Vic-20, BBC Micros and everything else. Currently there are more ZX81 computers are in households in the UK than another computer.

Disk drives had long been a problem for the European market, they are complex, expensive, and usually unavailable. Unlike America which used mostly Atari, Commodore or Apple disk drives, Europe and the UK were stuck with cassette tapes or other bizarre devices that offered some or none of the benefits of disk drives. Clive Sinclair swore he would not fit a disk drive to a Sinclair as they were far too expensive for the average computer user.

The Acorn BBC micro had an established disk drive user base early on, but schools usually paid for these. In fact, school was the first time that I ever saw a disk drive and that was attached to a BBC B micro in the computer room.

Commodore did of course offer the disk drive for both the VIC-20 and C64, but they cost more that the computer itself. Dragon data had endless problems creating one for the dragon32 and some of the cheaper micros simply offered them as a future option that would never appear. The Texas Instruments Ti99/4a must hold the record for the most expensive disk drive setup. As it needed a separate expansion case, controller card, 32K ram card and then a disk drive was needed too. Of course, you cannot read disk directories without also buying the disk manager module. As a package it would cost around £1000 on top of the price of the computer itself. It was inevitable that alternative solutions would pop up and pop up they did. Wafer drives, stringy tape, Microdrive, and even floppy tape drives would become available.

Texas Instrument is being squeezed by Commodore in a price war which starts to heat up in mid-1983. In response TI announce the new Ti99/8 home computer with 80K and built-in speech. It is a direct attack on the Commodore 64 and is both faster and has more feature than the C64. Should Commodore be worried? The C64 is the main source of income for the company, the VIC-20 is showing its age it is now three years old, a lifetime in computer terms. The new 16bit Ti99/8 has high resolution graphics, colour, and an upgraded keyboard. The Ti99/8 is the first of a new wave of computers from TI in which it hopes to compete against Commodore and Atari. The Texas Ti99/4A is currently selling well at the reduced price of £150 but slow software development is a problem. Texas Instruments have said that rather than kill off the Ti99/4a they will cost reduce it into a plastic shell which will be cheaper to produce. However, software is still a problem for TI and a large percentage of new software titles are made for the ZX Spectrum, Commodore 64, Atari, and BBC but not for the Ti99/4a. Perhaps increased sales will change that?

Memotech enter the computer business, Memotech the well know spectrum peripheral supplier has developed its own computer system and its on sale soon. The 48K Zilog Z80 computer will have high resolution graphics, 79 key keyboard and 32K available to the user. The computer will also boast different languages from the normal BASIC, including Logo, Forth and Pascal. Display will be 40 columns, but an 80-column option will be available as well as RGB output for better video quality. With 16 colours in high-resolution mode which is 256x192 and three channel sound the Memotech is an interesting computer and should be available soon.

Sinclair have announced a price cut along its range of 16 and 48K computers. The 16K spectrum can be had for under £100 and the 48K model is down from £175.00 to £130.00. This will add pressure on similar priced micros. Sinclair also cut the price of the ZX printer and ZX81 computer. In a case of bad timing ORIC computers have said that its ORIC1 will have a price increase as it cannot source enough memory chips to build the ORIC. Its price will increase from £99 to £150.

Commodore have cut the price of the VIC-20 to £99 and now includes the C2N cassette recorder with the purchase price. It was previously available at £45.95 and including the cassette recorder is a clever way to cut off the supplies of 3rd party cassette recorders that are currently available for the Commodore range.

Former BBC newsreader Kenneth Kendall[liv] has had his voice saved into silicon and it will feature in a new ROM for the BBC computer. The ROM along with the TMS-5220 from Texas Instruments will allow the BBC to speak. 165 words have been spoken and saved into silicon and can be yours for £55, if you own a BBC Micro that is. Kenneth's voice has been saved on a PHROM which is a Phrase Read Only Memory, and it can be controlled via BASIC commands on the Micro.

August 1983

Despite a massive advertising campaign and a name that everyone knows, Atari still manage to sell computers in ever dwindling numbers here in the UK, they are expensive and have less RAM than the newer computers on sale today.

Atari have finally listened or at least noticed the lack lustre sales here in the U.K and have finally updated the range with new and less expensive models. The new 600XL has 16kb ram and the 800XL has 64kb of ram, they are still largely the same computers as before but now offer greater flexibility in terms of cost they say. In fact, the newer models no longer must meet the tight FCC regulations and require less metal shielding than the previous 800/400 models.

Microsoft enter the computer market in a deal with the Japanese or more specifically the MSX group. The American company Microsoft has proposed a deal in which several companies create computers of similar if not equal specification, all will be 8-bit and must follow a pre-agreed set of standards. A Z80 CPU, TI9918 video chip and 32Kb ram and finally extended BASIC. So far, a total of 14 Japanese companies have signed up to the MSX specification and it could be a way into more lucrative markets like the USA and Europe. Software compatibility is the key to success here and the future looks promising.

Hollywood is at it again.

Romanticising computers with sketchy facts and ridiculous claims but here we go with the release of WARGAMES, a high school hacker gets access to "JOSHUA" which appears to be an online computer game. However, it quickly becomes obvious that it isn't a game but a military network that he has dialled into. Not realising he is playing a defence computer; the hacker accepts a challenge to play a game on the computer, but it turns out that this is not a game at all!

War games has become a classic film over the years and captures the early 1980s optimism perfectly. kids who came of age in the early 1980s had many reasons to wish they lived in the bedroom of Wargames' fictional hacker David, but the display seen on David Lightman's monitor wasn't generated by the IMSAI 8080 computer in his bedroom but instead, it was generated by a secretly hidden CompuPro 8086 system computer.

Commodore cut the price of the C64, previously sold in the UK at around £345.00 it can now be bought for only £243.00. Some dealers have said they plan to sell the computer for only £200.00. Price cuts across the Commodore range are set to drop the price of a computer, printer, and disk drive to around £600.

Commodore, say they have sold half a million units in the U.S to date. As usual the biggest dealers will benefit from the Commodore cuts and smaller retailers may suffer, all dealers buy at reduced rates from the manufacturer and hope to maintain a profit but large-scale cuts impact that profit and it's possible that smaller dealers may lose out.

Another month and another computer hit the UK, this time it is the COMX35 looking like a cross between a C64 and ZX spectrum the COMX35 features a build-in joystick – so it must be a games machine? The computer is powered by the RCA 1802 CPU. But is it any good? In a word no, it has eight colours and a non-standard BASIC. However, it has a larger picture area than the popular ZX Spectrum as it has no borders while keeping a similar resolution of 24x40 – the ZX Spectrum display is a mere 24x32.

It has become obvious now that games are the main focus of home or microcomputers now and everyone is trying to release software for the popular brands. The less popular machines are sadly not commercially viable for new software titles, and they are quickly forgotten about. Mail order or random magazine adverts' might be the last hope for these abandoned micros.

December 1983.	
BBC Micro	£399.99
Memotech 512	£315.00
Memotech 500	£275.00
Atari 800 48K	£249.00
Commodore 64	£229.00
LYNX 48	£224.99
Acorn Electron	£199.99
Atari 600XL	£159.99
Commodore VIC-20	£139.99
ORIC 1	£139.95
Sinclair Spectrum 48K	£129.99
Texas Ins Ti99/4A £99.95	
Atari 400 16K	£99.00

Computer game charts: December 1983		
1.Android attack	BBC Micro	Computer Concepts
2.Arcadia	VIC-20	Imagine
3.Mutant Camels	C64	Llamasoft
4.Crazy Copter	Atari	English Software
5.Damper Glooper	ZX81	Quicksilva
6.Flight Simulator	ZX81	Sinclair
7.Gridrunner	VIC-20	Llamasoft
8.Jet-Pac	Spectrum	Ultimate
9.Space Raiders	ZX81	Sinclair
10.Manic Miner	Spectrum	Bug-Byte

Christmas 1983 has arrived, and the first wave of the blood bath is happening. The Acorn Electron[lv] has finally arrived-in late August. And while warmly received by the press it is a little late to the party and too late to serve the Christmas sales rush. In the last few weeks of the year, accountants at various computer manufacturers have been adding up the cost of competing, advertising, and fighting within a global recession. Memory shortages and a higher-than-expected inflation rate are all having a serious effect on business.

Texas Instruments announced on late Friday that because of continuing heavy losses, they are ceasing the manufacture and sale of its 99/4A home computer, hoping its losses will be slowed. But they will continue to advertise the 99/4A but will slash prices to clear inventory. They will then, exit the home computer business for good. The last Ti99/4a computers will be completed in early 1984 and manufacturing in Texas will close. The upcoming Ti99/8 which was just about to be released has been cancelled as well as the budget Ti99/2. TI have said that they will honour warranty claims for the next 12 months. Share prices at TI rose on this announcement.

Texas Instruments has reported a loss of $110.8 million in the third quarter, following a loss of $119.2 million in the second quarter. It also said it took a $330 million write-off against earnings to cover losses and withdrawal from the home computer business. That followed a second-quarter pre-tax loss of $183 million for the home computer division.

- The fall of Texas Instruments computer division (1979-1984).

Texas Instruments had an early lead in the computer market and did enjoy better sales with the TI99/4a but then Commodore International released the VIC-20 home computer and Texas Instruments decided on a price war to maintain what they saw as their market share. However, things did not go well for Ti99/4a.

Disaster No1

TI had the misfortune to discover an electrical fault on the power supply that powered the Ti99/4a and they would have to replace them immediately. This would not only cause TI significant sales losses, but it would also stop any deliveries of new computers that do not have the newly revised power pack. In effect all sales of the Ti99/4a computer were stopped for a few months.

TI released this statement. In March 1983 Texas Instruments Incorporated said that it is conducting a voluntary program of providing transformer adapters free of charge to correct a potential defect recently discovered in one model of the transformers supplied with the Texas Instruments 99/4A home computer. Over four hundred thousand transformer units are at fault.

Not only this but Texas Instruments had entered a price battle with Commodore International but that wasn't increasing profits as expected, it would mean that the Ti99/4a's retail price was cut throughout 1982 and by 1983 it was heavily discounted in the UK.

Disaster No2

In February 1983, in order to remain competitive against growing competition, TI cut the price of the TI99/4a to dealers and the cost of a TI99/4A drops to about $150 at retail in the USA. Comparable price cuts occur globally. Sales increase but profits fall.

In June 1983, TI released the cost reduced beige plastic version of the TI99/4A. Removing the stainless cover of the original and using a cost cut motherboard to help reduce manufacturing costs. This version of the TI99 is version 2.2 and contains an updated ROM that will check for unlicensed cartridges and will block them from running.

TI is still desperately trying to recoup costs from licensed software in an effort to shore up the reduced hardware profits, but the release of beige model is followed by another price cut bringing the TI99/4a price to just $100 in the U.S. However, it's not all doom and gloom as TI celebrates with the news that the 1 millionth TI99/4a has been sold. This news is somewhat tarnished by the financial situation. Texas Instruments computer division would lose $100 million dollars in this second quarter of 1983 as they fought with Commodore International, both the VIC-20 and then the Commodore 64 are seen as competitors and are being fought in a head on battle for market share.

Disaster no3

TI then finally reversed its 3rd party software policy and software did slowly start to appear on the Ti99, but this was then reversed again soon after and adverts were placed in the press stating that any company writing software for the Ti99 without a license would be subject to a lawsuit.

Software abruptly stopped being released, games that were advertised were cancelled and support once again reversed for the TI99. Texas Instruments wanted 90% of all software profits, meaning developers received a tiny 10% this caused outrage and resentment in the industry.

At this point, the Ti99/4a was finally selling well and lots of TI own software was available for it. MB games had joined the list producing software for it, as were Atari. A rewritable ROM exchange software centre opened up in the U.S for costumers to exchange games. However, it was proving difficult to keep software developers interested in the Ti99/4a and some announced games would never be released. With the decision to drop the price of the computer to $99 with rebates, the public asked what's wrong with it? Why is it so cheap? This was the final blow for the TI99/4a, the ill-thought-out battle with Commodore resulted in the TI99/4a being sold at below its manufacturing cost. Although this policy can work and it is how consoles are sold today, it needs a steady income from other sources like software or hardware accessories, but TI had crippled both of these revenue streams. TI then decided to almost give away peripherals and software with the loss-making Ti99 in an effort to increase its market share. The thinking was that they could bankroll the loss-making computer division until they had cornered the market. Unfortunately, they hadn't bargained on Commodore's ability to fight them.

Texas Instruments closed the home computer division in early 1984. After a total of 2.8 million Ti99/4a computers had been built, along with an enormous number of peripherals and software titles too. Enough in fact that sales of the Ti99/4a continued into the late 1980s by wholesalers who bought up large stocks of bankrupt equipment, long after being orphaned by manufacture Texas Instruments.

The final sale price of the TI99/4a was $49.99 in the U.S, and in the UK from January '84 they were reduced to £88 and then finally £50 to clear stocks. It was well known in December '83 that the computer division would close soon, and the computer would be abandoned. The press quickly caught on and news broke quickly that TI were stopping production of the Ti99/4a, overnight development stopped, and new software titles are immediately cancelled. Computers appeared for sale in the second-hand sales for as little as £20.

Texas Instruments is not the first and is not likely to be the last company to get out of this highly volatile home computer war.

Osborne Computer Corporation, which made somewhat more expensive machines than Texas Instruments home computer division, has declared bankruptcy. Many other smaller companies are expected to fall by the wayside and even some larger companies might pull out of the business altogether, which is plagued by severe price cutting and rapidly changing technology that can make a product obsolete almost overnight.

Sinclair, Texas Instruments, Commodore International and Atari unit have been battling at the low end of the market, with computers selling for £200 or less. Both Texas Instruments and Atari have been plagued by heavy losses. Commodore, which has emerged the victor for now, also seems to be surviving but profits are very slim, with product reliability problems and product shortages how long can Commodore survive? Sinclair have seen sales boom at the very low end with the ZX Spectrum continuing to sell well.

Mattel have announced that the low selling Aquarius has been cancelled and that the Aquarius 2 has now been cancelled too. Mattel have said that trading in today's market is too difficult and that they are leaving the computer sector. As a magazine of the time put it, "The Aquarius suffered one of the shortest lifespans of any computer — it was discontinued by Mattel almost as soon as it hit store shelves, a victim of the 1983 home computer price wars". Just after the release of the Aquarius, Mattel announced plans for the Aquarius II, and there is some evidence that the Aquarius II reached the market in very small numbers (50 estimated) before being cancelled.

And finally, Cantab of Cambridge have gone bankrupt (November 1983) and its assets are sold to Boldfield Computing Ltd in 1984.

Chapter 9 - 1984

1984 would be a pivotal year in the UK as this was start of the national coal miners' strike and it would be a bloody battle that would tear families and communities apart. From March 1984 to March 1985 thousands of working men downed their tools and didn't get paid a wage for a whole year. Houses were repossessed and families were destroyed. Working men tried to protect their future and ultimately failed. These men, both young and old fought Margaret Thatcher's Conservative government but lost. Ultimately the huge UK coal mining sector would be culled, and cheaper foreign coal imported in an effort to supply the power needs of the country. This is a one of many steps to modernising or ruining British manufacturing, depending on your viewpoint.

My three elder brothers lost their wages in March 1984 and didn't return to work until 1985. In total twelve months without a wage or any income. But to think that I was allowed to buy computers at this time is staggering but I digress, while this had little to do with technology at the time it did have an impact on computer sales in the UK. A huge portion of the country was practically bankrupt.

Hard to believe as it is but in early 1984, software was coming out almost weekly for the ZX81, Sinclair Spectrum, BBC, and Atari. The TI99/4a, Dragon, ORIC and MSX machines were having a harder time. The new Commodore 64, while being popular in the USA – was harder to find in the UK and it was still expensive. Software was a problem for the new C64, but It was starting to appear, the Sinclair Spectrum was taking an early lead with British buyers.

News of hardware shortages created a panic in the weeks leading up to Christmas, it seems that even Commodore knew this as they announced that a night shift would be needed on the VIC-20 production line. The press of the day, seem to either embrace the panic and run with it or to be a little suspicious, after all a good panic is great for selling your stocks and making room for the new stuff. 1983 was undoubtably the year of the computer in the UK with computer mania being everywhere and everyone and their mother buy one micro or another. Would 1984 continue that trend?

Sinclair announced the QL, a little expensive for a home micro but perhaps a little cheap for a business micro and if business is the key to the QLs fortunes, where is the industry standard software like the spreadsheet program Visiclac? And what about a disk drive? No, it will have the failed Microdrive from the ZX Spectrum.

The Dragon 64 [lvi]arrives and looks the same as the Dragon 32. Dragon Data has refused to accept the challenge of innovative design offered by newer arrivals on the market such as the Electron or the Enterprise and instead of producing a new machine has concentrated on enhancing its old one. A 64K version of the Dragon is available for £229.

It is really a Dragon 32 with extra memory, an RS-232 port and auto repeat on the keyboard. These are loosely cobbled on to the 32 rather than being an integral part of the machine.

For the ordinary home-computer use there are too few advantages over the Dragon 32. The Dragon 64 is really a Dragon 32 with extra features stitched on instead of a new machine. Theoretically it has one of the very best eight-hit processors, the Motorola M6809F. which is halfway between an eight- and a 10-bit micro with many Instructions, If Dragon data can sell the machine in numbers, it may prove popular but with an unpopular CPU it could be a problem.

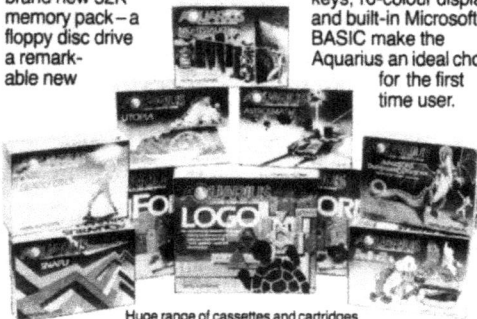

AQUARIUS™
HOME COMPUTER SYSTEM
More software - more hardware!

The best value full colour computer on the market – at around £50.

1984 is going to be an exciting year for Aquarius owners!

During the next two months, we are adding to our wide range – an excellent new four colour printer/plotter – a brand new 32K memory pack – a floppy disc drive a remarkable new

light pen – PLUS an even wider choice of games, and educational cartridges.

There's no doubt that the Aquarius is the best value full-colour home computer system available in Britain. 49 moving keys, 16-colour display and built-in Microsoft BASIC make the Aquarius an ideal choice for the first time user.

Huge range of cassettes and cartridges with more becoming available each month.

The instruction manual is one of the clearest ever written and our 'LOGO' cartridge takes you step by step to a full knowledge of computer language.

Manufactured and sold by Radofin Electronics (UK) Ltd..
Hyde House. London NW9 6LG.
Telephone: 01-205 0044 Telex: 923624 FIPLC G
Trade enquiries welcome.

Available through many leading retailers – including Harrods – Menzies – Carrafour – Asda.

Atari 800XL

146

Image source: mjnurney

- Microprocessor: MOSTEK 6502C
- Clock speed:1.79 MHz
- RAM 64K
- ROM size:24k
- Video:40x24 ,16 at 320x192, 128 colours at 40x 24, max colours 256.
- Audio: Sound Interface device – Pokey / 4 voices
- Atari BASIC in ROM.

The Atari 800XL[lvii] lands in the UK is also pretty much the same as the old 800 in most respects, except for having four extra graphics modes and two fewer joystick ports but it's cheaper to manufacture and looks much more modern. Like the 600XL, the 800XL. is very well designed and well-made machine. It should be, being essentially a reworking of the familiar Atari 800, first launched at the end of 1979. The thinking behind the XL range is, however, radically different. The original 800 was designed to be both a consumer product and a rival to its main competitor, the Apple II. It was designed to be internally modifiable by the average user. Thus, the 48K memory was on three 16K cartridges, with only one being supplied as standard.

While this thinking was laudable in 1979, it is out of date today, especially when the competition is not Apple but the Commodore 64. The Atari also has hardware sprites, which the Acorn BBC and the Electron micros lack, but which the Commodore 64 has. The Atari has four eight-bit sprites or "players" and four two-bit missiles which can be combined to make another sprite if required, this is fewer than the C64. The Atari graphics are about as powerful as the BBC computer and are like the Commodore 64 but Atari has the advantage of more modes and more colours than either computer. The graphics takes up much less RAM than the BBC computers modes and are much easier to use than the Commodore 64's graphics which are unsupported by its built in BASIC.

The Atari 800XL, Commodore 64 and BBC Model B are three micros that stand out as being far superior to the less popular Dragons, ORICs and the Lynx. These three have better hardware, better keyboards, better BASICs, more peripherals, and better software. The average user would probably be delighted to own any of them.

But if you must choose one:

The Atari has the best games at the moment as well as a wide selection of good software, languages, and peripherals, though there is extraordinarily little in the U.K so far. The real catch with an Atari is that the software is expensive. The Commodore 64 is cheapest of the three computers, it is well supported and looks the best bet for home and small business software, though it currently has less software than the other two. The catch here is that it has a very primitive BASIC.

While the Lynx has been available in 48K form since the beginning of 1983, Camputers has recently launched a 64K memory version with an enhanced ROM set, to be followed shortly by the 128K Lynx. The additional 4K ROM in the 96K Lynx is the first in a series of planned expansions for the Camputers microcomputer. The prices of the Lynx are as follows: 48K Lynx £225 and 96K Lynx £299.

When the Lynx was launched nearly a year ago, the price of the 48K ZX Spectrum was £175, only £50 less than the 48K Lynx which, when considering the keyboard, superior colour graphics and built-in monitor, was probably reasonable. Even when allowing for all the Lynx's bad points, the price of the Sinclair's Spectrum has now fallen to around £130 but the Lynx price has remained the same. However, it now faces stiff competition from the Electron and more seriously the latest offering from Atari and the bestselling Commodore 64.

The Atari and Commodore machines have a proven, although limited, CP/M capability and large libraries of quality software, if Commodore can quickly overcome the current reliability problems of the C64 and Acorn is able to manufacture the Electron in large numbers, life will be very difficult for the Lynx.

In conclusion, the Lynx has a poor keyboard and not all the RAM is accessible to programs. The cassette loading is poor, and it is an expensive games machine without a huge library of software to buy. As a business machine it cannot run CP/M – which business demands, this you need the 128K lynx and that is not available yet.

The mysterious ELAN / FLAN or Enterprise press release and semi-launch in January is somewhat subdued by the fact that the computer will now launch in April and not January as announced. The specs for the supercomputer are impressive but it is delayed yet again…

January would see Commodore cut the price of the C64 to £184.99, a massive drop from only a year ago. The VIC-20 is now selling at £134.95.

February greets us with full colour adverts for the new games from Imagine. How will these four master computer game writers be feeling in a few weeks' time? They have been brought together to pool their awesome talents to create the two most sensational, mind-boggling games ever imagined…Psyclapse and Bandersnatch. When such computer wizards as (from left to right) Ian Weatherburn, Mike Glover, John Gibson and Eugene Evans are locked away for weeks on end, anything can happen, will they maintain their sanity, or more to the point can you control your patience?

They may be smiling now, but they are about to encounter...

PSYCLAPSE COMMODORE 64
&
BANDERSNATCH. 48K SPECTRUM

How will these four master computer game writers be feeling in a few weeks time?

They have been brought together to pool their awesome talents to create the two most sensational, mind boggling games ever imagined...Psyclapse and Bandersnatch.

When such computer wizards as (from left to right) Ian Weatherburn, Mike Glover, John Gibson and Eugene Evans are locked away for weeks on end, anything can happen, will they maintain their sanity, or whats more to the point can you control your patience?

..the name of the game

Coming soon from Imagine...Psyclapse and Bandersnatch... the two most exhilarating experiences ever. Can you wait?

Imagine Software Limited, 5 Sir Thomas Street, Liverpool, Merseyside L1 6BW.
Dealer Enquiries Contact: Colin Stokes on 051-236 8100 (20 lines).

150

Sinclair QL

Image source: mjnurney

- Released: January 1984 (Available: May 1984)
- Price: £399
- CPU: Motorola 68008 @ 7.5MHz
- RAM:128K
- Display:256 X 256, 8 colours
- 512 X 256, 4 colours (up to 25 lines x 85 characters)
- Ports:2 network, 1 ROM,
- 2 serial ports, 2 video out (RGB, RF), 2 controllers, system bus
- Storage:2 internal 128K tape drives (Microdrive)
- OS: Q-dos / Super-BASIC in ROM

Sinclair release the eagerly awaited ZX-83 or the Quantum Leap as Sinclair calls it. The QL is a quantum leap in computing according to Sir Clive. Even if Sinclair customers used to wait for 28 days or more for Sinclair products, many are wondering if it really stands for Quite Late. Delays are now common on most Sinclair products. The standard QL has 90K RAM free for programs which can be stored and accessed from the pair of Sinclair Microdrive's. Unfortunately, these are not quite the same as the standard Spectrum Microdrive's although the Spectrum Microdrive cartridges can be re-formatted for use with the QL.

QL BASIC, or Super BASIC. As Sinclair insists on calling it, is a structured evolution of Sinclair BASIC rather than a radically new language. The QL was still waiting for a last version of Super BASIC at its launch as its not ready. The rubber-suspended keyboard is not angled towards the user, but plastic legs click uncertainly into the base to provide an angle.

At the time of its launch on the 12th of January 1984, the QL was far from being ready for production—at that time there was no working engineering prototype. Although Sinclair started taking orders immediately, he promised delivery within 28 days. However, because of its premature launch, the QL was plagued by a number of problems from the start. Early production QLs were shipped with preliminary versions of the firmware which containing numerous bugs, mainly in Sinclair's SuperBASIC. Part of the firmware was held on an external 16 KiB ROM cartridge until the QL was redesigned to accept the 48 KiB of ROM internally, instead of the 32 KiB originally designed.

The QL also suffered from some reliability problems of its Microdrives after launch. Based on a Motorola 68008 processor clocked at 7.5 MHz, the QL included 128 KiB of RAM, which is officially expandable to 640 KB. It can be connected to a monitor or a domestic TV for display. Sinclair recommended the "SINCLAIR VISION-QL" CUB RGB monitor for usage with the QL. When connected to a normally-adjusted TV or monitor, the QL's video output overscans horizontally. This is reputed to have been due to the timing constants in the ZX8301 chip being optimised for the flat-screen CRT display originally intended for the QL.

Two video modes are available, 256 × 256 pixels with 8 primary RGB colours and per-pixel flashing, or 512 × 256 pixels with four colours: black, red, green and white. Both screen modes use a 32 KiB framebuffer in main memory. The hardware is capable of switching between two different areas of memory for the frame buffer, thus allowing double buffering. However, this would use 64 KB of the standard machine's 128 KiB of RAM and there is no support for this feature in the QL's original firmware.

At £400, Sinclair believe that the QL will give the BBC Micro a tough ride although its lack of IBM compatibility in an increasing IBM compatible office may make businesses think twice before buying one. Sinclair hopes that by the sheer weight of sales, major software houses will have to write packages to suit his.

Neither the ZX Spectrum nor the ZX-81 will stop production for some time and Sinclair have not mentioned anything about price cuts. It certainly seems worth wailing for with 128K RAM, a 32-bit central processor, two built-in Microdrive's and all the interfaces - cartridge, RS-232, joystick and RGB - that Sinclair usually leaves out, for just £399. Even the keyboard is almost of typewriter quality and there are both reset and power on/off buttons. A first for Sinclair. By July, Sinclair was no longer having to bundle the QL with a Rom dongle – the new batch of QL's now coming off the Datatech production line were now revision 'D06'. Come the end of the month.

Sinclair said it would soon begin asking for original, dongle-supplied QLs to be returned, free of charge for a Rom swap. These were replaced with D06 or later QLs.

"Our intention is to stagger the recall of machines, and as yet we do not know how long customers will be without their QLs when recalled," a spokesman admitted. The 'Rom-swap' recall process began in August, by which time the company reckoned the turnaround time would be ten days but as with everything Sinclair this was rather optimistic.

ORIC Atmos.[lviii]

Image source: mjnurney

- CPU: MOS 6502 @ 1 MHz
- Operating system: Tangerine/Microsoft Extended Basic v1.0
- ROM: 16 KB
- RAM: 16 KB or 48 KB
- Sound: AY-3-8912
- Graphics: 40×28 text characters/ 240×200 pixels, 8 colours
- Storage: tape recorder, 300 and 2400 baud
- Connectivity: cassette, printer port, RGB, RF out, expansion port

The updated version of the ORIC arrives and it's changed its name to the ATMOS. Atmos may took like a flashy portable but under its chunky plastic typewriter keyboard lurks the old ORIC 1. Only' the ROM has been changed to protect the innocent. Peter Harding from ORIC, claims that all those bugs in the old operating system have been ironed out and cassette loading has been much improved.

Old ORIC software will still load but you first must enter a short program from the welcome tape which comes with the Atmos, and which simulates the old ROM. Another special program will suspend the error-checking facility during loading if you suspect at all that is making the program crash. At last, the other notorious fault of the ORIC — the sketchy manual has been corrected. Atmos buyers will get a full 270-page book together with a quick reference leaflet for beginners.

More than one year after the first deliveries, the ORIC has finally put right most of the teething problems that should have been corrected before the product went on sale. Peter Harding hopes to offer people who bought the original ORICs the chance to upgrade to an Atmos for about £50.

The Atmos should give the Electron and C64 a run for their money. Although it has poorer resolution and sound than either and lacks the sprites of the Commodore and the BBC BASIC of the Acorn, it has more memory available than either and at £170 is significantly cheaper but will the buying public agree?

At first sight the price is surprising since ORIC Is have been selling for as little as £130 for the 48K model recently. But Peter Harding attributes this to the January sales and attempt s to clear stocks of the old model. He says ORIC will not be making any more profit on the Atmos with its new keyboard, ROM, and manual than they did on the old machine.

"Which is the best home computer for games?"

Before answering your question directly let us consider what it is that makes one computer more suitable for playing games on than another. Broadly speaking three factors are involved: the computer's graphics and sound facilities, the amount of RAM it offers, and the number of software houses producing software for the machine.

This last factor is by far the most important and is related to the number of machines sold. Obviously, programmers are more interested in producing software for an established best-seller than for a newly launched machine; and the more programmers there are working on a particular machine the greater the range and quality of its programs.

Time is also important since it takes programmers time to discover how best to exploit a computer. Spectrum programs being released now are markedly superior to those of a year ago. It is for these reasons that the current range of Spectrum games are, by and large, better than its ORIC counterpart. Both machines offer comparable graphics and indeed the ORIC's sound facility is more powerful than the Spectrum's, But the Spectrum has been on the market longer and sells in far greater numbers.

Provided they reach a minimum standard - say 256 by 192-pixel resolution together with eight colours — a micro's graphics capabilities play only a minor part in deciding the quality of its games. Some highly playable games have been written for the Vic- 20 despite it relatively humble graphics capability.

Clearly the greater a computer's pixel and colour resolution the greater the potential will be for writing games of arcade quality. But that potential needs programmers to exploit It. The BBC micro is a case in point. It has the finest graphics of any home computer under £500 and has some excellent games to prove it; Acorn soft's Snapper for example is probably the best home computer version of Pac-Man, but only few of the recent games have matched the standard of Acorn soft's first batch of programs and the range of games do not compare with that of its nearest rival, the C64.

The C64, however, provides more RAM than the BBC for high resolution games therefore memory is also a factor here. Many of the more imaginative games require more than 16K. Manic Miner, for example, only runs on the 48K Spectrum and could not be converted for the BBC.

It boasts 20 different screen display and takes 16K to store the details for each screen. As indicated, the 48K Spectrum is undoubtedly the best machine under £150 for games. Its drawbacks are that its keyboard is unsatisfactory and will need to buy an interface if you wish to use joysticks, the sound is rather poor too.

In a higher price bracket, you should consider the Atari range or the Commodore 64. Games for the Atari like Star Raiders, Eastern Front, and the recent Pole Position would probably find a place in all-time games top ten. Unfortunately, most of these come on cartridges which are substantially more expensive than tape. After a slow start game are now flooding in for the C64.

(Source: YOUR COMPUTER, February 1984)

News of Commodores 264 computer has the press highlighting its strong points like the built-in speech and software. The Triple Four range of computers are the follow up to the Commodore 64. Editing on the 364 is easy as the computer will talk to you, giving spoken error messages. First to the market they say will be 264 which will be available in late spring in the USA and sometime after that in the UK. With 64KB ram and almost 60KB available in BASIC they will be an improvement on the Commodore 64.

The new computers will have 128 colours and Commodore is putting more software on ROM than any other company or so says Sig Hartmann of Commodores Systems Division. Commodore is also talking about introducing the new C128 computer, the next logical step in the Commodore 64 range.

The Coleco Adam when it finally arrives, will be the first computer to go on sale in the UK that supports Digital Research's CP/M language. Coleco rightly say that its CP/M compatible computer can run thousands of software titles and as they have developed a CP/M cartridge that loads CP/M into RAM allowing software to be loaded from cassette rather than disk.

With the launch of the QL, people are asking is the 32-bit CPU the future of computing? And perhaps more importantly is the 16-bit CPU already finished? Sinclair's new QL computer uses the Motorola 68008 CPU which is according to Clive Sinclair it is a 32-bit CPU but why should the bits matter? The processor does most if not all, of the work in an average computer, custom chips may take some of the load off the CPU, like the Atari 8-bits and Commodores 64 with their video and sound chips but the ZX Spectrum is wholly CPU powered with no co-processor assistance.

The Sharpe MZ 70, 64KB computer is on sale at £119.95 and with it the Sharpe MZ range becomes the 10th bestselling computer in the UK. Overtaking the Apple II, the abandoned TI99/4a and the Atari 800 in sales. Although the Sharpe's name is commonly believed to stand for (M)microcomputer (Z)Z80 it is probably taken from their first Z80 processor-based model to the MZ-2200 in 1983, the MZ computers included the monitor, keyboard, and tape-based recorder in a single unit, rather like Commodore's

PET series.

The MZ is notable for not including a programming language or operating system in ROM, unlike every other popular computer available today. This omission has encouraged a host of third-party companies to offer solutions like Hudson Soft who produce one of many languages and Operating Systems for it.

In an era when floppy disk drives were too expensive for most home users, the MZ's built-in high speed cassette tape drive is faster and more reliable than the cassette storage on most other competing computers.

Software incompatibly was a big deal in the 1980s, market leader Sinclair and their Spectrum had the most software available by 1984 but none of it worked on the commodore 64. None of Commodore's software worked on the Dragon 32 or ORIC, in fact no one's software worked on anyone else's computers. Bizarrely Commodore 64 software didn't work on the Commodore C16 and ZX81 software might or might not work on a ZX Spectrum. This was an Industry wide problem that was completely ignored by the computer manufacturers, they didn't care or show any interest.

Imagine buying lots of software for your ZX Spectrum, perhaps you run a small business and decide to move up to Sinclair's new computer, the QL. You might even have bought software and save databases on your micro-drive. Well, the QL uses micro drives, doesn't it?

Well, it does but they aren't compatible with the Spectrum and even if they were, the QL cannot read or understand anything even remotely Spectrum like. So, you've wasted your hard-earned money. Rather pitiful, isn't it? It seems there is no hope but to wait…The Japanese have a solution. A range of compatible computers from different manufacturers that all run the same software. Buy an MSX computer in Japan and any MSX compatible software will work, some computers even have enhancements that some software can take advantage of but as a whole every computer must meet a minimum standard of compatibility.

Sony, Canon, JVC, Mitsubishi, and Yamaha are just a hand of

manufacturers that will build and export millions of computers across Japan and overseas. Imagine being able to pull your game cartridge out of your Sony computer and pop it into your friends JVC computer! British and American computer manufacturers must wake up and take notice!

All MSX[lix] computers will have the same general specification:

1. **Z80A CPU or equivalent**
2. **TMS 9918A Video graphics**
3. **AY-3-8910 audio chip.**

All this equates to a 256x192 graphic resolution, 16 colours and 32 sprites with eight octave audio output. Microsoft are pushing for a computer standard, and the Japanese have listened with Sanyo already releasing the first MSX compatible computer. Memory is set to a minimum of 16KB which seems low by 1984 standard, but most computers have 64KB which is considered a standard now. However, all the computers so far have memory expansion slots, so the Ram can be expanded to 64KB later.

Home computers, whether we like it or not are the choice of the gamers, hackers, and businessmen alike but in one area alone the home computer stands tall and that's the entertainment genre.

Games are now becoming a million-pound industry with the arcades leading the way and home computer ports selling like hot cakes. One leader at creating computer games is or was imagine software from Liverpool. Imagine need no introduction for the games out there with titles like Arcadia (1982) Ah Diddum's (1983, Zip Zap (1983), Stonkers (1983), Alchemist (1983), Cosmic Cruiser (1984) and BC Bill (1984) but perhaps more infamously it was the much hyped and advertised "Megagames" that people will remember but of course these two games never appeared. Rumours of problems at imagine circulated in late 1983 when a bill for £50,000's worth of advertising had not been paid. Mounting debts during 1984 didn't help and when more bills went unpaid, imagine sold its games rights to Beau Jolly to raise funds.

Unfortunately for Imagine, the BBC had started filming a documentary of the company. Showing the workings of a high profile and successful software business, the wheels as they say fell off in spectacular fashion when the receivers were called in to secure the property when the BBC film crew were on site.

On 28 June 1984, a writ was issued against Imagine Software by VNU Business Press for money owed for advertising in the UK magazine, Personal Computer Games and the company was wound up on 9 July 1984 at the High Court in London after it was unable to raise the £10,000 required to pay this debt. From the ashes: Imagine had intended to develop six Megagames, the most well-known of which were Psyclapse and Bandersnatch. These games were designed to push the boundaries of the 8-bit computers of the era, so much so that additional hardware was to be designed and built to enhance the computers features. The games were advertised heavily in magazines and would have retailed at around £30 – an expensive price tag when the average price of a game at the time was much less.

During the BBC documentary it was revealed that Psyclapse was little more than an idea and design drawn on paper with no programming actually done. The name was later used by Psygnosis software. Most of the concepts originally intended for Bandersnatch eventually appeared in another Psygnosis game, Brataccas on the 16-bit computers but nothing would appear on the current 8-bit machines. This torrid end to a very successful software business showed that the new gaming and computer industry was not immune from disaster, even computer manufacturers were finding it harder to make money and with the UK in a recession – money was tight and spare cash for exotic and possibly unfathomable computers was in short supply.

Commodore was all over the news, the rein of Jack Tramiel had ended, and a host of upper management has left soon after. Jacks' son Sam Tramiel, Tony Tokai and Greg Pratt who had orchestrated the purchase of MOS Technology have all left the company. However not everyone was leaving Commodore to join Jack Tramiel at whatever his new company was going to be, General Alexander Haig had been appointed to the Commodore board of directors, apparently his skill and knowledge will be an asset for Commodore…

Atari announce 1,000 layoffs which coincides with a reported offer from Dutch company MV Phillips would are rumoured to want to buy Atari but only if staffing levels are drastically cut.

The 11th ZX Micro fair is announced, at the Alexanders Palace in London on the 28th of April, Doors open at 10am and you can stay all day for £1.25p. The show will be used to show the new QL computer to the public. The Computer Fair at Earls court kicks off to a good start and proves to be extremely popular with the press in attendance to see what Sinclair is up to. The first thing that the keen eyed among the attendees would notice, was that the Sinclair QL was shown working without the infamous ROM addon that was needed on early models. For the first time in public, Q-Dos seems happily confined within the black plastic case, perhaps Sinclair should have gone this route rather than rushing the QL into production.

The attendees seem impressed with the QL, and it appears to be a very popular attraction. Commodore also garners favourable reviews of its new Commodore 16 and Plus4 computers which appear on the Commodore stand. The plus4 seems to be the most popular with its large 64KB RAM and a price of £249, it is seen as a QL rival, despite the Plus4 being based on older technology than the QL.

Acorn is also in attendance, showing the Z80 CPU addon of the BBC microcomputer. This enhancement comes with 64KB of ram and allows the use of disk-based CP/M. Dragon data seem to keep a low profile despite being at the show, financial problems, and a general concern over the future of the business didn't seem to stop them showing the new Dragon64, disk drives and the OS-9 Operating System.

Also showing new hardware at the show was Tangerine ORIC who have their new Hitachi 320KB disk drive and a Prestel terminal program to allow downloading of software over modem.

```
CHOOSE TEAM TO MANAGE -
NUMBER            NAME
1                 Arsenal
2                 Aston V.
3                 Brighton
4                 Coventry
5                 Everton
6                 Ipswich
7                 Liverpool
8                 Luton
9                 Man.City
10                Man.Utd
11                Norwich
12                Notts.F.
13                Swansea
14                Spurs
15                Watford
16                West Ham
Type team number of the team you
want to manage (or 99 for more
choice)
                        (h=copy)


L
```

The No.1 Football Game

Football Manager

Kevin Toms at a recent retro show Retcon in Greenford, London. Kevin described how he created football manager. I started writing it and then friends played it, and they seemed to enjoy it a great deal. I couldn't get them off it. It had taken me about a year to write it on a part time basis. Friends found it to be very addictive, which is where the company name came from. I decided I was going to launch it as a commercial product and start selling it. Initially as a mail order service.

I wrote the game over 1981 and launched it on the TRS-80 in 1982 and the ZX81 16KB version came soon after. WHSmith's then ordered 1000 games, it was then that I knew I needed to leave work and do this full time. The football manager game was released on many platforms : BBC B, C64, ZX Spectrum, ORIC 48k, Dragon and the humble ZX81 with a 16KB ram expansion of course.

Sadly, it never appeared on my Ti99/4a!

Amstrad CPC 464

- Zilog Z80 4MHz
- 64KB RAM
- 16 Colour palette
- AY-3-8912 3-voices & 8-octaves
- BASIC in ROM

Amstrad unveil its new CPC^{lx} becoming the latest company to join the home computer revolution. Amstrad seem to of watched what everyone else was offering and then streamlined the operation. The CPC doesn't come with a buddle of unsightly cables with incomprehensible connections, in fact the power supply is fitted to the Amstrad monitor and the data recorder is fitted to the keyboard. This will impress parents who fear connecting and setting up a new computer, the Amstrad is a breeze and probably the most simple and elegant on the market to date. Amstrad might be on a winner. With 64KB of RAM the CPC seems well appointed, the project apparently started in 1983 with a 6502 based computer but that was cancelled, and a Z80 CPU was chosen.

Amstrad say the Arnold project has been a remarkable success and the CPC 464 will be on sale in limited numbers in September 1984.

Clive Sinclair goes on the defensive about the recently launch but seldomly delivered QL computer, claiming that Sinclair is better than many other companies at meeting its promised delivery times. He complains that complaints about delivery schedules are damaging and unfair! He issues a pledge to customers that Sinclair will not let people down and that the QL will be delivered.

Why? He asks are Commodore not being pulled over the coals for not delivering computers that it unveiled in June 1983; Acorn have only just started delivering the Electron which have been delayed for months and the IBM PC was three months late to market but no one moans about them.

Sinclair's QL is now in a head-to-head battle with Acorn as Clive Sinclair once again sets his sights on the education market. The BBC Micro was good for its time he says but the time will come when its ready to be replaced and the QL is the logical choice. Asked how he was going to replace the BBC Micro in schools? Clive says "No problem, it's just a case of working from the top, down, the QL will be used swiftly, becoming standard in universities. They need the 68000, it's much more powerful than a BBC".

One could ask, why was the QL launched so early and with known bugs? Sinclair thinks he can sweeten the deal by offering a free RS232 lead with every late QL. In fact, if you are one of the first or first to receive the QL, you might notice that the computer has a strange add on. It seems Sinclair couldn't get all of the BASIC language on to the QL ROM and so a plug in ROM is provided to make the QL work. Clive has hinted that the early machines could be exchanged but when pressed he offered no extra details. *(Source Personal computer news issue 65)*

Dragon Data have called in the receivers as they have massive amounts of unsold stock and with too few sales to keep the company afloat. However, some good news is on the horizon as Tandy have expressed an interest in buying the company. The company blames a too volatile UK market as the main reason for Dragon's demise. Apparently the Dragon32 and 64 are still selling well but the company simply ran out of cash. 81 of the remaining 152 staff have been made redundant, at its peak before the Christmas break. Dragon did employ 270 staff. Dragon isn't the only computer company in trouble, Camputers the makers of the Lynx machines have agreed to call in the liquidators after an angry exchange at last week's creditors meeting. Accountancy firm Cork Gulley was chosen as one accountant to sort out the financial mess that Camputers are in. The company owes £1.8 Million in debt of which £877,000 is owed to Camputers parent company Camputers PLC. Surprisingly Camputers assets amount to only £94,250.

Jack Tramiel seems to be back in business as he forms TLL. The electronics company seems tight lipped on its plans, but a new 68000 based computer has been rumoured.

In happier news Commodore supplied glitz and glamour at London's Novatel Hotel, even the news of middle management walkouts didn't dampen the spirits of the new computers arriving soon. The new Commodore C16 and Plus4 models were accompanied by several bits of new hardware but not the much-rumoured Byte Hyperion portable PC that they have been working on. The new computers that were on show were the C16 (129.99 retail) with 16KB of RAM, which looks just like a Commodore 64. The other machine, the Plus4 (£249.99 retail) is more unusual for a Commodore computer as it resembles one or two of the current Japanese MSX machines. Commodore have released a new data cassette recorder (1531) which retails at £44.95 and a printer, the MCS 801 which will sell for £399.99.

Renault get in on the computer craze but rather than fitting speech or a Z80 CPU to their cars[lxi], Renault have decided to give every purchaser of the Renault 9 – a Sinclair Spectrum. Not only that but it comes with a software pack to keep you entertained.

The rise of the IBM clones continue with the arrival of the Advance 86A, an IBM compatible computer that is being sold by WH Smiths, among others. The 86A is a 16-bit 8086 computer with 128kb of RAM. 64K ROM and colour output. Is the era of the 8-bit over already? The Apple II, TRS80 and Commodore Pet arrived in 1977 and are often called the trinity that started an industry, perhaps the 86A is the start of a new era.

Tandy have released the overpriced and underperforming MC-10[lxii] computer in 1983, retailing for just £99 and now just over six months later it had been dropped. The ZX81 or Vic-20 like computer was supposed to be a budget version of the colour TRS-80 but it did not find buyers.

The last stocks of the MC-10 will be sold off at less than £40 or so Tandy say. No replacement machine has been announced to take over from it, however Tandy Chairman John Roach has suggested a "adequate home computer could be released soon for around £500 to £1000" The system may come with a monitor, disk drive and software.

More Tandy news, Tandy releases the TRS-80 colour computer 2[lxiii] but keeping the name of the original TRS-80 from 1977 might be a mistake as the two computers share absolutely nothing in common and are not software compatible in any way. The colour computer is aimed squarely at the home user. Easy connection to the home TV and a lofty 64KB of RAM, Tandy hopes the new computer will help fight off the tread of Sinclair and Commodore.

The CoCo 2 is about 15% faster than the original CoCo (Colour Computer) and at £160.00 but as the CoCo 2 offers colour and resolution on par with computers cost half that price it doesn't seem especially competitive. But what could make the CoCo 2 stand out is the new OS-9 operating system, which is designed by Microware System Corporation, and it's based on the UNIX operating system. Costing an additional £70 for the 6809E version it could be a compelling purchase. Upgrading again to the BASIC-09 (another £70) and requiring a minimum of two disk drives (£250) it quickly becomes an expensive proposition.

If you should go for the OS-9 operating system, then you will have a full hierarchical directory OS with files and multiuser features. Directories organised in family tree like sorting and attributes for files like read/write.

As summer draws on and Britain enjoys the sunshine, Mastertronic try to beat the summer sales drought by launching the £1.99 cassette range. Mastertronic claim to have sold 250,000 copies in the £1.99 range already but as Mastertronic work on the sale or return system it remains to be seen if selling games in garages and off-licences is a good business model?Alan Sugar finally joins the extensive list of computers with the Amstrad CPC 464. It arrives late in 1984 and Amstrad hope to burst open the computer market, just like they did with the Hi-Fi market a few years ago. Amstrad have the money, engineering skill and dealer network in place to do it too. On paper the grey wonder looks like it could compete if not, beat the like of the Sinclair Spectrum, Commodore 64, ORIC etc. It has 64KB RAM, a real keyboard, a monitor for superior picture quality and the possibility to run CP/M. The built-in data recorder takes the hassle out of loading cassettes and ensures a standard. Add to that the AY-3-8912 sound chip and you have a well specified computer for all the family. The colourful keyboard is designed for new computer users and has helpfully coloured keys that demand your attention. The computer looks good, functions well and is easy to use but will the public and software houses make a success out of it.

Time will tell…

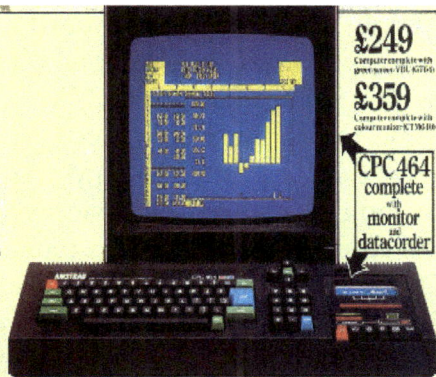
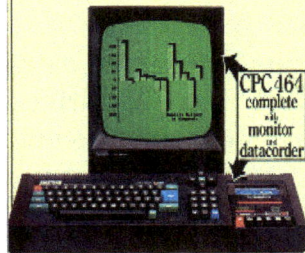

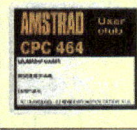

The Triumph Adler Alphatronic PC arrived and attempted to convert us in to using CP/M, who needs BASIC? Not the snappily named Triumph Adler Alphatronic that's for sure but then the Alphatronic is not your usual home computer. Armed with 64kb RAM, a Z80 CPU and a dual personality, it claims to be both a home computer and a business computer. However, the Alphatronic will need a disk drive to use the CP/M operating system, and it costs £330, the computer starts at £347.

With an 86 key keyboard and assigned function keys the computer definitely means business; it has an 80-column screen which is essential for CP/M. It comes with graphics of a similar style to the Sharpe MZ computers, meaning it doesn't not have user defined graphics and that is a real problem for the gamers among us. Sound is basic to say the least and the computer is confined to beeps from a piezo speaker. BASIC is included in its 28KB ROM but it also includes a monitor program. The BASIC included is Microsoft BASIC or at least a version of it and is somewhat like the Dragon 32KB.

Will it be a success? Probably not as a games machine as the graphics are poor and the sound is dreadful. The disk drive is needed for business use, and this jumps the price to a bracket that includes much better machines.

The Japanese are finally coming!

Meetings have been taking place behind closed doors across our green and pleasant land and the topic of discussion is the MSX computers. Various computers are due to arrive on our shores by the end of 1984 and apart from the panic at various computer manufacturers, software companies on the other hand seem excited by the prospect of writing games that will work on multiple computers with little or no modification. Yamaha, JVC, Sony, and Mitsubishi are expected to launch computer in the coming weeks. High street chain stores have agreed deals to sell the computers and now software houses are being asked to create software for them, although the first public appearance will be at the September PCW show.

Sinclair has shared his belief that the Sinclair C5 electric car can usher in a golden age of electric, low-cost vehicles. His Sinclair Vehicle Project is committed to producing low-cost town runabouts says SVPs Managing Director Barrie Wills – former chief executive at De Loren Motors.

The first Vehicle to be produced will be the lower cost MK1, built at the Hoover factory in Merthyr Tydfil. A cross between a motorbike and a car he says, and they are aiming for 100,000 vehicles a year.

September 1984.

Dragon finally ends manufacturing and have cancelled all new development days before the company collapsed. While new machines were recently shown at Earls Court its now over as the receivers have been called in. Eurohard SA have bought the remaining stock for £1 million and will sell them in Spain from next year.[lxiv]

Enterprise may finally arrive in the shops by the end of September, or so says Mike Shirly of Camputers. The much-delayed computer may be powerful and feature rich, but it is so late that any great lead it may have had could be lost as other companies bring forward more powerful machines. Even if new hardware doesn't arrive for some time from Commodore or Sinclair, the current popular machines are giving other companies a hard time by cutting costs almost monthly. It was only a few months ago that Elan claimed the first Enterprise would be in the shops by April.

The first MSX arrives on UK shores, the Toshiba HX-10. Overall is seems the reviewers consider it a well-built computer that is a pleasure to use. Better than the ill-fated Spectravideo and strangely it appears to be a little faster than other MSX computers to date and with a full keyboard too. Perhaps when software starts to appear the MSX standard could be the computers to own, but then it will come down to price.

As 1984 ends, the onslaught of new computers starts to slow down as it becomes obvious that the UK and indeed global market for new computers has cooled somewhat. The big players have settled down to the now, well-practiced procedure of procedure of announcement and then possible delivering new hardware before cost cutting the older stock, this applies increased pressure on the less popular machines, which will then either stop selling or they must cut costs too. Which some can seldom afford to do. Both manifesting leaders, Sinclair and Commodore have reduced prices in 1984 and are expected to do so again in 1985.

However, a new addition to the UK, is the Tatung Einstein. A British computer manufactured by a Taiwanese company for a Shropshire based company and named after Albert Einstein. The Einstein is a mid-range business computer with a built-in 3-inch disk drive. The BASIC was developed in Torquay, so we can say it's mostly British. The computer is an uninspiring plastic box that looks sturdy enough for a monitor to rest on. The non-standard disk language of the Einstein is Xtal BASIC which is not only non-standard but has many alien commands that a common computer would not have. While it's not a bad or poor version of BASIC, it being non-standard will mean that is harder to develop software for and it could be a problem in the future. The computer is being released at £500.

SONY

聖子のパソコンHB-55に新しくHB-75が仲間入り。
64KB RAMを実装して、さらに充実したヒットビット。
絵が描けるカラーフロッタープリンターも、まもなく登場。

HB-75

MSX

UK Computer prices in 1984.

Commodore SX64	£799.99
Sinclair QL	£399.99
Acorn BBC B	£399.99
Acorn Electron	£199.99
Commodore Plus4	£299.99
Memotech MTX	£275.00
Atari 800XL	£199.99
Spectravideo	£199.95
Sinclair 48k Spectrum	£139.99
Atari 600XL	£129.95
Commodore C16	£99.99
ORIC 16KB	£55.95

Commodore have provided details of their new modem; the new modem will cost £99 and will be available for the Commodore 64 and SX64 and includes a year's free subscription to Computernet. Computernet connects directly to other Commodore users via a mini-Prestel system, providing shopping and telebanking services.

Commodore Plus4.lxv

Jack Tramiel with a 364 and 264 (plus4) in the background.

Source: https://www.nytimes.com/2012/04/11/technology/jack-tramiel-a-pioneer-in-computers-dies-at-83.html

Commodore drops the first new computer this month, the Plus4 computer on to the unsuspecting public in late 1984. This new 64KB computer is neither a Commodore 64 nor is it compatible, but it has a better version of BASIC and it has essential built in business programs for the small businessman. The 112 colour, 64k computer is fitted with BASIC version 3.5, which fixes many of the problems of the Commodore 64, it also allows the user to have more free memory in BASIC.

Gone is the dull coffee brown of the C64 and in is the new black case with a white keyboard, it all looks very modern and well built. It's a slim looking computer in a case as most of Commodore machines are but this one is sleeker and better looking than other Commodore machines. One slight problem could be the zero compatibility with the popular Commodore 64, the 64 is established and while it can't match the wealth of software that the Sinclair spectrum has – it is starting to catch up in the UK. This leaves the new computer with a problem; do software houses support 2 commodore computers, or do they choose one? But that's not all from Commodore, not one but two computers land. This time it's the turn of the new C16, looking strikingly similar to the C64. The C16 computer is in the black livery style that Commodore considers to be the new 1980s colour scheme. Compared to the Plus4, this computer looks like a black C64 but under the case, the C16 and the C64 could not be more different. This certainly isn't a Commodore 64 with 48KB of ram forcibly removed. The new C16 is as different to the C64 as different could be, in truth the C16 is a close relative of the Plus4 with its TED display chip rather than the powerful VIC2 graphic chip and SID sound chip that the C64 has. The C16 can be thought of as a VIC-20 replacement, offering more RAM, better BASIC and more colours that the VIC-20 but nowhere near the graphical power or audio fidelity.

Australia, not a name that springs to mind when we think of computing but none the less; Australia have named a computer – the Sega SC3000H computer of the year! Now Sega are not known for making personal computers or computers at all, apart from their arcade machines and incredibly good they are too but are Sega doing joining the rather hectic world of home computing with the SC3000H. So, what is it? Well Sega are well known for their superior arcade games like Buck Rodgers, Zaxxon and the seminal Frogger but a home computer? Well let's have a look, the Sega 3000 is a neat, rubber keyed and slim in profile. It looks a little a Commodore plus4, even including the prominent arrow keys of the Commodore machine. It has two joystick ports and a large hole in right hand side to accept cartridges and it needs one as the computer has no ROM to boot up. A cartridge-less machine will display a blank screen. So, what's inside this new machine? Well, the tried and tested Z80 CPU and the Texas Instruments TMS-9929 – which is the same as the TMS-9918A which give the computer the following modes and colours.

Sinclair ZX81	£30
Tandy MC-10	£50
Sord M5	£50
Mattel Aquarius	£50
Atari 600XL	£89
CBM VIC-20	£89
Tandy colour computer	£99
Dragon 32	£99.95
Atmos ORIC	£99.95
Sinclair Spectrum	£129.95
Aquarius 2	£129 (50 units est.)
Commodore 64	£199
Acorn Electron	£199
Memotech MTX	£239
Amstrad (Green SCR)	£240
BBC Micro	£399
Sinclair QL	£399
Amstrad CPC (colour)	£349
Tatung Einstein	£499
Advance 86A	£400
Alphtronic	£347

This also means that the TMS9918 does not have any scroll registers, and so scrolling must be done by software and not hardware, an important omission. 15 colours are provided by the TI chip and this pretty average for 1984. The TMS9918 Video Display Processor (VDP) was used in systems like MSX, Coleco Vision, TI-99, and Sega SG-1000/SC-3000.

Sadly, the computer suffers from slow BASIC, but the cartridge games are excellent if expensive and none of Sega's classic titles are available on cassette. The sound on the machine is also lacking having only one noise and three tones, so it will never be a joy to listen to. Sega are to release the computer imminently, but no price has been set in the UK.

Sinclair launch the much-anticipated Sinclair Spectrum+[lxvi] model with a software bundle and a new colour manual. The plus model is a new injection moulded keyboard with a much-needed reset button but apart from that it is the same Spectrum that we know and love. Sinclair call it a professional keyboard and that they are very keen to finally have a robust keyboard for the spectrum model. The keyboard looks like the new QL model but lacks the function keys, having said that it does add a few new keys to the Spectrum. Sinclair say the plus will cost £180 and that the older model will be sold into foreign markets. Sinclair say that they have the new units in stock, so for the first time you won't have to wait 28 days or more for a Sinclair product. Sinclair expect to be making 200,000 computers a month.

Commodore offers you £1 million! Commodore is launching a software extravaganza by giving away £1 million to the winner of the game Spirit of the Stone, a treasure hunt game on the Commodore 64. The new £15 game and book have a series of puzzle games which give clues to the where abouts of 40 talismans that are hidden on the Isle of Wight. Commodore have teamed up with the Isle of Wight tourist board to offer this great prize and no doubt boost the tourist trade as well.

Commodore is adding 50p from every game sold to a fund that will supply the million pounds to the winner, Commodore will need to sell a lot of copies…

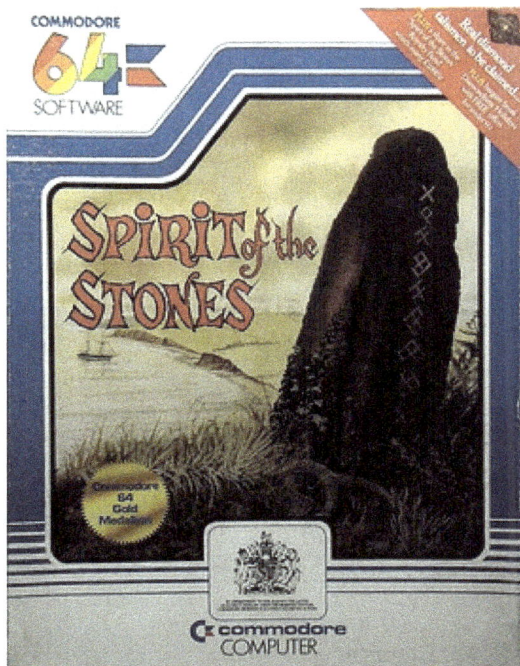

Image source: mjnurney

And with that we close 1984, we can quickly look at the UK computer market by looking at the computers for sale in late '84.

Retail prices for 1984. These prices can only be used as estimates as the retail price changes month by month and retailer by retailer.

New computers for (late) 1984	
Commodore C16	£140
Enterprise 64	£250
Commodore Plus4	£250
MSX (various)	£250+

Chapter 10 -1985

January Gaming top ten titles.			
1.	Airwolf	Elite	Spectrum
2.	Booty	Firebird	Spectrum
3.	Bruce Lee	US Gold	C64
4.	Combat Lynx	Durell	Spectrum
5.	Decathlon	Ocean	Spectrum
6.	Elite	Acorn soft	BBC
7.	Eureka	Domark	C64
8.	Fall Guy	Elite	Spectrum
9.	Ghostbusters	Activision	C64
10.	Havoc	Dynavision	C64

January 1985 starts off with a piece of history being made, the first mobile phone call. Britain's first mobile phone call was made on the Vodafone network, on 1st of January 1985 by comedian Ernie Wise - one half of the British comedy duo Morcombe and Wise.

Sinclair is back! But not with the expected ZX Spectrum upgrade that we all want but with an electric car that no one wants. Sinclair launches the C5[lxvii], an electric trike on to a cold and unimpressed press at the launch event in January 1985. The electric tricycle, capable of a top speed of 15 mph was launched by the computer wizard Sir Clive Sinclair. It is designed for short journeys around town and can be driven by anyone over the age of 14. However, the £399 vehicle, driven by a battery-powered hoover motor at only 2 ft 6 in high and six feet long, has already raised safety concerns. The British Safety Council says the vehicle is too close to the ground and the driver has poor visibility in traffic.

The fact that it cannot drive up a gentle incline has caused some concerns as press testing the car found out at a snow-covered launch event.

Meanwhile controversial pop band Frankie Goes to Hollywood have signed a deal via their record label ZTT[lxviii] (Trevor Horn) for a game to be made with the software house Ocean. The £10 game is due to be released in only a few months' time or so they say.

Clive Sinclair hits the newspapers again as he been involved in an altercation in the Baron of Beef[lxix] public house with Chris Curry of rival computer manufacturer Acorn. The two millionaire boffins had a set too in the pub over the Christmas period. Sir Clive Sinclair, apologised Monday for his behaviour in the Friday night brawl, which began when he slapped his rival Chris Curry with a rolled-up newspaper. Apparently, Sinclair confronted Curry about a newspaper advert for Acorn, in which the reliability of Spectrum products was questioned. Clive Sinclair reportedly called Curry 'scum' and physically attacked him with the rolled-up newspaper. Curry said Sinclair slapped him several times about the head and face.

Curry, 38, said he fled to a nearby wine bar with Sinclair hot on his trail. 'I was forced to retaliate with a right-hand blow,' Curry said. 'He was extremely aggressive and rude to me, and he was calling me names,' Curry said. 'I tried to placate him, but it was no good.

Meanwhile Acorn releases an avalanche of peripherals for the Electron and BBC computers, disk drive for the electron and a second processor for the BBC using the tube interface.

The electron disk drive requires the Plus3 expansion unit to be plugged into the rear of the Electron and it costs £229. The disk drive unit has a 300KB storage capacity and uses the now common 3.5-inch disk.

Engineers at Shugart have created a laser disc unit that holds a staggering 1,000,000KB or 1 gigabyte of data. The disc is a write once affair so don't expect Commodore or Atari to offering drives anytime soon and with a retail price of £5000 its unlikely to appear on a home micro for quite some time.

Jack Tramiel of the new Atari has unleashed a flurry of information on upcoming Atari machines that Jack says will dominate the market and no doubt create a headache for Commodore. Jack resigned from Commodore in January 1984 for reasons that were not clear at the time, but he now heads up Atari which was, a year ago on the brink of collapse as they were losing $2 million a day. Atari have unveiled four families of computer, the first of which is based on the XL range, will be redesigned, and cheaper to produce. There will be 64k, 128k and a portable 256k version with a 5in screen and a special, music enhanced version, or so Atari marketing say.

A new range of computers from Atari will be based on the MC68000 Motorola CPU, taking on the likes of the QL but for around £300, Atari expect to beat the QL on every level. Jack has said that the computers will be shown at the January Consumer Electronics Show in Chicago and will be shown in the UK, later in the spring.

The return of the Enterprise.[lxx]

- Enterprise Computers
- Release Date: June 1985
- Processor: Zilog Z80A @ 4 MHz
- Memory:64 KB
- Storage: Cassette
- Operation System:EXOS Basic

After a delay of almost a year, the Enterprise computer is on sale but only via Prism mail order. It should be available on the high street soon but with most computer shops carrying advertisements for months the good will for the Enterprise could start to fade. Customers have been trying to buy the ailing computer for months now and have turned away to other manufacturers. According to Enterprise the delay has been caused by the "Dave" video chip which apparently is or was bug ridden. With 48k and a build in word processor the micro sounded terrific value a year ago but now it is still a great machine but not as great as it once sounded.

Coleco has finally killed the - all in one computer, the ADAM. The concept of an all-in-one computer with disk drive, printer, and computer for £500 caused a stir and looked like an amazing deal that no other manufacturer to beat. Announced in 1983 it sounded amazing but delays, quality problems and a launch date that disappeared into the distance, rather like the Acorn Electron and Enterprise. It all seemed too much for Coleco, on its final launch in the UK, the price had risen to £800 and with little software or interest the lofty ambition of the ADAM project has now been finally quashed.

The Megagames that never were...

Many things are often talked about but never seen, UFOs for instance or that huge cheque in the post but one thing that was endlessly talked about in 1984 was Imagine software's Megagames – the games that were so big and powerful that they needed additional hardware for your computer.

Imagines former programmers David Lawson and Mike Glover, now of FireIron are about to produce Bandersnatch for the Sinclair Spectrum. So, what was or is Bandersnatch? It was envisaged as a film in which you controlled the main character, communication could be via a speech bubble on screen or even real speech. Realistic animation, background music and immersive atmosphere are all needed to create the film like environment but with most computers at 48 or 64k this sound unlikely but that is where the extra ROM came in, with an extra 64K of data on the ROM which could be used of special effects it might have worked? We will have to see if it arrives on Sinclair's machines.

Sinclair have a new Microdrive pack on the market called the ZX Expansion System. It has the ZX Microdrive, an interface and a software pack. The software contained within is Tasword2, Ant Attack, Games Designer, and an empty blank Microdrive cartridge. All this and an RS232 port for networking for only £100 which is a bit of a bargain.

Another choice for software storage is the similar type of device called the Wafadrive from Rotoronics, this device has two drives rather that the single Sinclair offering. Data is stored on an endless tape as per the Microdrive, but it is slightly slower but with better BASIC command options. The Wafadrive has optional sizes of cartridge too, 16k,64k and 128k. Also priced at £100 and with a word processor this is a good option for the cassette cursed user.

Wafadrive image: mjnurney

For the well off, the next choice is probably the Disk Drive. Sinclair himself famously hates the disk drive – declaring it overpriced and complex but it is the standard data storage system for the modern era, the days of cassette are over already. Beta Disk form Technology Transfer allow you to fit a cheaper BBC disk drive to the ZX Spectrum, although you may need a power supply for the disk drive.

ORIC appears to have resurfaced, asserting its advanced computers that are likely to be released in France and the United Kingdom in the near future. Despite facing financial ruin in 1984, ORIC has regained its confidence and unveiled new machines and future plans.

So, what is the key to ORICs future? Well, the ULA or uncommitted logic array it seems, this chip combines multiple chips that the computer needs and combines them into one larger chip that is faster and cheaper to produce. However, the devil is in the detail as they say, a fault no matter how minor can cause havoc as the chip cannot be modified later. It will need to be redesigned and have a new production run. This is the curse of the ULA, Acorn's Electron suffered with its ULA design as did the Enterprise 64. Cheap to manufacture but difficult to design.

Sinclair cut the cost of the ZX81 and ZX Spectrum by using a ULA and it worked out rather well, other companies have not been so lucky. ORIC say that the first new computer will be the Stratos, and it uses the ORIC command set to include compatibility with the older machines. ORIC also say they have a QL beater in the works too.

Jack Tramiel is on the war path again but this time it's with Atari rather than Commodore, Jack has announced that the Atari 800XL is to be cut immediately to £99 in the UK and the new American Atari machines have now been given revised prices too.

1. 800xl $120
2. 65XEM $160
3. 130XE $200
4. 65 XEP N/A
5.

Atari have their QL beater with the Atari 68000, starting at $500 called the 130ST [lxxi]which comes with 128kb of ram. A $300 version will be released called the 520ST which will have 512kb of Ram.

Acorn, have new machines out too, the ABC computers. Acorn expects to have these on sale next month in the UK. Combining a slim BBC computer, viewpoint spreadsheet and a monochrome screen it should cost about £1000. Price cuts are announced for the BBC computer range and Acorn have finally admitted that the Electron was a sales disaster last Christmas, saying that they are not even close to being in the same league as Sinclair and Commodore.

Speaking of Commodore, the latest machine from them is the C128 with 128k and a C64 mode. With much improved BASIC and the ability to run CP/M programs due to the computer having a Z80 CPU in addition to the 8502 CPU. The C128 will be on sale soon at $250, it was unveiled at the January CES in Las Vegas.The king of computer delays and disappointment, the Enterprise computer is now on general release. First demonstrated in September 1983 and now on sale in February

1985, this is a record that makes Sinclair look good and the Acorn Electron just mildly late. When first announced the computer looked like a winning machine with superior specifications and lofty ambitions but now all these months later the outlook is less promising. Reviews of the day consisted of the following comments. The keyboard is disappointing, with a spongy feel that will not endear it to the typists out there. It looks flimsy and cheaply made. Edge connectors are used at the rear rather than the more professional sockets which are more the standard now. There are some ports like joystick, RGB and printer which is all good. The PSU has no power switch, but a reset is provided. Internally the Z80 uses a 22bit address bus which allows up to 4 megabytes of switched ram. Dave, a custom chip is used to handle the address bus and sound generation. The Z80 runs at an impressive 4hz – compare this to the pedestrian C64's 1MHZ.

Nick, the custom chip that caused months of delays is the video chip. It is a complex chip so delays may have been foreseen. The video chip can assign ram to video and define parameters such as height and width of a window and this window can be thrown around the screen with minimum effort. Hi-Res and 80 column mode are here as well as attribute mode which combines the two. There is even an Interlace mode that doubles the screen resolution. All impressive stuff indeed. With 256 colours and nice sound the Enterprise is an impressive machine but if it had been released a year earlier then it might have been a sensation in the UK market. It's now up to the software houses to offer support and for the public to buy it. It remains to be seen if it will be popular of not.

March - Troubles aplenty.

Hushed voices and mischievous glances from Acorn employees as the sales figures of the Electron show a steady decline, but that's a decline on an already slow selling computer. Sinclair gives the news that we all expected, that the QL isn't selling well at all. Just 50,000[lxxii] units sold in its first year on sale, which in comparison to the ZX Spectrum which recently celebrated its 5 millionth sale – the figures look dire.

In fact, 1985 looks to be a bad year, early signs seem to show that the slow recovery of the economy and the falling sales of microcomputers may be too much for some companies to ride out.

Sinclair still sells more computers in the UK than anyone else and they have done so since late 1981 when the ZX80 and 81 moved over for the ZX Spectrum. Acorn has big problems, its shares fell from £1.93p last year to only £0.23p recently after which Acorn's stock shares were suspended. Poor Christmas sales and a disastrous expansion in the U.S market cost acorn dearly. The aging BBC micro is due for replacement and the new ABC range goes some way to achieving this. But 1985 may be a crunch year for the ailing British company.

Sinclair have issues as well; the Spectrum is still selling well but it's an old computer now and the like of Commodore and Atari are hot on its heels. The QL isn't selling and currently Sinclair have only these two computers on sale. The dead in the water QL and the old ZX Spectrum, new machines are desperately needed but Sinclair attention seems to be elsewhere, his vehicle operation seems to be his main focus now.

ORIC has finally failed and so has Prism who distributed software for the ORIC and Sinclair machines. Enterprise who had signed a deal with Prism have sought an alternative supplier. Barry Moncaster who only a few months ago was full of ambition for ORIC, has sought a management buyout of the company. Marketing director Bruce Everiss formally of Imagine software said that if he had, had a crystal ball he certainly wouldn't be here now.

Price cuts!

A huge £50 price cut has been announced on the Spectrum 48k+ and Acorn have responded with £70 cut on the price of the Electron, both machines are now on sale at £130. Sinclair have hit out at Commodore by claiming that the Microdrive loads and saves faster than Commodore's flagship disk drive the 1541. Commodore meanwhile have said that the C64 will not be cut in price when the C128 hits the market later this year.

Sinclair and Atari square off in a verbal fight as Atari accuses Clive Sinclair of sour grapes when he calls the Atari ST disappointing to use and late to market. Atari's Robert Harding fired back, saying that Sinclair had tried and failed with the QL.

March 1985.

Acorn is on the brink of collapse[lxxiii] with £47 million of debt, its shares have been suspended and with a poor Christmas and a failed £10 million expansion into the US. Things are looking grim, but all is not lost as Italian computer maker Olivetti have bought 49% in the company for £10 million. The deal does not affect the BBC deal to brand the Acorn Micro and the BBC Micro.

New chairman Alex Reid will take control of the company with Herman Hauser and Chris Curry reporting to him. The next year will prove hard for Acorn but with Olivetti's backing they might be able to pull through. As things stand now 120 staff have been laid off and the Electron manufacturing will be cancelled due to excessive unsold stock of the computer. Acorn says a disk drive packaged with the Electron may be available soon. Meanwhile the new ABC computers will only be sold to specialist stockist rather than by the usual retail outlets.

Atari's new computers from Jack Tramiel, will have a new disk drive too. Atari have offered a disk drive for only £250 for the 8-bit range. Commodore slash the cost of the Plus4 by half, the £300 machine can be had of under £150, this is dangerously close to the £130 Sinclair Spectrum and Acorn Electron. Atari's 800XL is now offered with the £200 1050 disk drive, complete with home filing and a demonstration disk. The new bundle from Atari is £250.

Commodore have announced the Amiga and Z-8000 computers to be launched later this year, no doubt a direct competition to the new Atari ST models and QL 68000 based machines. Commodore continues to drive the market by reducing the Commodore 64 to £160. The ORIC meanwhile is reduced to £50 to clear stock and the BBC model A is being sold off at £150.

Clive Sinclair seems to be increasingly disinterested in the computer division as he announces a 250-mile endurance run in a Sinclair C5. The never-ending journey will take the C5 from John O'Groats to Lands' End – the length of Britain. Meanwhile Sinclair has given more details about the next Sinclair vehicle, the C10.

The Sinclair C10 will be a two-seater vehicle with a top speed of 30mph and a 40-mile range and to top it all. The C10 will be followed by the C15 which should achieve 80mph with a range of 100 miles by the end of the decade.

Serious and well-heeled Amstrad owners can now join the disk drive club. The flexibility, fast loading, and capacious disk at last makes its debut on the CPC range. The disk drive consists of an interface which plugs in the back of the CPC computer and a ribbon that connects to the disk drive. The disk drive is made by Hitachi and is a 3inch drive, while less popular than the Sony 3.5-inch drive it is finding its way on to many computers at the moment. When the disk drive is powered up, all cassette controls are taken by the disk drive and AMSDOS is loaded by default. AMSDOS takes a relatively small 1,280 bytes of memory. Serious users can now load CP/M from disk and as the Amstrad system uses cassette commands it means that all existing software should be compatible. Available at launch from £199.95

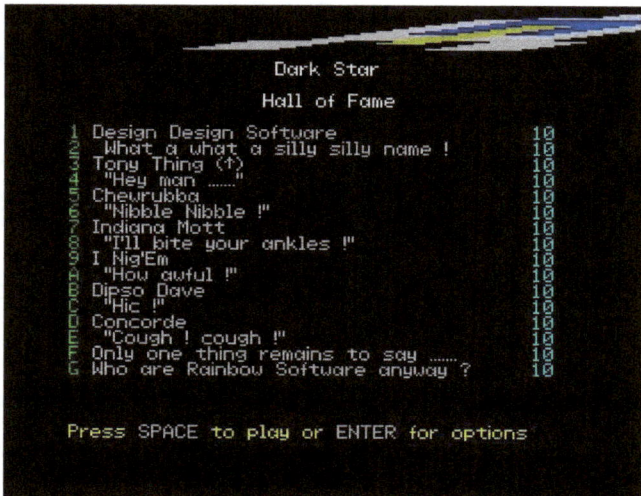

Regarding Amstrad, the classic game Dark Star has been converted by Design Design to the Amstrad CPC. This arcade, wire frame shooter closely resembles Star Wars and Star Raiders on the Atari. As a strategic arcade shooter, it demands skill to play effectively.

May 1985

Acorn have announced the BBC B+[lxxiv], initially things are not looking good as consumer manager Peter O'Keefe has resigned. The redesigned BBC B+ has 64K with its BASIC and OS now on one chip and with built a built in Western Digital WD 1770-disc filling system it means a disk drive can be added with ease. The one worrying aspect of the of the new BBC Plus is the high price of £500. When compared to the Amstrad CPC which costs £50 less and comes with a colour monitor, it could be a tough sell.

Sir Clive Sinclair is currently jumping lines of double decker buses on TV in his quest to sell the QL computer, but his gigantic leaps have done little to move the ever-growing stocks of QL computers that people just aren't buying.

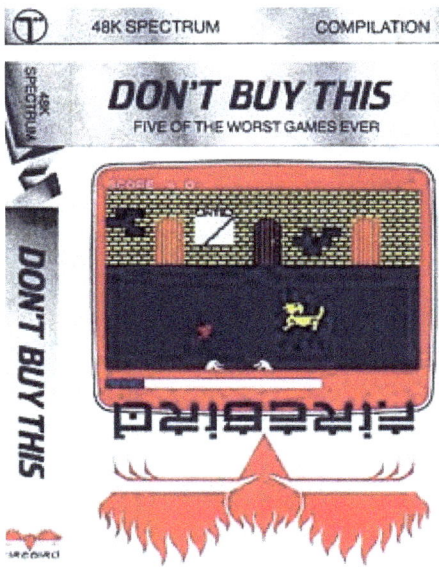

In the software world, Firebird have turned the compilation series on its head by launching the worst games on one cassette tape. Following the amusing title – Don't buy this!

The company has added a copyright notice to the game. It reads "Copy this tape if you don't mind wasting a tape!"

Firebird disowned the game upon release, with Firebird's marketing manager James Leavey claiming that the game "wasn't released — it just escaped It was released on 1 April 1985 under Firebird's Silver Range for £2.50.

This collection has the following dazzling games to impress your friends...

• Fido 1: The player controls a dog named Fido who has to try to defeat moles and birds, protecting a garden for several levels. Fido also needs to keep eating in order to stay alive. In the later levels, enemies such as a low flying canary and a cat which throws projectiles at you.

• Fido 2: Puppy Power: Features similar gameplay as the original Fido, but Fido can now move up and down instead of just left and right. In addition to Fido being able to defeat enemies with its tail, used as an attack in the previous game and Fido can now shoot laser beams from its eyes in order to destroy other enemies and gain health, in a similar way that real dogs do...

• Fruit Machine: The player controls an animated, low-resolution slot machine with reels that spin rather slowly. The instructions describe the game as a "mysterious, original new game that requires skill, timing, nerve and absolute concentration". It also suggests that you should play the game in the middle of the night. Imagine a slot machine (one armed bandit) that is slow, unresponsive and delivers no possible chance of winning real money and that is what, we have here.

• Race Ace: A racing game where the player controls a light blue race car that can only turn 90 and 180-degree angles. The game is impossible to win, regardless of the speed setting of the player's car because the computer-controlled cars advance more quickly every time the player turns. The controls have the tendency to freeze if another car enter your screen space.

• Weasel Willy: A game where a purported weasel, which has the appearance of a human in-game? So, a weaselly Willy? Anyway, you must avoid trees that look like broccoli and his own rather large footprints. The trees spawn in random locations whenever a level starts, so the weasel can be blocked by trees, preventing the player from being able to play the level. The weasel may even start a level with a tree occupying the same space as he does, causing immediate loss of the level. Inspired by Robopods on the Ti99/4a? Very possibly but nowhere near as fun to play.

June 1985

The Amstrad 664 [lxxv]arrives with its toned-down colours, a 3-inch disk drive and 64K of RAM. Alan Sugar can do little wrong at the moment and the 664 is a promising upgrade to the CPC464. The built-in disk drive is a 150k single sided drive, 3-inch unit, rather than a cassette drive. Gone are the garish and rather childish colours of the 464, being replaced with a more serious grey and blue colour. The keyboard is set slightly lower in the case, providing more comfortable typing and with huge blue arrow keys for editing or gaming the 664 has you covered.

A few new commands have been added to ROM and you have the choice of CP/M or AMSDOS to play with. The cassette commands have been kept and now operate the disk drive, this should minimise the overlap between cassette and diskette software. The 664 uses the now slightly elderly Z80 CPU and the choice of a 3-inch disk drive is slightly odd, when the new computers are choosing 3.5 inch. Both Apple and HP have chosen the 3.5-inch disk as a standard and the 3-inch drive neither competes on capacity or price at the moment. The 664 is available with a monochrome screen at £339 or with a colour screen at £449. How well the computer will compete against the new Atari and Commodore machines is difficult to judge.

Atari's 130XE with not 130KB but 128KB arrives from Atari. The

MOS6502 based computer is equipped with 128KB of ram, diagnostic ram check and 11 graphic modes. Four sound channels and a rather nice keyboard for only £170. Atari have created a 256-colour video computer with large ram and a ready-made software collection and that's a good deal. The 130XE has two joystick ports, a cartridge slot, SIO connector, reset button, a serial bus and video out.

From the Atari's SIO you can connect a disk drive, printer, touch tablets and so on. Atari say that a 3.5-inch disk drive on its way as is a hard disk drive system. Combine this with 400 and 800XL compatibility and you already have a vast range of software ready to go. Whether the software industry plans to support 128k it is another thing all together. At the moment, there is no 128k software available.

Commodore 128k[lxxvi]. The 128k machines seem to be a 1985 sensation, is it to breathe life into the depressed and stagnant home computer market? Probably yes but is it useful to have 128k? well maybe, yes? Commodore seems to of thrown everything including the kitchen sink into the C128. Imagine a Commodore 64 with 2 modes of operation, one mode has the original C64 modes, speed, and sound for compatibility. The other mode is faster, with 80 column graphics, but with reduced sound quality and CP/M software compatibility. Interestingly It cannot use the new C16 or Plus4 software, so are these computers going to be dropped by Commodore? These is no TED (C16/Plus4) mode on the C128.

In C128 mode, the computer is faster with enhanced BASIC (version 7), 80 rather than 40 column display and a high-speed disk mode for the new C128 disk drive. Gone are the days of waiting for a program to load on disk but sadly this feature is not available in C64 mode.

The narrative from Commodore is that the C128 will offer every feature that your computer may need but in truth it has some limitations. Will your old 1541 disk drive speed up on the C128? Well, no it won't, and your new high speed disk drive will slow down to a crawl in C64 mode...

Also plugging a Commodore 64 cartridges into the C128 will trigger C64 mode and remove any of the new features until the cartridge is removed. Why was this done? Well, the C64 is a complex collection of custom chips that will never work faster than they were designed to do in 1982.

Users needing 80 columns will need to add an extra video screen as 80 column is not displayed through the same video out signal as the 40 column c64 mode is. 80 column mode is enabled by a new button on the keyboard.

The end of Sinclair? As late 1985 rolls along the turmoil in the computer industry continues, Sinclair cannot seem to sell the ill-fated QL, even though it now has peripherals a cheaper price and is quite usable. The non-standard storage and quirky keyboard are putting business off, but Sinclair seems to ignore this. However, it comes to a head in August as debts mount at Sinclair, one of the first worrying signs is that Sir Clive Sinclair has announced that Robert Maxwell is a "great bloke" (wealthy?) after a statement was issued implying that Mr Maxwell wishes to invest in and offer financial support to Sinclair Research. Sinclair's creditors might be happy about that as the golden years of Sinclair producing a new computer each year seem to be behind him. Timex at Dundee have dismissed 400 staff at their ZX Spectrum manufacturing factory. It is rumoured that Sinclair currently have £34 million of stock in warehouses that they must sell as fast as possible to prop up the ailing companies' finances.

The Bank of England [lxxvii]had planned to organise a rescue for Sinclair, but this has not happened yet, they may well be waiting for the £12million cash injection from Maxwell. In the meantime, Clive Sinclair has stood down as chief executive of Sinclair Research to concentrate on research projects.

Mikro-Gen now plan to sell the games based on the Megagames idea from the bankrupt Imagine Software. Mikro-Gen will use an interface with joystick ports and a Rom socket, Mikro-Gens games will be supplied on rom and cassette and only when both are present will the game run. Shadow of the Unicorn will be the first game released and could lead to a new way to defeat the software pirates, but will the game be any good?

Acorn's woes continue after its shares were reinstated on the stock market, and then suspended again after they fell immediately to a low of 11 pence. According to Acorn the home computer market has shrunk and become fiercer. Acorn currently has 70,000 unsold Electron computers in stock and the BBC Plus computer is not selling either, despite a recent £30 price cut.

Commodore plan to cut the price of its peripherals, like the 1541 disk drive and C64 modems. The Commodore modem comes with one year's subscription to Compunet and costs £229. The internet age has arrived.

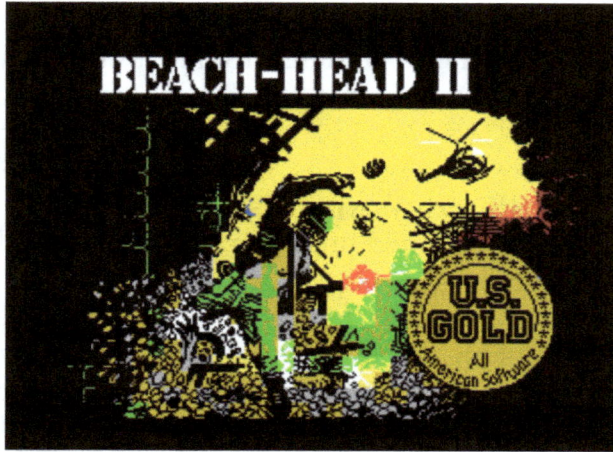

Software to the rescue. US Gold / Ocean / Centresoft have such a combined force and bank balance that they have said that they might make an offer for Sinclair Research.

Next year's new software is getting ready, the likes of Solo Flight 2, Beachhead 2, and Pole Position 3 all on the horizon. Marketing is already being prepared well in advance of release. This advanced planning is an effort to maximise profits and to obviously generate interest in new titles.

September.

Sinclair joins the 128k race. The rumoured Sinclair 128k has a real audio chip, the AY-38910 as used in the Amstrad models. Hoover in the meantime have issued Sinclair with a writ for £1.5 million in regard of Sinclair C5 manufacturing and unpaid bills. Bill Jeffery has been appointed to replace Clive Sinclair.

Atari's ST 260 is on sale and from next month the new 520ST will be on sale in a package including a monochrome monitor. Various software houses have signed up to the new machines while some have said that they will continue to support the current 8-bit machines, others have not been so positive about the 8-bit market. Ocean, Firebird and Llamasoft have agreed to support the ST. Both Atari and Commodore have machines on the way that will enhance the computer experience. With faster speeds, colours, and sound – will the 8 bits survive?

Acorn is still alive (just) but with Olivetti's financial support, Olivetti now own 80% of the company in a deal which has cost Olivetti £4 million. Acorn still owes over £8 million in creditors debts and the work force has been cut from 450 to 275 staff. The RISC CPU is the only shining light in Acorn's manufacturing at the moment and will no doubt be the reason in Olivetti's increased share of the company. The BBC micro sales have fallen flat, and the Electron is now dead as commercial product.

Amstrads CPC464 was launched a year ago and has been very successful, especially for a new computer. Alan Sugar has come back with the recent 664 and now the 6128, a 128k CPC computer this time. Amstrad is wasting no time and shows that they can adapt to the ever-evolving home computer market as quickly as any of the more established manufacturers. The 6128 takes over from the 664 which will be dropped from production immediately. Is the 6128 just a 664 with more ram? Well, yes, it is, it looks the same and operates in the same way too. The cursor keys have moved on the keyboard to become more accessible. Apart from the inclusion of CP/M plus it is very much business as usual and why wouldn't it be, the 664 was a capable machine.

October

Software houses have been secretly sent the new Sinclair 128K+ computers as Sinclair called them. The prototype machines have external ROMs that are obviously unfinished. With a QL style plastic injection moulded keyboard the 128 looks like a slightly larger Spectrum plus. It has a large heatsink on its side that reportedly gets rather warm.

Acorn revamp the poor selling 64k BBC B+ with the new BBC B 128k model. The new model will sell for £499 but not from WH Smith who have decided not to stock the BBC computer. However just a few days later, Acorn says that after 4 years in production the 32K BBC B microcomputer will be discontinued in the UK.

Despite still being badged with the BBC logo and adopted by almost every school in the UK, its time is up. It seems Acorn have already stopped production to focus on the new 128K plus model. Time moves on and the 32k machine wasn't selling very well, but then neither did the 64k plus model...

On a brighter note, Acorn has a £1,000,000 order for the BBC 128K computer from Canada, while that may sound impressive – the company have huge debts and stocks of unsold Electrons. Dixons come to the rescue and have just agreed a deal to buy some of the unsold stock of Electrons. Rumour has it that they are being sold at below manufacturing cost price just to clear warehouse space. It's a good deal for Dixons as the make a healthy profit from the deal.

December

Tatung say that they are working on a new model of their Z80 based Einstein – the Einstein 256k, by-passing other companies 128k models completely. The new model will be available next year and will be compatible with current 64k model which has been reduced to £400 including the monitor. While sales of the Einstein started well, they have now slowed down as a result of a fairly high price and poor software support.

With Christmas coming soon, most computer companies are desperate to see the end of 1985 and look forward to a brighter and hopefully more profitable 1986. The new 128k machines will no doubt generate – "new sales" and help restore a somewhat stale market. So, after the blood bath of 1985 If you haven't bought a computer yet which one, should you buy? Here is a rundown of available computers in the UK.

• Atari 800XL – Great graphics and sound and with good software support it is sure to be a winner this Christmas.

• Atari 130XE – More memory from Atari but apart from that it is essentially the same computer as the 800XL.

• Commodore C16 Incompatible and non-upgradable, a disaster from commodore – by the C128

• Commodore 64 The classic C64, second only to the Spectrum in software support but with superior colour graphics and sound.

• Commodore plus4 – With built in software that is already outdated, the Plus4 is well made but overpriced and obsolete already. Not compatible with any C64 software and has little support in the industry.

• Enterprise 64– Technically superior computer but it's too little, too late to create an impact. Limited software and poor sales so far.

• Spectrum 48k – Horrid keyboard (all models) and often limited colour graphics and its sound output is horrendous but it's cheap, successful, and popular but buy the Plus model.

• MSX – One specification for all models – a great idea but sadly the standard is yesterday's technology, and it can be pricey here in the UK.

• Electron – The BBC micro's little brother. Its slow, unloved, unpopular, and now unsupported by Acorn. Although great deals can be had as Dixons push the machine at a cut price. Software support is improving.

• Memotech – 500 and 512 models are well made and have a high specification, but they cannot find software support although if you add a disk drive you can run CP/M for business.

- Amstrad CPC6128 – Newest of the CPC line and with 128K it is sure to be a winner. Cheap and will no doubt be popular.
- Commodore C128 – New from Commodore, advanced features, CP/M and a C64 compatibility mode to use your old software. Surely a big winner next year?

Is this the end of the line for Sinclair vehicles? Just as 1985 closes – so does Sinclair's ill ventured electric dream. TPD who took over from Sinclair to handle the failing company has itself gone into liquidation with debts of £1 million, Sinclair personally lost £8 million in the business but bizarrely he has now shown interest in the assets of TPD, whose assets are currently valued at just £500,000. Sinclair may well return if he buys the inventory, and we could see the unpopular C5 back in the shops in 1986!

1985 was a turbulent year for the UK computer industry, many established names have gone forever, and some are on a fragile footing as profits slip from their fingertips. Two of the biggest UK companies Acorn and Sinclair are fighting for survival.

The Americans have flooded the UK with cut price computers, especially Commodore but now Atari are fighting back with the new ST and XE models. Atari have always been popular, but they have never had the impact of Commodore and especially the C64. Atari are currently having trouble as they slip further down the UK sales list.

So where did the British go so wrong and wrong so quickly? One word. Expansion or at least ill-fated expansion. Acorn spent million trying to crack the USA market, but the Americans already have Apple, Commodore, Atari and for businesses – IBM and its clones. Just where Acorn thought the BBC would fit is anyone's guess, but the answer is plainly nowhere as their plan failed miserably. Their desire to compete in the Spectrum's gaming space was a mistake too; the Spectrum is too cheap and to combat that they created the late, costly, and slow Electron. Who wants a slow computer? Was It better than a Spectrum? In many ways yes but wasn't as cheap or as established as the ZX Spectrum. Too little too late perhaps. Being first is very important.

How could you sabotage the Sinclair Spectrum empire? Simply by using Sinclair himself. Sir Clive Sinclair is a magnificent inventor but an extremely poor businessman, he even says so himself. And of course, the doomed C5 electric car. It consumed millions of pounds and produced few sales and much ridicule but even it could have been a success as a university campus run around or as a holiday camp runabout - it may well have succeeded, allowing Sinclair to build the next more useful model, the C10. Sinclair's fixation with the C5 cost the computer business dearly but then he practically killed Sinclair Research by launching the awful QL.

Sinclair C5.
A new power in personal transport.   *£399*

Chapter 11 - 1986

1986 Software Chart.		
1.	Yie Ar Kung Fu	Imagine
2.	Kung Fu Master	US Gold
3.	Formula 1 simulator	Mastertronic
4.	Elite	Acornsoft
5.	Winter Games	Epyx
6.	Hypersports	Imagine
7.	BMX Racers	Mastertronic
8.	Commando	Elite
9.	Finders Keepers	Mastertronic
10.	Action Biker	Mastertronic

Will lessons be learned in 1986? Will the computer industry blindly continue to sell obsolete hardware, or will new hardware propel 1986 into the future with new stunning software to suit? Surely the likes of Acorn who have been burned twice already, once with the poor selling Electron that they are now practically giving away and then again with the aged BBC computer. If it wasn't for Olivetti saving the company (twice) last year. Acorn would be gone now, sold off to the highest bidder.

Clive Sinclair, once the darling of the Britain's tech industry has gone, the QL is on life support and the ZX Spectrum struggles on with its old 1982 hardware. When will the new 128k machine arrive? Surely Sinclair cannot continue to sell the old Spectrum 48k.

America's Commodore International lost millions last year[lxxviii], selling computers that no one wanted. The C16 and Plus4 are incompatible with the gigantic C64 software pool and are poor sellers to boot. The C64 soldiers on alone but maybe the C128 will help keep Commodore in second place in the UK.

Only Amstrad managed to go from strength to strength with new CPC models and a very quick hardware cycle with new models already here. Software support is improving too on the Amstrad machines which can only be a good thing. Europe is proving to be a profitable area for them too, with the Schinder brand selling the CPC in Europe.

The Tramiel family have taken the failing Atari and breathed new life into it, with new machines and an upgrade path to the 16-bit too. Commodore launched the expensive Amiga last year, but it seems in short supply, and it is more for the business market than the ST from Atari which seems to be able to cover all tasks from games to music and business.

January.

WHSmith's have cut the price of the Sinclair Spectrum plus to £99.95 in an effort to clear remaining stocks left over from the Christmas season. Meanwhile the new Spectrum 128k is expected to land this year and it is desperately needed, the Spectrum is looking very much like yesterday's technology. Curry's is offering the Spectrum for £129 which includes a cassette player. Not to be out done, Commodore is offering another of their famous trade in deals – much loved by Jack Tramiel era. Take a C64 to the shop and get £50 off the price of the new C128 which currently sells for £220.

Sinclair and Commodore have made huge losses in 1985, especially up to and possibly over the Christmas period. Sinclair's sales figures for the first quarter of 1985 were bad, showing a loss of £18 million. Commodore on the other hand, have gone one better and made a loss of £30 million in the 3 months to September '85. Could Commodores decision to buy the Amiga of been a costly mistake after all? It has no software and is not compatible with the hugely popular C64.

Sinclair may blame stockists who bought in bulk and then held on to stocks for slowing his over optimistic sales predictions. Up to 400,000 Sinclair machines are held in warehouses in early 1985. Commodore on the other hand have developed new computers and they need to recoup that investment by selling millions of them. The problem is that the computers they have made are not selling. The plus4 and C16 are generally regarded as a flop that no one wanted. Industry analysists have claimed that Commodore simply cannot afford to continue doing this as they simply don't have the finances or the high share price to sustain it.

Currently Sinclair (without Clive) is trying to raise £10 million to stop the company failing. Robert Maxwells bid for Sinclair has fallen through and his offer has been withdrawn. Sinclair needs the money to build the new 128k machines and pay off its substantial debts.

On January 23rd (USA) Apple announce the 16-bit Macintosh, a Motorola 68000 computer with a high resolution black and white graphical windowing system that is a million miles away from the BASIC text screens of the current computers. The Macintosh comes with 128k and a double sided 800k disk drive, and a mouse too. No cassette loading here.

Acorn are fighting back the malaise with a new BBC model, this time it's got 128K and it's called the master system. The master system is a series of computers with different specifications for different budgets, the lowest model is the Master 128 which sells for £499. It contains View, Viewsheet and it has ADFS – the Advanced disk filing system. The next model, the master 512 uses MS-DOS via a co-processor. With a GEM operating system from Digital Research and the top tier model is the Master Turbo which uses a faster co-processor and a special version of BASIC called Hi-BASIC, running at 4MHZ.

Commodore is to end all UK manufacturing with the closure of the Northamptonshire Corby plant[lxxix]. 250 staff are being made redundant as manufacture of the C16, Plus4, C64 and C128 come to an end. Commodore tries desperately to stem the huge financial losses of last year. Commodore had a disastrous 1985 that only improved over the Christmas period, will that make up for the poor decisions of the previous 11 months? Commodore seems to have lost money on the new TED series of computer, which are not selling well at all and the PC range (PC10 & PC20) computers have not perform as well as expected either. Include the purchase of the Amiga computer and you have all the ingredients of a financial disaster. Can Commodore recover quickly enough in 1986 with the guidance of new management?

Sinclair Spectrum 128

Image source: https://en.wikipedia.org/wiki/ZX_Spectrum

- Processor: Zilog Z80A microprocessor at 3.5469MHz.
- ROM: 32KB ROM, arranged in 2 pages of 16KB.
- RAM: 128KB of Dynamic RAM, arranged in 8 pages of 16KB.
- Graphics: 256 × 192 pixels, 16 colours, attribute based.
- Sound: AY-3-8912 3 channel, 8 octaves.
- Keyboard: 58 plastic keys above a rubber pad and plastic membrane.
- I/O: Software controlled RS232 serial port. Keypad Port. Tape In (ear) and Tape Out (mic). Expansion I/O port. MIDI port (RS232).

Finally unveiled in the UK after being previously sold only in Spain, however now it lacks the external number pad that was available to the Spanish. The Spectrum 128 looks like an elongated Spectrum plus with a black heatsink on the righthand side but obviously furnished with 128K ram and an AY sound chip for proper audio sound at last. Sinclair have yet to announce the UK price but being positioned above the Spectrum 48k and below the QL, one would expect about £150? The QL is selling for £200 at the moment but for how long is anyone's guess as it continues to sell poorly.

Commodore finally releases the Amiga computer, looking like a C128D with a built in 3.5-inch disk drive. Commodores poorly kept secret was apparently designed in parallel with the C128 but was only released to the public recently.

Only Boots have these deals at these low prices.

NEW SPECTRUM 128 STARTER PACK,
BOOTS EXCLUSIVE COMPUTER DEAL PRICE £199.99.

NEW SPECTRUM 128 MICRODRIVE PACK,
BOOTS EXCLUSIVE COMPUTER DEAL PRICE £249.99.

AMSTRAD 8256,
BOOTS EXCLUSIVE COMPUTER DEAL PRICE £469.95.

No-one offers computer deals quite like Boots. Drop by and check out the very latest in hardware and software. At very low prices.

SPECTRUM 128 STARTER PACK

Spectrum 128 Computer	£179.95
Boots CDR 265 Data Recorder	£19.95
Joystick/Interface	£18.90
Total Price	£218.80

BOOTS EXCLUSIVE COMPUTER DEAL PRICE £199.99
SAVE £18.81

*Plus 3 vouchers each worth £4 off Spectrum 128 Software costing £5 or more at Boots (see pack for details).

SPECTRUM 128 MICRODRIVE PACK

Spectrum 128 Computer	£179.95
Interface I	£49.95
ZX Microdrive	£49.95
Total Price	£279.85

BOOTS EXCLUSIVE COMPUTER DEAL PRICE £249.99
SAVE £29.86

*Plus 4 FREE microdrive cartridges.

AMSTRAD 8256

Amstrad 8256 Personal Computer including Locoscript Word Processor	£458.85
Supercalc II Spreadsheet	£49.95
Total Price	£508.80

BOOTS EXCLUSIVE COMPUTER DEAL PRICE £469.95
SAVE £38.85

*8256 Complete Word Processor System includes monitor and printer. Disc Drive for fast and secure loading and saving of information. *Supercalc II - the best spreadsheet programme available for the 8256. *Locoscript software offers many features including a choice of typestyles.

Boots

Are Amstrad moving away from the CPC range? Alan Sugar has recently returned from Japan where he has managed to secure another batch of 3-inch disk drives, the elusive drives and disks are proving hard to find in the UK. Rumours abound that an Intel based Amstrad is on the way.

So, what is arriving on UK shores in 1986? Well Jack Tramiel of Atari is planning not one but a series of new Atari ST computers. Like to 1040ST which is the same as the 520ST but with double the ram and the 520STFM which features a TV modulator, allowing you to connect the computer to a domestic television set. This new model is expected to replace the original 520ST at some point but not straight away.

Curry's, Dixons, and Argos have shown interest in the new models after refusing to sell the 520ST as it was too expensive-it retails at £750 currently. Atari have also announced a high-speed hard drive for the ST which will retail at £850 for the 20MB version.

What is driving the new models of computers? Why are they pushing increased ram on the 8bits but not increased processor speeds? Why are so many computers stuck in the past-without a disk drive? No serious or even non serious user wants to load from cassette now and 1986 could be the year of change. Bring on the disk era.

Prices of ram have fallen to a new low, manufacturing costs of disk drives have also fallen. In fact, the cost of manufacturing computers on the whole has fallen.

The ZX Spectrum
Expansion System. Only £99·95

Sinclair's complete alternative to floppy discs...

Source
https://www.pinterest.co.uk/pin/572731277588268761/

Rise of the (128k) machines.

Let us start with memory prices, since 1982 ram prices have steadily fallen in a predicable manner but during 1984 and into 1985 memory prices continued to fall as more and more manufacturers started producing ram and with that the amount and density of ram increased too. Production has refined and RAM stocks have finally increased. This has been a driving force behind the 128k craze at the moment, it's a cheap headline grabbing addition to a computer.

Increasing CPU speed is much more complex than adding RAM.

It is difficult to increase ram as 8-bit CPUs generally cannot access more that 64kb or 48kb of ram. A solution had to be found and now it has, the memory is segmented into sections or pages and the sections are added together to create the entire 128KB. When the computer needs at access a different memory location, an extra page is used loaded and 128KB can hold a lot of memory pages.

Of course, the other elephant in the room is software, are Sinclair expecting people to load 128K programs from cassette? This would mean a load time of about ten minutes, and that's not ideal. So will software appear on the Microdrive, well probably not as Microdrive sales have been slow and it remains an unpopular option so that leaves us with disk drives. Will Sinclair finally drop the unwanted and relatively unreliable Microdrive and release a disk drive? It must be the only option.

Acorn on the other hand have upped the specs of the previous BBC models and have given us the Master 128K. 35K is allocated to system tasks and other useful programs like extended graphics, terminal communications and DFS. BBC BASIC v4 and View are included too. While many of these features could be added to the 32k BBC B, Acorn have added them in to an all-in-one package for the first time. Not forgetting that the 1MHZ bus has been upgraded to 2MHZ as well. An Amiga like feature has been bolted on too and that is the genlock video feature, this allows the BBC to display graphics over a video signal. Useful for video text and headings. Acorn have even managed to make the

128k master largely compatible with the older models too, allowing a great deal of software to ready to run on the new machine.

Amstrads new CPC6128 is still the same Z80 powered CPC we know and love but now it has 128k and a disk drive which will load the software so much quicker than cassette, so let us time how quick it is...

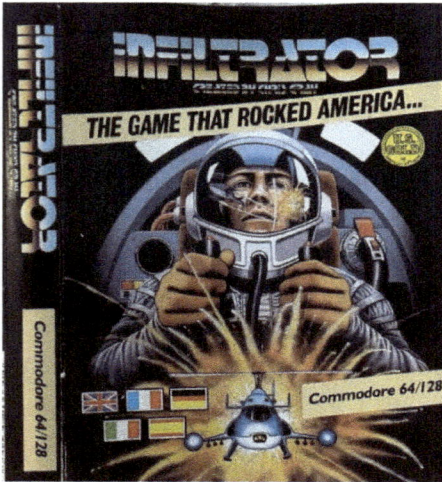

Infiltrator is produced by US GOLD and was written by Chris Gray.

This is a multi-load game and a fine example of everything that was wrong in the cassette based 8-bit era.

Because our computers had limited memory and slow data access, designers had to use tricks to try and create large, interactive video games. Infiltrator used a multi-load system to load sections of the game, one section at a time. But while this is probably acceptable the first time you play – it quickly becomes very tiresome, as we will see. The practice of cassette data storage is a throwback to a different time when tape loading was cheap but never fast. The Americans avoided most of this by adopting cartridge and disk-based solutions much faster than the UK and Europe.

Infiltrator displays a loading screen after a few seconds, this is a nice large graphical interpretation of the games name and then it continues to load. It then stops again, to play a brief introduction - a briefing of the mission and then we continue to load again. The game then loads up the first level and we can play can start. The game is irrelevant, it is the loading time comparison that we are interested in. For this example, we will use the Amstrad

CPC6128 and compare it to the Commodore 64.

Cassette loading is at a glacial pace, taking 4 minutes to load up to the introduction screen after which it then loads the first game level, in total this takes 7 minutes on the Commodore 64. By comparison, the disk version loads the up to the introduction screen in 17 seconds and then it takes a total of 55 seconds to load up to the first game level when the player is sat in the helicopter, ready to play. So as a quick calculation, in this instance the Amstrad disk version is approximately 6 minutes faster to load.

Infiltrator's cassettes use a fast loader routine by default – novaloader but it still takes 1 minute thirty to load the briefing screen and just under 6 minutes to load the first level. The disk version takes 1 minute 18 to load to the briefing screen and then a further 4 minutes and 22 seconds to load the first game level. Disk is so much faster.

Although this pales in comparison to Movie Monster from Epyx, this beauty takes 2:47 to load the introduction screen which in this case is a rather nice cinema facade where you can select which movie monster to control in the game, and then which city, and then finally which scenario to play before the cassette spins into life to load the cinema trailers of other games from Epyx.

This takes the loading time to 6 minutes, the cinema trailers show upcoming games from Epyx and the story of our game, if you play as Godzilla then it's a tale of nuclear bombs waking the beast by a detonation under the sea and with a headache and a bad attitude he heads to San Francisco! After a short intermission, the game will then continue to load. We are now at 9 minutes since we excitedly popped the cassette into the Commodore datasette, we are now asked to turn the cassette over and insert side B, press play and continue. where we wait another 12 minutes for the game to finally load.

If anything shows the dire need for faster storage-it is this! Commodore, Atari, Tandy and Amstrad have embraced the disk drive, even the less popular machines like Dragon, ORIC and Ti99/4a all have disk-based solutions. Only one company refuses to use disk. Sinclair.

C64

Melbourne House

"BEAT THIS"

Jeoffrey Thompson
WORLD KARATE
CHAMPION

The way
of the

exploding fist

So, back to the Amstrad CPC 6128[lxxx].

With the cancelling of the short lived CPC664, Amstrad went on to produce the 6128, supporting 464CPC software and CP/M Plus too, it comes well equipped. The standard features are all present like joystick, printer port, second disk drive port and a serial interface is available at extra cost. With 128K available to CP/M it means that popular CP/M programs like WordStar will work, something that the CPC664 could not manage as it had memory allocation problems in CP/M. One point to note is that while CP/M will load on the CPC, it will need to be supplied on 3inch disks and not the more popular 3.5- or 5.25-inch disks that are now standard. Amstrad prices are £279.99 for the green screen version and £399.99 for the colour monitor version.

Atari's 130XE[lxxxi] looks like a mini-Atari ST but it is based on the A8, Atari's 8-bit system rather than the more modern Motorola based 68000 ST. Atari have added an extra 64k of ram to the 800XL and come up with the 130XE, as the falling price of ram have made this an economical upgrade option that most other manufacturers have opted for. The extra ram is added above the 64k memory range that is normally used on the 64k machines and some code poking is needed to access this in BASIC. Other than the extra ram, the Atari machine offers nothing new, and it could well be left out in the cold as software developers focus on the 64k user base rather than the 128k. It could well be another Commodore 128k situation, why bother writing software for the new 128k 8-bits when the 16-bits are just around the corner and after all the 128k machines have yet to create a user base. It is possible the 128k computers will be a final hurrah unless some new extra features can be added to new models. Cost cutting could help as the 16-bit machines are still extremely expensive but perhaps culling the 64k machines and forcing the 128k into stores might help.

Commodore were one of the earliest computer companies on the scene and has a reputation as an innovator and cost driver in the marketplace. Without Commodore, Apple and Atari would have no CPUs to power their computers. So, Commodore knows their stuff, right? Well yes and no! 1985 was a bad year, an unbelievably bad year for Commodore and the miss-steps might continue with the C128. While initial sales are ok, they are nowhere near the C64s sales and while it seems a bit of a bargain for the first-time buyer or more serious user, what does it offer to Commodore 64 users?

Well, the answer is that just now, not much. In C64 mode it allows the user to use none of its new features and the new Amiga must be more of a serious long-term machine than this. It will probably be the last 8-bit Commodore computer although some software houses have pledged some support the C128 but how much is anyone's guess.

Sinclair have their own issues at the moment, the QL is proving unpopular, and sales continue at a snail's pace. Initial production problems are now over, and you can buy one from the shops and that is the problem. Most shops have stock and some of the big retailers have too much stock, it is the same for the ZX Spectrum as well. The new 128K machine from Sinclair offer new features like real audio and the larger 128K ram, monitor out and midi. So, is 1986 to be the year of the 128k computer? Well, yes, it most definitely is. If you are a first-time buyer or a user looking to upgrade, the 128k machines are they machines to buy. It is not worth buying the earlier models unless they are reduced to a bargain price. CP/M is supported on most 128k computers but not all and the same goes for disk drives. All CP/M is supplied on disk but not all 128k computers have readily accessible disk drives, it is a catch 22 situation and that goes for software support too. The most upgradable micro is the BBC Master, but if you need a 16-bit CPU at 8-bit prices then the unloved QL might be the one for you.

Commodore may pull it out of the hat with the C128 if software arrives for it but for now Amstrad seem to have the most sensible package in the CPC6128.

A Master Class.[lxxxii]

Acorn started by getting things the wrong way around, they won the BBC computer contract while not having a working fully built computer to show. With the clock ticking the BBC 'A' rose and evolved into the popular BBC model B. We now have the Master series of computers and it is just in time too. Financial problems, poor management decisions and products that do not sell quickly have all reduced Acorns profits to a negative and without Olivetti's backing Acorn would have been closed. But Acorn is back, the Master series is now five computer models to suit your needs and costs.

Using a CMOS built 65C12 CPU that is low powered and of a more modern design when compared to the original MOS designed 6502 anyway and with expansion galore, the Master could well be the saviour of Acorn. It now has a keypad, internal ROM's containing VIEW and VIEW sheet, Terminal and ADFS disk filing system. The 128k has segmented RAM as all 128k computers have. 64KB is available as usual and then four pages of 16KB ram, all adding up to 128KB. However, some software does have issues loading on the new 128k machine, Acorn say that these programs use illegal memory address. One example given is that of 'Elite' but all BASIC programs will work correctly. An updated version of Elite is on the way for the Master computer.

The new Spectrum arrives!

Four years have passed since the Sinclair ZX Spectrum launched and things have moved on, including Clive Sinclair himself. An estimated two million Spectrums have been sold so far and a new model has just landed. The Spectrum 128K was developed during 1985 in conjunction with Sinclair's Spanish distributor. Why did it take so long to appear in the UK? Well Sinclair have a lot of unsold Spectrum 48K computers to sell and it seems no one will buy them once the 128k arrives. Anyway, Sinclair decided to work with the Spanish when developing it, as the Spanish government wanted all computers to have a minimum of 64k and to be able to display BASIC instructions in Spanish. Sinclair worked with Investronica to develop not a 64k machine (which the Spectrum sort of is already) but a 128k machine.

The first thing to notice is the large heatsink on the righthand of the computer, this cools the 7850-voltage regulator which is bolted on to this to keep cool. The next features are the very un-Sinclair like connectors, Sinclair computers are notorious for being minimalistic. The ear and mic sockets have moved to the left of the case. A QL type RS232 phone like socket has been added to connect midi or printers. A monitor socket has been added – a first for a Sinclair computer rather than using and tuning a domestic tv, although they can be used. Another telephone type socketed is here and that is for the external keypad – although released in Spain (as was the spectrum 128k) it will not be available on the UK machines.

The motherboard is completely redesign with a new ULA chip by Ferranti, 128KB is fitted, again using 16KB pages as is the normal procedure in bank switching memory.

A General Instruments AY-3-8912 is fitted and this diverts all sound to the tv or monitor rather than having a piezo beeper speaker on the computer. Sinclair have changed the ROM too, to a 32K ROM and this is next to the CMOS low powered Z80 (Z-8400A).

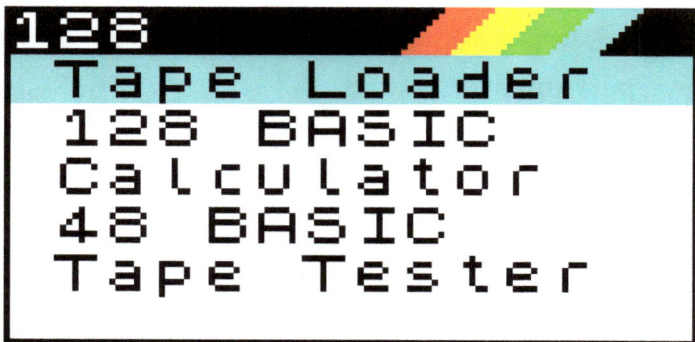

A cursor-controlled menu now greets the user, rather than the rather dull copyright message of old. It has five options of:

The tape loader will start loading 128k software, the option to use to load your new 128k games. It is possible to use this mode for 48k software but realistically 48k mode might be better. 128 Tape tester is used to test the volume of your cassette tapes and setting the volume correctly. A bar will appear with a block on it, adjust the volume to get the block as far right as possible, this should be the correct volume level for loading. The calculator is a simple calculator that has no special or scientific functions at all, which is a pity as they could have been included. A colour test is included too, it is less obvious. Reset the computer while holding down the "break" key and a series of vertical lines will appear with eight paper colours and 8 ink colours. Your tv set should be adjusted to the optimal settings on this page.

128 BASIC is the latest version of Sinclair BASIC that has done away with the single key press data entry for the first ever, the much loved and hated key entry system has gone for good thankfully.

Missing features are Microdrive's or connectors to fit them, it still has no joystick ports and more worryingly no option for Sinclair disk drives – which don't exist of course as Sinclair refuse to make them. Oddly, Sinclair include the old Spectrum plus colour manual with an addendum booklet of 14 pages which clarifies the 128k features.

SPECTRUM 128
EL SUMMUM

Spectrum, como líder, marca un nuevo hito en la historia de los ordenadores familiares.

El Spectrum 128.

Gran capacidad de memoria. Teclado y mensajes en castellano, teclado independiente para operaciones numéricas y de tratamiento de textos...

Sinclair e Investrónica han desarrollado una auténtica novedad. En ningún lugar del mundo, salvo en los Distribuidores Exclusivos de Investrónica, podrás encontrar el nuevo Spectrum 128.

Sé el primero en tener lo último.

SPECTRUM 128. NOVISIMUS

DISTRIBUIDOR
EXCLUSIVO

investronica

Tomás Bretón, 62.   Camp, 80.
Tel. (91) 467 82 10.   Tels. (93) 211 26 58 - 211 27 54.
Telex 23399 IVCO E.   08022 Barcelona
28045 Madrid

220

The ZX Spectrum 128KB in its Spanish guise, well before the UK launch

Commodore has a habit of announcing products and then killing them off sometime later but bizarrely they seem to release computers that no one wants, and then they cancel the more interesting computers. Commodores LCD portable, shown at CES would have been a wonderful machine and the first portable Commodore computer – we cannot really call the SX64 portable as it needs mains power. The other Commodore machine that was announced but strangely absent until now was the C128D.

Commodore may have messed up 1985 but they plan to correct the good ship Commodore in 1986, the C128D is part of this plan. While it is only a C128 in a case with a 1571 disk drive added and a carry handle is some of parts is more than that. The C128D is on sale at £499.99, it has the new 128K designed 1571 disk drive which has burst mode. A detachable keyboard which is much nice than a C64 and all the connections of the C128.

It is an attractive computer, very much in the Amiga style and it makes a compelling case for software houses to get their act together and make software for the 128 range. Comparing the C128D to its nearest rival – perhaps the CPC6128, the Commodore machine seems better built and is nicer to use. In use it is much nicer to use than the enormous C128 or the clunky C64, the only downside is the attaching of cables or inserting a cartridge as they are at the rear of the computer and a monitor is in the way.

April.

Herman Hauser seems to of decided to call it a day at Acorn as he has moved to Olivetti. Mr Hauser has become the director of advanced research and may soon be moving to Italy.

Sales figures are in for the Christmas period, Sinclair seem to have the upper hand in the UK with 37 percent of the market. The Sinclair ZX Spectrum+ is the biggest seller according to Audits of Great Britain. Sadly, the good news of Christmas fails to lighten the financial woes at Sinclair, news breaks that Alan Sugar of

Amstrad has bought the Sinclair brand, name, and all remaining stock of Sinclair computers.

April 7th A press conference has been held in which a smiling Clive Sinclair shook hands with the delighted looking Alan Sugar, Sir Clive announced his immediate withdrawal from the home computer industry. The Sinclair/Amstrad brand may be guaranteed a brighter future under Amstrads management but there is little doubt that some of the flare has died in the deal.

Alan Sugar has announced that Sinclair branded computers will be aimed squarely at the lower entertainment section of the computer market – possibly a clear sign that the QL will be cancelled any day now. Amstrad say that they will improve the quality of Sinclair machines and certain models will the cancelled or redesigned immediately. The most obvious change will be the creation of a Sinclair computer that resembles the CPC range with a built-in data recorder. A probable cancellation of the Sinclair 128K computer is expected and a replacement Amstrad looking Sinclair 128k model is expected soon.

As Sinclair will occupy the lower end of the price bracket it is expected that the Sinclair computer or computers will be sold as single units without monitors like the Amstrad CPC range.

Sinclair or rather Amstrad have a large stock of QL computer to sell on but production is expected to be cancelled, and no further units are to be manufactured. Amstrad have a rumoured advanced computer in the works but whether this is a Sinclair or Amstrad machine is not clear but if it is to be a 16-bit machine then it is unlikely to be a Sinclair computer.

In this purchase Alan Sugar has captured a large section of the UK computer market and could potentially make life hard for the American and Japanese importers, there is no doubt that Sugar is a shrewd businessman. Sinclair's stocks of unsold computers could well cover the cost of buying the Sinclair business without another Sinclair computer being manufactured. Alan sugar paid a mere £5 million for Sinclair.

So where does that leave the current cost of computers?

Amstrad CPC6128	£279.99
BBC Master	£499
Atari 520ST	£399
Atari 130XE	£139.95
Commodore 16k	£49.99
Commodore C128	£269.99
Sinclair QL	£199
Sinclair 48K plus	£120
Commodore Plus4	£200
Spectrum 128k	£155
Enterprise 128k	£249.95

June 1986.

Commodore maybe high on the announcement of the UK release of the Amiga but all is not well at Commodore HQ. Financial pressures, poor sales and a bad Christmas have all come back to bite CBM. The company has just recorded a pre-tax loss of $36.7 million on sales of $182.3 million dollars[lxxxiii]. Chris Kaday of Commodore UK says that despite the poor financial status at present the company is going from strength to strength and people still want Commodore computers, The C64 and C128 are so popular that people need not worry. Mr Kayday is particularly upbeat about the Amiga which was released in the UK in May at £1500.00 with a colour monitor. Apparently 50 dealers have already signed up to stock the new Amiga. Mr Kayday seemed more cautious when pressed about the C64, C16 and plus4 computers, although rumours are rife about a new super 64 computer that has more memory and enhanced graphic modes.

The personal Computer World takes place and the biggest and boldest show new hardware and software in London. The show has grown from a small hotel to a huge corporate event and being a September even it allows companies to show off what will be the hot item for Christmas.

Acorn, IBM, Amstrad and others all have computers and updates available, so let us have a look at some. Acorn show the final production version of the BBC Master 512 MS Dos computer, and they also show the rebadged Olivetti M-1, another IBM clone and as a surprise to all - Acorn announce a budget BBC computer for £600! Rumours again and this time its Commodore and the C64C computer, a new C64? Or a C64 in a 128k style case?

Some say it will come with a windowing menu system, GEOS maybe. More realistic is the idea of a new case for the old C64 with a cost reduced motherboard. Commodore is expected to cut the cost of the C64 even further to finally capture the UK market now that Sinclair have cut the retail cost of the ZX Spectrum.

Amstrad show their IBM PC clone in a move that will probably interest business but worry CPC users. Amstrad will not doubt place the PC at the budget end of the market in an effort to keep the American clones off the market. It is also possible that the Sinclair brand could be brought back but on a PC clone rather than the usual home computer.

Atari are in fine form, having a huge stand at the show with the Atari Village. The village has more than seventy software publishers all showing their new Atari software. Atari have the ST on show and its 8-Bit computers but that is not the only software on show...

Durell Software is showing two of its new titles, Turbo Esprit, and Thanatos by Mike Richardson. Turbo Esprit sees you driving the titular Esprit across busy cities hunting down drug runners and escaping hitmen. Elite Systems show a demo of the impressive looking Scooby Doo on the Spectrum. Gremlin Graphics show two new games, Trailblazer and Avenger and Hewson have the impressive Iridium on the C64 and soon to be Spectrum. AlleyKat, City Slicker and Firelord will be available soon.

Mastertronic unleash Flash Gordon, the 1950s sci-fi classic but due to the complexity of the game Mastertronic say it will be a multi load only game on the Commodore 64.

September.

Apple plan to release a Commodore & Atari killer in a plan to shake up the market. The more sceptical among us could say that Apple have been caught napping with the ancient Apple II looking tired and somewhat neglected. The Apple II has never sold well in Europe and its always played a secondary role to the all-conquering Commodore 64 but to be fair, the Apple II is one of the slowest sellers in the UK.

The rise of the new 16-bit Atari ST and Amiga machines have left the Apple II looking like a very poor deal indeed. The Apple II's only strong points are the wealth of software and upgrade options for it but then no upgrades can lift it up to the ST or Amiga level or even the Commodore 64 or Atari 8-bits.

Apple have responded in a rather clever way, not by lowering the Macintosh price but upgrading the Apple II with proper graphics and real sound. Not only that but the ram and CPU have been upgraded too.

For a man in a shadowy world who does not exist, Michael Knights photo and his car will be plastered all over Oceans next release. Ocean have decided to finally release the much-delayed Knight Rider based on the popular fantasy crime fighting TV show. Ocean also say that another TV show game, Street Hawk is almost ready too. Ocean software is currently riding high on the success of The Great Escape, Parallax and Miami Vice and do not seem to be slowing down any. Ocean software is not just TV shows as they have film releases like Cobra and Top Gun on the way too.

Amstrad are back in the news with their new baby and its slightly familiar. When Amstrad paid the bargain price of £5 million GBP for Sinclair Research it was clear that Sinclair was making poor decisions and had lost its way. The Spectrum+ improved the former Spectrums laughably poor keyboard but did nothing else, the Spectrum 128k offered new sound and extra ram, but it was not available in huge numbers and the back log of older Spectrums hampered its sales. Then we have the QL, a computer that looked like a spectrum but cost more and was aimed at business, but business did not want it.

Amstrad have now brought the Spectrum back and it looks like an Amstrad CPC, it looks the same and will compete in the same sector as the CPC. This very odd juxta position is a little strange but hopefully Sinclair fans will buy the new 128k machine in droves, allowing the more expensive CPC to occupy the more expensive ground as a home and business computer. Amstrad have added a cassette deck into the design of the new Spectrum, just like the CPC and given the Sinclair/Amstrad Spectrum +2 a grey colour rather than the traditional black that Sinclair favoured. It now sports a proper keyboard with keys that actually press down and spring back up as you would expect. Rather than sticking or falling out like those on the Sinclair plus.

A similar menu is included just like the old 128k from Sinclair, but now with an Amstrad copyright message. The computer sports mostly the same I/O at the rear but this time it has Joystick ports, something a Sinclair machine never had. Finally, the Sinclair+2 computer looks well-made and is a pleasure to use. Surely Sinclair users will be all over this.

In an effort to prove that Amstrad know what they are doing, games can now have a seal of approval with the Sinclair Quality Control check. The first game to be deemed worthy of this accolade is Moonlight Madness from Bubble Bus software.

As the summer turns into winter in the UK a new fleet of IBM clones start to appear. The familiar drip of clone machines has now turned into a deluge as cut-price Intel and AMD machines arrive on our shores. Prices range from eye watering to mildly stinging but they all seem to point to one thing. The PC is coming but, it will not be for the home user. Not just yet. These machines cannot compete with the Atari ST and Amiga but that is not what they are for, not yet any way. These machines are firmly in the dull office machine bracket. Computers like the Tandy 1000EX, Comcen and ARC Pc are all Intel 8088 at 4.77MHZ or 8MHZ with

256KB ram. Amstrad have what is probably the best PC clone at the moment with the PC1512 for only £399. Running an Intel 8086 at 8MHZ and with 128KB of ram.

Rumours are that Nintendo want to enter the UK market with some sort of games console. Nintendo are already making a console in Japan, and it appears to have lots of games for it but as yet there is no official word of a UK release.

Einstein a-Go-go.

When Tatung launched the Einstein in 1984, it was quickly disparaged. It had more bad points than good ones. Tatung claimed that the computer was a good CP/M machine and it did eventually sell in reasonable numbers. It seems that Tatung have listened and created the Einstein 256, a complete redesign of the computer and now it's aimed at the home market rather than business. But is it any good?

Selling for £399 complete with a monitor the Einstein looks a good deal, it is a smaller and a better-looking machine. Sound is provided by the AY chip as used in Sinclair 128k and Amstrad CPC. The colour palette is an impressive sixteen colours from a palette of 512. It has 40 and 80 column display modes and more sprites than a Commodore 64. It still uses the Z80A CPU allowing the computer to use CP/M as well as the Xtal Dos operating system.

Will the 256 succeed where the original failed? Who can tell, as always software support is needed and as the older computer had about five hundred titles and these will run on the new machine or so they say, it will be up to companies to provided new, exciting software if it has a chance to compete? The original Einstein, launched in 1984 has sold an estimated 20,000 units but they will have to do much better than that for it to prove successful.

Chapter 12 - 1987

Gaming Charts 1987:		
1.	Gauntlet	US GOLD
2.	Hits 10 Vol3	Beau Jolly
3.	Paperboy	Elite
4.	Trivial Pursuit	Domark
5.	Space Harrier	Elite
6.	Konami coin-ops	Imagine
7.	Footballer of the year	Gremlin Graphics
8.	Hit Pack Elite	
9.	Five Star Games	Beau Jolly
10.	Cobra	Ocean

1987 brings a change in the computer market, the never-ending optimism and relentless pile of new computers now slows to a slow drip. The need to push 8-bit hardware or to introduce new 8-bit machines is starting to end as the 16-bit era looms on the horizon. The enthusiasm for spending millions developing a new computer that may or may not break even has all but gone now. Rumours of Super Spectrums or new Commodore 64 machines seem forgotten, the MSX tidal wave turned into a minor ripple and the oddball computers that the British love so much have all but vanished now. A few stragglers hang on, a few MSX machines are still on sale but with the likes of Sinclair, Commodore, Amstrad and Atari there is little room for any other machines. Companies that have survived this long are trying to recoup the monies already spent and any new machines may well be 16-bit. The 8-bit dawn is moving into a close. Software is changing too; the big box and big money games are slowing giving up the dusty software shelf for new smaller and cheaper titles. The budget game is making a stand and is quickly becoming a firm favourite with the younger consumers, helped by the fact that numerous software houses are releasing new and re-releasing old software at £1.99 and £2.99. Why wouldn't you buy a former £10 game for only £1.99? and in the end if it is not particularly good, you can always pop down to the newsagent or petrol station and buy another one.

The once thick and dense issues of 8-bit computer magazines are feeling the pinch too, with the word count falling month on month as the advertisers move over to the Amiga and ST world. Crash magazine for the Spectrum for example had 160 pages in issue 10 (1984) but the last issue (92) had only 68 pages.

The consoles are coming…

Atari have announced that they will be releasing a console version of the Atari A8 computer system. Or in simple terms, the 800XL will be appearing in a plastic box without a keyboard and the point of this is to stop the Japanese from taking control of the lower end of the market. Atari say that they will have a console ready soon for about £75. Will it stop Nintendo and Sega?

Mattel have issues a press release saying that they plan to introduce the Nintendo console into the UK, very soon but details seem somewhat vague.

Sega have said that their Sega Master System will be launched in the UK for £99.99. Sega say that Outrun and Enduro racer will be available on their console at launch. Sega's Master System can display thirty-two colours on screen out of a palette of 64 colours in a resolution of 256x192.

Apple bring glitz and glamour to Islington's Business Design Centre – with Apple World and manage to attract over 9000 visitors, while trailing behind the Commodore or Sinclair shows that we are used to it is an important step for Apple if they are to make a mark in the UK.

Atari announce price cuts across its ST line up with the 520ST-FM being cut to £399.95, the original ST, the 520ST is now down to only £259+vat, although you will need a disk drive to use with it. The top-of-the-line ST, the 1040ST-F is now down to £899.95.

Apple must be doing something right as profits are up, as of December 26th profits rose by 24 percent. Net sales were $662.3 million and net earnings of $58.5 million. The Apple IIGS is proving a remarkable success or so they say.

Commodore prepares the new Amiga 500. Commodore seems to have not one but two new Amiga computers to show and they say that they will be released in the UK shortly. The new Commodore Amiga A500 will have 512KB of ram and sell for $700 which is about £500. Commodore says that the new Amiga will be a powerful machine for the home and small business user, particularly in graphics and sound. The other Amiga appears to be a business model that can be upgraded like the IBM PC. Commodore have taken their time at reducing the cost of the Amiga, but this may tip the scales in the Amigas favour over the Atari ST and Apple Macintosh.

April.

Commodore have done the impossible! They have reported a profit. The remarkable turnaround sees the American giant report a $21.8 million profit compared to a loss of $53.2 million in the same quarter last year. The success is partially down to the Commodore 64 which, with price cuts continues to sell well. The Amiga which did not sell very well at first for a variety of reasons (too expensive and no stock from Commodore) is now selling well and with the new A500 and 2000 model sales are expected to increase year on year.

Sir Clive Sinclair's new venture, Cambridge Computer ltd show off the new Z88 portable computer. Once again Sir Clive bucks the trends and goes his own way with a super lightweight handheld portable, it is about the same size as a A4 piece of paper, runs on batteries and has 32k of ram. The LCD screen has 80 characters by eight rows and uses the tradition Z80 CPU. Sinclair says that it will include a suite of software (they are not ready yet) and will run for 20 hours and has a standby time of one year! Price £199.95

Atari trump Commodore by releasing their sales figures and things look good, the Atari ST is selling well, and the older 8-bit line continues to sell but in lower numbers than expected. Atari's first quarter shows an increase, with sales of $65 million an increase of 45 percent. Shares have risen by 45 percent – an increase that should make Jack Tramiel smile.

Silica Systems are now selling the 520ST-M for £259, the 520ST-FM for £399 and the newer 1040ST-F for £599.

Domark are visiting the new James Bond set at Pinewood to get the low down on all the action for their upcoming computer game. Timothy Dalton is the new Bond, and his character will feature in the new game. Domark say the action game will be out in July for the Amstrad CPC, PCW, Spectrum, Commodore, Amiga, ST, BBC micro and MSX.

Remember the mighty Memotech MTX512? Well now you can have this computer for £49.99 + £5 post and packing. The Z80,

64KB computer is being sold off by various retailers who are trying to clear left over stock but don't expect new software or any support.

Activision manage to make money for the first time in four years. The company reports a profit of half a million dollars. Activision say it is down to carefully selected games that are popular rather than the bigger titles that many months or years to produce.

Commodore issues a warning about illegal imports of their new Amiga A500. In a move that is reminiscent of the old CBM Pet days when dealers discovered that the USA Pet could be used in the UK by just changing the power supply. Well, it seems the importers aren't even doing that and are Importing 220v machines rather than the UK 240v. Commodore say that customers must check before they buy them as Commodore will not repair illegally imported computers.

Talking of Commodore, let us have a look at their current range and pricing in the UK.

Commodore.

C128	£390
C64	£164
A2000	£1095
A1081 Monitor	£349
A22860 PC Board	£699
A500	£499
A1010 Disk Drive	£249
A501 TV modulator	£21.73

Commodore PC Range

PC10	£997
PC20	£1397
PC40	£2247

Atari

1040STF	£565
520ST	£210
520STF	£322
SF314 disk drive	£173
SF354 ½ mb upgrade	£129

Sinclair is back or rather Amstrad-Sinclair is back! The new ZX Spectrum 128k +3 is here! Do you remember the Spectrum dream from Uncle Clive? The colour ZX Spectrum, a computer for serious applications, to learn with and to program on? No, me neither but I do remember the ZX Spectrum 48k computer with the funny rubber keyboard that was great for playing games on despite Sinclair's best efforts to prevent that. So, five years later the Spectrum finally has an official disk drive, it might be a 3-inch drive but it's better than a Microdrive and way better than cassette. Opus brought us the first disk drive for the Spectrum and that was the more popular 3.5-inch version too and with a parallel port and Kempston joystick port, but it was not an official Sinclair product and was never endorsed or supported sadly.

The +3 is the same computer as the +2 or 128K computer that Sinclair made more or less. The plus3 is a black computer, harking back to the Sinclair machines of old and moving away from the dull Amstrad grey colour. Some audio fixes have been made by Amstrad to fix the problems that were introduced on the +2. The +3 has two 16KB ROMS, one is for the Amstrad / Sinclair BASIC, and the other is the disk operating system (+3DOS). Memory bank switching was improved allowing the ROM to be paged in and out of the address space, this was done to allow the use of CP/M.

The following changes were made to the +3.[lxxxiv] Removal of several lines on the expansion bus edge connector (video, power, and IORQGE); causing some external devices problems. One solution was to use the 'FixIT' device that could be used on the VTX5000 modem.

Reading a non-existent I/O port no longer returned the last attribute, causing certain games such as Arkanoid to be unplayable. Memory timing changes: certain RAM banks were now contended causing high-speed colour-changing effects to fail. The Spanish keypad scanning routines from the ROM were removed helping some older 48K and 128K games were incompatible with the machine. The ZX Interface 1 was also incompatible due to differences in ROM and expansion connector, making it impossible to connect and use the Sinclair Microdrive units. There was a regression in sound quality from the previous 128K models – an error with a resistor placement meant sound was distorted.

Commodore has released the new Commodore C128D[lxxxv], yes, the new C128D. You might think that the C128D had been released already but no, this is a new version-the highlights of which seem to be that the carry handle has been removed. This enormous case redesign is enough for Commodore to announce that it is a new model and not the C128 that was released nearly two years ago. Commodore says that it has extra video ram as well. While it still has 128K, a Z80 and CP/M it retails at a frankly ridiculous £399. The Atari ST is currently being sold for £299 and it outclasses the C128 in every area, the fact that an Atari machine is faster and cheaper than a premium Commodore product must amuse Atari's Jack Tramiel.

Commodore appears to be losing its way once more, despite the Amiga's initial sales surge and the continued success of the C64. Commodore's mismanagement has once again hindered its progress. While it appeared that Commodore was finally eliminating unsellable computers and rectifying its internal issues, this was not the case. Turmoil ensued as their former president, Thomas Rattigan, was recently fired and subsequently sued Commodore for millions of dollars.

Despite Commodore's successful turnaround, resulting in profitability and debt repayment, this achievement did not appear to hold significant weight when U.S. sales continued to decline, leading Commodore to rely heavily on the United Kingdom and Europe for funding. This peculiar situation mirrors the current predicament faced by Atari.

November.

Commodore has announced a £100 discount on the retail price of the new Amiga A500, exclusively for registered Commodore users. This offer is similar to the one previously used for the original Amiga, now rebranded as the A1000. Commodore has reported a $28 million profit during the 1986/87 fiscal year, indicating a potential turnaround in their fortunes.

Despite previous setbacks, Commodore has demonstrated a knack for overcoming challenges. However, this success has been achieved through significant cost-cutting measures and a diminishing profit margin. It remains uncertain whether this strategy can be replicated in the future.

As with many instances of near-disaster, Commodore's recent successes have been precarious. The Amiga possesses superior capabilities compared to the Atari ST and IBM PC, but its market reach is severely limited. To achieve broader success, Commodore requires a substantial software portfolio.

The U.S. market is significantly larger than the UK and Germany, which are Commodore's primary markets. Commodore U.S. must urgently address its shortcomings and expand its presence in this market if it wants to suceed.

December

The sound of low, deep rumbling near Dover isn't new shipments of updated 8-bit computers – far from it but the sound of digging as the channel tunnel is started. "I Should Be So Lucky" is released by 19-year-old Australian actress Kylie Minogue who is already hugely popular with British audiences for her role in the TV soap Neighbours, which debuted on the BBC fourteen months ago.

UK Inflation remains low for the sixth year running, standing at 4.2% for 1987. The UK economy as a whole is in better shape with overall unemployment falling below 3,000,000 and youth unemployment is now below the 1 million. Overall economy growth for the year reaches 5.5% – the highest since 1963.

Sir Clive Sinclair has managed to secure the market capital needed, some £2.8 million to continue in his new Silicon venture.

Sinclair's wafer scale integration got off the ground some 18 months ago when Barclays Bank gave a cash injection to Anamartic, a subsidiary of Sinclair Research. Tandem, the U.S computer manufacturer have added a further £1 million dollars and Italian SGS have added more to the pot. The idea of Wafer-scale integration, which is a system of building very-large integrated circuit networks that use an entire silicon wafer to produce a single "super-chip". Anamartic is 13%-owned by Fujitsu Ltd and 19% by Tandem Computers Inc. The funding shows that Sinclair is still in demand, and he may well have new products to shape the computer industry.

Banned in Germany!

Palace Software is encountering difficulties with the German censorship authorities due to the ban on its game, "Barbarian." The Bundesprutstelle fur Jungendgefahrdende Schriften, a German government department, has deemed the beat-em-up game contains excessively violent content because players can decapitate their opponents. Compounded by the realistic audio effects on the Commodore 64 and Amiga, the game has been added to the banned list. Palace Software has announced that "Barbarian 2" will feature monsters instead of human opponents to reduce the gore and potentially expand the game's market reach in Germany.

Amstrad has set its sights on the United States and intends to expand its presence beyond the limited market of the United Kingdom. Over the past few months, Amstrad has been actively expanding its global reach by establishing offices in Italy and Spain. In September of this year, Alan Sugar acquired Vidco, a new U.S. distributor, for a sum of $7.5 million. While Amstrad maintains a strong presence in the United Kingdom and parts of Europe, it currently lacks a foothold in Germany. However, this situation is poised to change as Amstrad aims to acquire Schneider, a German computer manufacturer. Although their contract is scheduled to expire in 1988, Amstrad intends to open its own distribution center in Germany to challenge Schneider's dominance in the market, which seeks to sell more advanced computers than Amstrad currently offers.

Atari's financial performance continues to improve, with recent figures indicating a substantial 130% increase in profits. This growth is primarily attributed to the successful sales of the Atari ST, which has garnered significant demand. The company's sales have reached such a level that it is currently facing supply constraints with several distributors reporting low or no inventory. Atari's Bob Gleadow remains optimistic, aiming to sell over 100,000 units during the upcoming Christmas season.

While Atari has announced a temporary halt to price reductions for the ST machines, the company plans to introduce upgraded models with enhanced specifications in the near future.

Chapter 13 - 1988 and on...

I have decided to combine the final two years of this book into a single chapter. The primary reason for this decision is that no major computer company was willing to manufacture a new 8-bit computer in 1988. The technology had become obsolete. While it was possible to repackage computers, companies such as Sinclair (Amstrad), Commodore, and Atari did so. However, these repackaged computers were not new or an upgraded continuation of a product line. Instead, they were repackaged or re-cased machines with older technology. The world continues to advance towards 16-bit and 32-bit computing, but the costs remain high. Only Atari has managed to create a cost-effective 16-bit computer with the ST. Commodore is lagging behind with the Amiga, but the Amiga 500, released in 1987, will change that.

The 8-bit computers are still selling well but are now regarded as budget options with most 8-bit machines being sold for less than £150 but that is not the whole story. The 8-bit machines have a huge software library that is plentiful and cheap to buy. The Sinclair Spectrum, Commodore 64, Atari and Amstrad machines can all be bought on any high street and will probably be supported for the foreseeable future and new software is coming thick and fast at the moment but as the decade ends so will new support for the 8-bit machines at least from the bigger software houses, although budget software may fill any remaining void and probably target children and young teens.

Microprocessor technology is changing rapidly the older 8-bit designs are now too slow and too limited for the advanced software that is coming out now.

Atari have the Abaq 32-bit transputer technology, a reduced instruction set computer chip or RISC chip that will transform the Atari range, but it will be expensive to produce.

The transputer that Atari are working on is the British Inmos T-800 CPU running at 12 MIPS, compare this to an IBM PC-AT which runs at about 1 MIPS. (Millions of instructions per second).

In the last 10 years something thirty computer manufacturers have either folded or ceased to produce computers. Jupiter Ace, ORIC, Mattel, Texas Instruments etc have all gone and can only be found in dusty warehouses via mail order. Falling memory prices mean that the days of the ZX81 are long gone, we will never see a new 32,48 or 64k home computer on sale again. Atari have shown that 1mb or 1024KB can be achieved at a reasonable price now and other companies have to follow or need to exceed this to survive.

American chip manufacturer Motorola has built the 32-bit super CPU – the 68030 which they say is twice as powerful as the Intel 386. Systems should be available for about £2000 with the new processor, compare this to the Acorn Archimedes which is selling for £700. Motorola expect the 68030 to enter production the first quarter of 1988. Motorola are wasting no time and are currently working on the 68040.

Microprose is celebrating victory after managing to get their game – Gunship reappraised and possibly removed from the German blacklist which effectively bans its sale in Germany. Microprose have other titles on the blacklist, both Silent Service and F15 Strike Eagle.

Defender of the Crown is being developed on the Commodore 64, the 16-bit wonder game has just arrived on the Atari ST and is being squeezed on to disk for the C64. Debuting on the Amiga a couple of years ago the graphical powerhouse is a great demonstration of the advanced graphics on the 16-bit platform but can Mirrorsoft pull it off on the C64?

MGT reveal the mysterious SAM Coupe computer, often called the super spectrum. MGT are no strangers to the Sinclair market as they have been making hardware for Sinclair machines or years, but the creation of a computer is a whole different ball game. MGT will not give an actual release date yet as the computer is not finished but it is expected by the end of next year.

1989 would usher in the age of the cheaper 16-bit computers for the new decade, the PC was starting to catch up and the 8 bit was being slowly dropped in favour of lucrative deals with the consoles of Sega and Nintendo. Various companies managed to scrape in to the 1990`s, Mad-Catz with its peripherals like game pads, steering wheels and soon to be titans of the pc industry, Opti and Plextor. In February SKY TV was launched in the UK, and we would be glued to MTV for first the few exciting years. Nigel Mansell wins the Brazilian GP and Nick Faldo wins the Masters Golf Tournament completing sporting events that will appear in various games coming soon. James Bond returns in Licence to kill, the sixteenth Bond film and the second with Timothy Dalton. Margaret Thatcher, along with American president George Bush and Soviet leader Mikhail Gorbachev, declare the end of the Cold War. 40 years after it started and finally, the Ford Escort is Britain's best-selling car for the eighth year running, managing more than 180,000 sales.

From a gaming point of view, 1989 was a momentous year to own one of the popular home computers but this had mostly been trimmed down to two or three systems. The Commodore 64, the Sinclair Spectrum and then the Amstrad CPC. Atari and Acorn were still selling but the strong software support that they had once enjoyed had generally ended by now, only certain big price games, movie licences or budget games come to the rescue. Practically all other machines were abandoned.

Arcade hit APB would appear on the C64 and ZX Spectrum and Amstrad PC. Arkanoid would make a surprise appearance on the Apple II and the TRS-80. Buffalo Bill would buck the trend and support computers that were almost completely forgotten like the Acorn Electron. It would also appear on the more obvious platforms like the C64, ZX Spectrum, Amstrad CPC.

The Acorn Electron would only see five commercial releases in 1989, Ballisitix, Buffalo Bills Wild West Show, Camelot, Perplexity and Superior soccer. The Apple II would have around 30 titles released. The MSX would have about 80 games. While the TRS-80 would have 4 releases, while these would be TRS-80 colour computer games and not the original TRS-80 version. The Atari 8-bit range would get a rather poor 4 releases, Adventures of Robbo, Kenny Dalglish soccer manager and Kick and finally Scapegoat by Level 9 computing.

The big software sales of the year would be on the Commodore 64 – 186 titles, with 166 on the ZX Spectrum 48/128k and 153 on the Amstrad CPC. These 3 home computers would be the last of the big 8-bit computers that made serious money in the UK, these numbers are estimated as they do not include mail order or special offers or multi pack games.

The once prolific developers slowly either died away or moved to other platforms. Activision for example only released 2 games for the 8-bit systems and that was Predator on the NES, Shanghai 2 on the MSX. The Bitmap Brothers would release Speedball on the C64 and then they moved to the 16 bits. Broderbund released Centarui Alliance and Lode Runner on the CPC and Apple II and C64. Cinemaware were almost completely on the 16-bits except for The Three Stooges on the NES and Defender of the crown for the C64. Codemasters bucked the trend with ten games on various 8 bits like the C64, CPC and the ZX Spectrum. Fantasy World Dizzy, Advanced Ski Simulator, Fast Food and Grand Prix Simulator. DMA designs of Grand Theft Auto fame created the shoot-em-up Menace on the C64. Epyx released a wealth of 'Games editions' of various platforms with Summer, Winter and World Games appearing on handhelds, 16 bits, consoles, and the CPC, ZX Spectrum and Commodore 64.

As the 8-bit world slowly declines, magazines, software and hardware manufacturers move to the 16-bit machines, leaving the 8-bit systems behind but it's not over yet; not quite. Commodore UK continue to push the Commodore 64 and with that push, Christmas sales are surprisingly good considering the onslaught of consoles.

There is plenty of life left in the older computers, Atari spend £2 million on a TV campaign which includes the XE. Bob Gledow of Atari say that it is money well spent. Atari currently have 67 game centres in the UK and hope to have 110 by next year.

Imagesource:
https://en.wikipedia.org/wiki/SAM_Coup%C3%A9#/media/File:SAM_Coup%C3%A9_(whit e_bg_and_shadow).jpg

SAM Coupé [lxxxvi]is an advanced 8-bit computer with ZX Spectrum compatibility but with more advanced features too. The Sam Coupé has many hardware and system designs which are more typical of a 16bit home computers.

- powerful BASIC dialect (like Spectrum's Beta BASIC)
- disk/net interface (based on Spectrum's Disciple/+D)
- huge memory expansion
- 6 channel sound, graphics modes and advanced colour palette
- extended (PC-like) keyboard and mouse.
- MIDI, parallel, serial connection

Sadly, the SAM Coupé came too late to market – launched at the peak of the Atari ST and Commodore Amiga, it was mostly compared to these 16bit machines. But it is purely an 8-bit computer only but a very complex one that is still somehow, compatible with the Spectrum 48k. To call the Coupé a 'Super Spectrum' is tantamount to blasphemy in SAM circles. It's a lazy phrase really, because only one of the computer's four video modes mimicked the idiosyncratic output of the Sinclair machine, thereby allowing the SAM to run Spectrum software (with a software emulator).

The SAM finally launched in 1989 when the Spectrum hardware was seven years old and really beginning to show its age. All Amstrad had done since acquiring Sinclair was bolt a tape player and disk drive onto the existing 128K model in a bid to prolong the machine's life. No actual improvement in processing power or graphics had been done. It had worked up to a point, yet some publishers were starting to talk about dropping 8-bit support and focusing on the 16-bit formats instead. Spectrum owners looking to upgrade were naturally drawn to the Commodore Amiga, Atari ST or a PC-compatible, so the idea of a powerful new computer in the same league as the 16-bits, yet still able to play all the old Speccy games, was pretty damn persuasive. It also guaranteed that plenty of positive SAM editorial appeared in the Sinclair magazines.

When designing the SAM hardware, Bruce Gordon was clearly influenced by the work and principles of his former employer. Like the ZX81 and Spectrum, the SAM's innards incorporated several off-the-shelf chips and a custom ASIC (Application Specific Integrated Circuit). This design helped reduce the chip count and drive down manufacturing costs, thereby enabling MGT to undercut the competition by a considerable margin.

Just as Sinclair Research had done with its computers, the SAM was to be launched in 'core' form, with the idea being that extra memory, storage solutions and other expansions could be bolted on as and when. "With the Coupé, your computer can grow with you," stated the advert.

"BATMAN is here![lxxxvii]

In the summer of 1989 one film captured the imagination of film goers and computer gamers across the world. Tim Burton's Batman would be a summer Blockbuster, starring Michael Keaton as Batman, Jack Nicolson as the Joker and Kim Bassinger as Vicky Vale.

The darkly atmospheric film captured the mood of Batman in true 80s style with an upbeat soundtrack by Prince and a video game by Ocean Software, it sounds simple, but Ocean would have to pay handsomely for the rights to the film. Games based on TV shows or Film were usually poor, didn't sell well and gave little back for the investment in the license but that didn't matter as the film studios cared little for video games. Batman would be different, as the film studios had noticed that Robocop sold by the millions – fortunately that was an Ocean game too and the head of Ocean was Gary Bracey, and he knew had to obtain a licence for a game.

Gary would ultimately pay $1 million dollars for the licence, the highest ever paid to date, so sure were Ocean that the game would sell that they paid for it. In return Ocean would have exclusive access to the filming and locations and the all-important licence.

Ocean would make a mini-game style that featured numerous but distinct levels.

The first level was the Axis Chemical plant, and this was a beautiful looking platform level with Batman fighting his way from one end to the other, before seeing the Joker fall into a vat of acid.

The second level was a traditional race section but with Batman throwing his Bat rope before turns in the road, this swings the Batmobile tightly around the sharp corner.

The third level was a puzzle level that was mostly disliked by players, but this involved Batman trying to work out which consumer products were poised by the Jokers Smilex.

The fourth level featured Batman flying the Batwing and cutting the balloon tethers that hold the poison filled balloons. Moving on the final level Batman climbs the Cathedral in an effort to shoot the Joker before he climbs to the top and escapes in a helicopter. You only have one shot at this!

Batman would go on to sell in huge numbers across all platforms.

Batman © Ocean Software 1989.

But. Ocean were in for a shock when David Pleasances' Commodore UK team approached Ocean Software and asked for exclusive distribution in an upcoming Amiga 500 pack. Mr Pleasance convinced Ocean to allow Commodore to solely include the game in the Amiga pack before allowing the game to be sold in retail. It is often said that David Pleasance and his teams Batman pack sold almost 200,000 Amiga 500s because of the included Batman game.

The end of an era and the inevitable end of the 8-bit computer. No manufacture could seriously release an 8-bit now unless it was with a super-fast CPU or with memory allowing megabytes of ram and thousands of colours on screen and then be cheap enough to undercut the likes of the 16-bits from Atari and Commodore.

With Consoles were now firmly established, and the 8-bit era was starting to fade but that's not to say that it was all over, far from it. Atari would continue to push the XE line and Commodore would push its C64 with some very creative games bundles into the 1990s and up until the doors closed at Commodore in April 1994. Commodore and Amstrad even tried making a console version of their aged computers. This was obviously a huge disappointment. The Atari ST continues its dominance, selling at £260 but the Amiga 500 has started to turn the tide in Commodore favour as the Amiga generates lots of press and starts to win the hearts and minds of artist and gamers alike. The Amiga 500 is currently on sale for £346.95. The Sega Master System is still on sale and sold by Virgin and the Nintendo NES is selling well but more slowly.

The Commodore 64 reaches new heights of programming power with the likes of Stunt car racer and Turbo outrun pushing the almost ten-year-old hardware further than ever before. The 8-bits have their final hurrah with some great games and hardware peripherals, some of the best-looking games that were available, were made at the end of the decade.

In rainy old England, there were two factors at play which slowed the rise of the console for just a little while longer. The first was the economic recession in the UK during 1991. This was caused by high interest rates and falling house prices as the Conservative Government lost control of the economy, Interest rates of 15% slowly reduced inflation but were critical in causing a collapse in house prices and lower consumer spending. This directly affected the public's interest in shiny new electronics. The UK economy shrank by 4.3% and there was a double-dip recession after a slight recovery at the end of 1991. This was unwelcome news for Japanese and American importers. The other problem for console makers was the dominance of the home computer scene. Atari and Commodore users were more likely to buy the new Atari ST or Commodore Amiga than a console. The only exception may have been the Gameboy from Nintendo as neither Atari nor Commodore offered a handheld system – yet.

Arguably, the other issue could have been the serious use of computers vs just gaming on a console. After all GEOS was available on the Commodore 64 and TAS word could be used on a ZX Spectrum or if you were writing your next Blockbuster then maybe the Amstrad PCW.

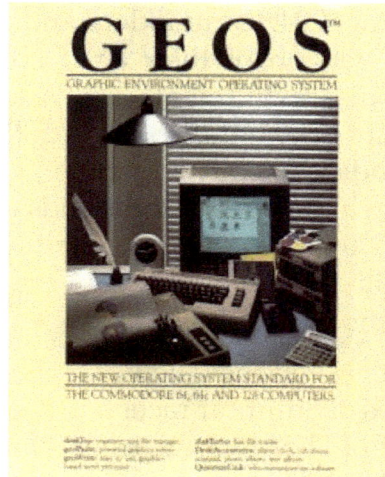

Chapter 14 - The School Playground

The school playground was a harsh place. Buying the wrong computer could result in ridicule that almost verged on the edge of bullying. Imagine buying an obsolete computer! What would your school friends say? Just because a computer sold well initially, it certainly did not mean that it was going to be hugely popular or that it would be well supported by software houses. No software equals no sales. The ZX81 sold over a million units until it was discontinued in 1984, does this mean it was popular? Probably yes but not by 1984 standards. However, in 1981 and 1982 it was extremely popular; but it was also very quickly abandoned as people didn't know what to do with it or it didn't do what people expected it to do.

It is almost impossible to launch a new computer and guarantee it to be a success, some companies thought they had the Midas touch and that anything they made would sell by the million, no matter how poor the product. Some of the biggest companies suffered from this in-built lunacy and some companies like Commodore suffered from this much more than others. A common ploy was to saturate the market with a computer, advertise it and then gradually lower the price. If it didn't sell, then the price would be cut and then cut again until units sold and new stock could be sold to retailers, but retailers would often refuse new stock of a cost cut unit as they could never believe the MRP, which often changed monthly causing them to lose money or at best break even.

Buying a computer on a whim or having mum and dad make a snap decision that is guided by the salesman at your local computer store could be a disaster.

Unfortunately, this is exactly how a vast number of computers were sold to the public, usually through a mix of ignorance and total uninterest. Imagine asking a salesman in 1983 or 1984 what the best computer was?

The world was your oyster, a multitude of poor performing, and obsolete computers littered the market then and most shops had a warehouse full of this unsellable rubbish that they were desperate to sell to the public and the salesmen got a commission on the sale too. It is difficult to show the overlap in sales as Commodore sold the VIC-20 from 1980 to 1984, with some shops having stock into 1985. For example, the Ti99/4a was still being sold, well into 1988 although only by mail order.

Home computer - estimated sales				
CBM 64K/ 128K 17-30 million*	MSX 9 million	APPLE II 4.8 million	AMSTRAD CPC 2.5 million	ZX SPECTRUM 48K / 128K 4+ million
TI99/4A 2.5+ million	TRS-80 2.4m	COMMODORE VIC-20 2+ million	ATARI 400/800 2 million	
BBC MICRO 1.5 million		ZX81 1.5 million		CBM C16/PLUS4 1 million
COLECO ADAM 250,000	ACORN ELECTRON 200,000	ORIC ONE 210,000	ORIC ATMOS 210,000	ENTERPRISE 80,000
ZX80 50.000	DRAGON 32/64 40,000*		Sam Coupe 20,000	AQUARIUS 20,000

*The Dragon 64 was still being sold in the USA up until the 2000s, long after the parent company had collapsed.

The Commodore 64/128k sales figures are taken from the Commodore bankruptcy auction sale provided by Commodore International to Mr David Pleasance (UK President Commodore UK) and include every version of the C64 and 128 hardware and its variations.

The school playground was a melting pot of different opinions, attitudes, and activities. The energetic kids played football and beat up the geeks, the more adult chased girls, and the geeky brigade, well we talked about computers, games, model making and TV shows and of course whose computer was the best and what grand plans our favourite companies had coming up in the next few months. Our knowledge came from computer magazines, we had nothing else. No internet or forums in which to discuss our topics, just magazines and they were notoriously bias in many articles.

For example, one magazine would seem to favour Commodore, another Sinclair or Amstrad and so on. Some would favour certain games companies or specific programmers and others would simply favour whichever company paid for the most advertising in that month's magazine. It was business, plain and simple or so it seemed.

Regardless of what computer was actually the best or had the most memory or even had the better graphics, ultimately all that mattered to the teenager at school; was what had the best games? And which games looked just like the arcade version of that game. In all honesty none did but we lived in hope.

Technical aspects of hardware mattered little as we didn't know what they meant, we thought we knew but we didn't. Some minor hardware information was particularly important, like how much RAM did it have and what was the sound like? how many channels of audio, how many colours? and possible how much did the games cost.

One conversation went like this...

How much RAM does your TI99/4A have?

72KB I said (it didn't but I'd read that in an advert from TI)

72KB ?? they said in astonishment...

Well, that 72KB is pah rubbish, its rubbish ram that is.

The Spectrum has a massive 48KB and that's better!

Someone said that the Commodore 64 had bigger RAM at 64!

…A lone BBC owner said they had 32KB and that it was still better than a Spectrum or a Commodore 64.

I could not argue – I didn't know what RAM was, I knew it was a kind of sheep and that computers had RAM, but some had memory as well, some even had ROM or ROMS. I was confused. I wondered off into the playground…Money or lack of money was an ever-present problem for the 1980s teen and for me especially so, we just did not have much but then neither did many of kids at school. I am sure they don't have much now but I'm certain it is a lot more than we had…

I distantly remember a few intense arguments and they went something like this…

Have you got Chuckie Egg?

Yes, I said, on the Spectrum.

Oh – he said.

Why, I asked? The Spectrum doesn't have real world physics like the BBC version, does it?

I don't know, I honestly replied.

Oh yeah, the Spectrum and C64 version is rubbish! the BBC is better, it's got real falling physics.

Now for those that do not know, and I was one of those poorly educated people in the eighties. The game Chuckie Egg by AnF Software is a simple but fun platform game. I.e. you climb and fall as if on a real platform. Well, it seems that Chuckie Egg had a 'fall-mechanism' for the player on screen, and the enemy birds too.

You see you play as Henhouse harry and your job is to collect eggs from the hen house without the hens pecking and killing you. As all standard hen houses had in the 80s, it was equipped with ladders, platforms and lifts that carried the player up and down various sections of the screen.

The 'fall-mechanic' that I was being told about was in fact a semi-real-world copy of gravity and the required physics to achieve this in mathematical form.

You see if the player happened to fall through a gap in the floor and brush the edge of another floor or obstacle, the player would ricochet at an angle in the opposite direction that they were originally falling and this would continue until you either landed safely on a solid floor and could continue or you fell in to a gap and died or hit an enemy hen and also died. It was a harsh and terrifying task, collecting eggs in the 1980s.

This game is possibly part of the reason Edwina Curry felt so strongly about eggs back then.

The game versions fall broadly into two groups - those with realistic physics (e.g., the BBC Micro and Amstrad CPC versions) and those without (e.g., the ZX Spectrum version and C64). Although there is a substantial difference in play between the two, levels remain largely the same and all the 8-bit versions have been accepted as classics.

To be honest the game, while being a good example of a platform game is hard to play and very unforgiving as pretty much 99% of games were in the 80s. This wasn't because we were hard core gamers back then, no it was often to hide that fact that many games were extremely short to play, often having half a dozen levels to play in total. So, ramping the skill level extremely high could mean that a game was played for years without the player ever reaching the later levels or ever reaching the last level at all.

For example, players often find climbing ladders extremely hard, spending inordinately lengthy periods of time stepping left and right at the foot of a ladder, trying to get Harry in just the right position to let him climb the ladder.

A simple trick is to run towards the ladder and hold the Up or Down key as Harry approaches and then Harry will immediately start climbing as soon as he reaches the edge of the ladder. It's a simple trick that took me a few hours to find all those years ago and after working that out I could often manage to get to level 3. I rarely progressed further that level 3 as it had moving platforms or lifts and jumping at the perfect time to land on one eluded the youthful me, it still does and yes, I still suck at Chuckie Egg.

They say nostalgia is a powerful emotion that generally leads to a disappointment. Computer games epitomise this hugely.

Sometimes it's better to fondly remember a game that it is to play it again, but I would say that is the not the case with Chuckie Egg, with its garish colours and beeping sound is just the same as you remember it. Great fun, go play it.

A problem happened with computers back in the 80s, you see you cannot upgrade them. No matter how much you want to, you cannot. The only exception to that rule was the 16KB (kilobyte) models of the ZX Spectrum which Sinclair would upgrade for you, or you could buy and solder in a little upgrade PCB or manually add ram chips and buffers or whatever it was needed. Later in life the C16 from Commodore and the C116, models could be upgraded to 64KB. A huge leap from the 16k fitted by the factory but this wasn't really a normal upgrade in the 80s. The Commodore C128 was the first home computer was ever advertised as being upgradable by the user.

So – RAM, what's the deal?

Well, the Commodore had 64KB, we know this as its written on the box and on the computer itself. However, no one, not one single person ever mentioned the fact that the C64 had only 38,911KB free of memory on the boot up! Turn the computer on and you are greeted with 38,911 BASIC bytes free. Why the Spectrum kids didn't jump all over this revelation I don't know! It didn't change the fact that the C64 did actually have 64KB, but it would been fun to argue because I'm sure that no one would have known why it only had 38,911KB free in BASIC mode.

Why did it only have 38,911KB free in BASIC? Well, it's simple really, yes, the computer had 64KB but 38,911KB is the normal value available in BASIC, since parts of the ram (in BASIC) is occupied by the BASIC rom, kernel, I/O logic, and screen memory.

But this is only a limit for BASIC programs, programs that are written partly or completely in machine language can access almost the entire 64K if they need to. A good example of this is the game, Planet X2 by David Murray (The 8-Bit Guy on YouTube). David manages to move code from the normal C64 memory layout to other areas giving him almost the full 64KB of RAM for his game code to run. Usually, a C64 game can only access something like 60KB as the absolute maximum as 4KB is needed for the computer at access I/O commands like the keyboard and such.

Let's get technical.

The Commodore 64 CPU is capable of addressing 65,536 bytes (locations from 0 to 65535 decimal) this is because the address bus is only 16 bits wide. The C64 has a 16-bit address bus which can have values from 0 to 65535 on it - that's 65536 unique addresses which we see written as 64KB. Each of those addresses' points to one byte (8 bits).

But the Commodore 64 has 64K RAM memory and a 20K ROM. It also has a special 4K I/O area where the chipset is addressed, (VIC-II, SID, CIAs) That adds up to 88K, so how is it possible for the Commodore 64 to address all of that memory?

As we all know, the 6510 CPU has a special I/O address line that allows you to select the memory configuration of the Commodore 64. This way, BASIC and or KERNAL ROMs can be swapped out and replaced with RAM for instance, freeing up 16K of RAM. So is 64KB readily available in BASIC? well no not really but even if it was, the BASIC on the Commodore 64 is so poorly developed that's its quite pointless to use for any sort of video game anyway.

The ZX Spectrum on the other hand had its own issues. It was only a 48KB machine and therefore greatly inferior to the Commodore 64. Well, that was how the school playground conversions went anyway, the other point of contention was the sound on the Spectrum, which was and still is quite dreadful, especially when compared to the C64. Let's not forget the colour clash, an avalanche of bleeding-coloured edges that the Sinclair Spectrum gave its users for free when it drew alternate colours on screen.

The Spectrum set aside 6912 Bytes of RAM to be used for a display file and an attribute array. The attribute array stores colour information for each character block, while this is an excellent space and RAM saving solution; it is slightly limiting for advanced graphics usage.

An absence of hardware sprites combined with the fact that Spectrum's display system was optimally designed to contain two colours per 8×8-character block, had ongoing problems for amateur games programmers, becoming known as 'Colour Clash'. This is when moving sprites with distinct colour information around the screen to an underlying character block, colours of either the character block or the sprite will be changed to match each other.

This led to what was technically known 'rubbish graphics' in kids' language. That is not to say the Spectrum had poor graphics, far from it.

The Spectrum had some great looking games and to my mind often a higher resolution or at least better drawn graphics than the Commodore 64 on many an occasion which used its medium resolution a little too often.

In my Texas Instruments days my friend had an Acorn Electron – more on this later but for a short period of time it was a big seller and seemed to have a promising future. This Sinclair killer from Acorn had both educational, technical and arcade type games aplenty. Compared to my Ti99/4a it was a whole new world, and I liked the games a lot. I cannot remember any particular game, except for Frak! if I'm honest, but they did have a very BBC Micro feel about them. For a brief period, I did want an Electron but on returning to school, I was reliably informed by the Spectrum crowd that the Electron was rubbish, and I better buy a Sinclair 48k. So, I did.

So what games were we playing and arguing about in the playground? Well, many but here are a few.

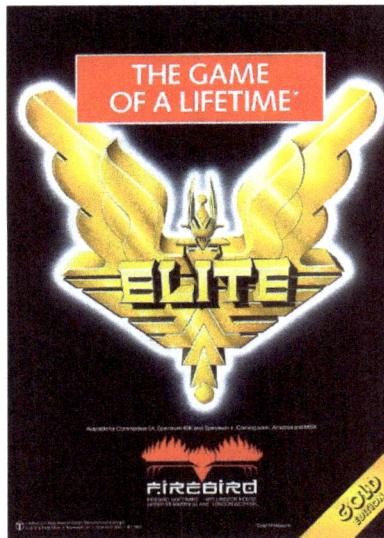

THE GAME OF A LIFETIME*

Elite.
Firebird Software
1985
BBC Micro, ZX Spectrum, C64, Amstrad, Amiga, ST and most computers ever made.

Elite (the space trading game) was another game that demanded argument. Was the fast wire frame graphics of the Spectrum smoother or the flicker bound C64 better? Which version slowed down, and which had the best sound? It was a tough call. Starting life on the BBC micro, Elite was converted for the Commodore 64 and ZX Spectrum after the initial BBC release and was much anticipated by the press of the day. Many other versions would follow for most popular computer systems.

Elite is famous of being piracy protected by the infamous and troublesome Lenslock protection device - a clever way of preventing piracy by supplying a plastic rectangle lens which is used to decrypt the access code letter for the game by placing the plastic device on your TV screen. In essence, after loading you need to look through the lens onto the screen in order to see the code letters which must be input before the program will work just as normal. Inputting the wrong code will force the computer to reboot!

Elite on the Amstrad CPC, ZX Spectrum and Commodore 64.

Elite sees you docked in a space station, with your trusty Cobra MKIII spaceship ready to trade, steal, help or hinder police forces across the galaxy. It is essentially up to you the player whether you are to trade goods, drugs or slaves. You can attack pirates or the police and raid other ships as you travel on your merry way. Your rating in the game will increase, the more successful you are. The ultimate goal is to become Elite, you start the game as Harmless.

The graphics are excellent and of a reasonable speed, and, unlike previous versions of Elite, they don't flicker. Remarkably the 48K Spectrum version had 5 missions compared to the rather low number of 2 of the C64 and BBC versions. Elite runs quite a bit more slowly on the Commodore 64, this is caused by a combination of the CPU - the BBC runs at a higher speed, and that vector graphics are harder to program on the 64, than say a

Sinclair Spectrum.

There are more than enough improvements to compensate. For a start, all known bugs in the BBC game (and there are plenty) have been eliminated, secondly, thanks to the 64's larger memory, the entire game is present in memory all the time, a considerable improvement on the BBC cassette version which had certain features cut down. More importantly the C64 version contains some new features: there are extra 'special missions' that can occur if you prove yourself worthy in battle.

Unique on the C64 version, are the Trumbles. These cute little furry guys will reproduce on your ship to fill the cargo bay and your ears with a cacophony of breeding squeaks. They could eventually stop you earning cargo and even start appearing on screen where the cute little bug-eyed bundles of fun may get in your way during a heavy battle or difficult docking. How you acquire them, and how you eventually get rid of them remain two of the universe's closely guarded secrets. Only C64 owners will know the answer to this!

Sitting in an art lesson in school, I asked a casual question. Does your C64 play music when the car drives in Spy Hunter? Yes, I thought they all did – of course it does, I was told.

This wasn't the answer that I was looking for. You see my spectrum version didn't play music, not a single note was uttered from Sinclair's rather cheap black box!

Spy Hunter is a conversion of the popular arcade driving and shooting game, played from an overhead point of view with a little red racing car zooming along a racetrack. The arcade game featured a big steering wheel in which to control the car but sadly this wasn't an option for the computer versions. I don't actually remember steering wheels being a thing for computers.

Your car is equipped with machine guns (James Bond style) to help you get past the numerous enemies out on the scrolling road Occasionally you will come across a weapons van, I'm not sure what triggered the van but it appeared randomly maybe, and if you drive into the back of the van your car becomes equipped with a second weapon such as smoke screen, oil slick, or missiles most of which I rarely used as you are too busy trying to smash the car in to the landscape. What do you mean it doesn't play music? That's the best bit -I was told. It starts when you drive into a weapons van. Your Spectrum is rubbish, why don't you get a C64? I have lots of games you can copy.

And so once again I was ridiculed for owning a Spectrum, I did love my Spectrum and the games were great but yes, the sound sucked big time.

We would spend copious amounts of our lunch time chatting about games and girls, games were easier to get to grips with by a long way. A vital part of our knowledge came from computer magazines of the era, and I would buy them whenever I was suitably lush with pocket money.

Between school yard debates and magazine articles we could mostly find the best games to buy although most of mine would be budget £1.99 or £2.99 games, with a few full priced games at birthdays, Christmas and so on. Full priced games hung around the mythical £9.99 sort of price, although a few big, boxed games on the top shelf seems to reach an unfathomable £12.99 or more. I never got any of those.

I had a conversation with the local computer shop employee in 1985, it went something like this. Me- "why are games so hard?"

Him- "It's because people complained, so they made them hard."

Me- "oh ok."

I never once questioned who this 'they' were or why they deemed games to be far too easy? I sucked at games; I still do but now I understand why. In truth there was no 'them' it was all a ploy to usually hide short or dull game mechanics.

It is after all much easier to make a 3-level game than a 20-level game and if the 3-level game is so hard that most people will never see level 3, then what's the point of making a 20-level game anyway? This was a simple ploy that budget games used extensively. Bigger budget games usually had multiple levels that were talked about at great length in advertising although most of us would never see the later levels in those either. Infiltrator is one such game.

In Infiltrator, you are Captain Johnny "Jimbo Baby" McGibbits, the Infiltrator of the titular title. Your mission, should you choose to accept it, is to complete three separate assignments, each comprised of a flight into enemy territory, a ground mission, and the flight out. As an Infiltrator, success will hinge on your ability to remain hidden from the enemy, sneaking in and out of hostile territory, fighting only when forced to.

Your attack helicopter is the Gizmo DHX-I Attack Chopper, nicknamed "The Snuff master" and before you hit the skies, you'll have to take a little time out to learn at least some of its capabilities.

Start by turning on the battery and initializing the computer system. Pressing I, starts your engine. Use the joystick to control movement, while the keyboard arms your various offensive and defensive weapons systems. Pressing the fire button on your joystick, launches your attack.

I distantly remember buying this game, I even remember the bus journey into town. I remember buying it and I remember sitting down on the bus – number 247 to Upton, I sat by the window, on the top row of a double decker bus. I was literally rolling about laughing as I read the manual for this game, you see it was the game that rocked America after all.

- For the sake of completeness here is a small snippet of the manual.

It had been only a few months ago that you, the one and only Johnny "Jimbo-baby" McGibbits, had flown your DHX-1 Attack Chopper fearlessly into enemy territory, infiltrated the diabolical Mad Leader's military installation, and spared the world from death, destruction, and despair. The evil mastermind, hell-bent on world take-over, had been utterly thwarted at your hands. You returned from your mission to a hero's welcome beyond anything even you--discoverer of the anti-starvation drug – Hungadin.

The manual continues in a similar vein for a quite some time, it is printed on a huge fold out piece of paper that contained mission brief, helicopter controls and such like. I knew this would be awesome.

Once the tears of laughter had subsided, I was almost home, the journey of about 40 minutes from town to home had passed by in a flash. Just a short walk later and I was home. Popping the cassette tape into my new Commodore 64 and waiting the obligatory 5,6 or 7 minutes for it to load...more if it was an annoying part loader. Load the music and pretty picture, load the menu, load the intro, and then load the first part of the game. This happened a lot in those days and a good twenty minutes could be spent watching the counter run up from 000 to whatever on the Commodore cassette player. Careful note had to be taken of the counter position in case of emergency reloads or error.

Anyway, back to the game, after loading the thing you sit inside a helicopter cockpit, press keys to turn the battery on, start the engine and elevate to a certain height before even beginning the mission.

Anyone of these operations carried out in the wrong order or at the wrong time will end the game as the helicopter falls from the sky and its game over. But the sound was good, and the graphics were great, it was all I needed to lord it over my Spectrum owning pals. They seemed unimpressed but I knew, I knew it was great.

The following Monday morning I went straight in to 'Infiltrator mode' have you played the new game; Infiltrator I asked? Nope was the answer, its brilliant said I. I then went into detail about the realistic graphics and sound, the funny manual and how it was the game that rocked America. In truth the game was impossibly hard, the controls were awful, and the game punished you for failure. It was standard fair for the 80s, none of this hand holding that gamers get these days. No help guide or rest area to hide in to regenerate your health in those days. It was hard. Extremely hard.

I found out later that the game didn't rock America at all, it was just an advertising slogan that meant absolutely nothing, I was more just a little disappointed. This is another game that had many playground conversations, have far have you got? did you manage to start the damn engines and take off? Did it load?

The last year of my high school life was filled with computer games, films we watched on VHS and girls we liked. It was a fun time to be alive. I left school in 1987 and conversations about games and computers would be put on hold but only for a brief time as college loomed. College would start at the same time as my 16-bit adventures and that would be life changing but I hung on to both my TI99/4a and my Commodore 64. Partly for nostalgia and partly because they were worthless in 1988. Thanks Jack.

Chapter 15 - Sales Figures

Where possible I have tried to collate sales figures, year by year. This has proved to be a difficult task to find definitive numbers. The following figures were taken from online archives, Your computer magazine and Wikipedia. Some home computer sales started in the UK in or around 1979, Atari and Apple arrived around then but Sinclair would appear in 1980 but there seem to be no reliable sales data. Most tables seem to be from 1981/1982, and it is here that we pick up the dates and sales figures.

Top selling global hardware in 1981/2 (thousands of units)

1	Atari 2600(VCS)	Atari	5,100,000
2	Game & Watch	Nintendo	4,600,000+
3	Coleco Arcade		3,000,000
4	Intellivision	Mattel	1,100,000
5	Timex Sinclair 1000		750,00
6	Atari 400 / Atari 800		600,000
7	C64 / VIC-20		600,000
8	TI-99/4 / TI-99/4A T.I.		600,000
9	ColecoVision		550,000
10	Nelsonic Game Watch		500,000

Top selling global hardware in 1983 (thousands of units)

1	Game & Watch	Nintendo	5,300,000
2	Atari 2600 (Atari VCS)		3,000,000
3	Commodore 64 (C64)		2,000,000
4	ColecoVision	Coleco	1,500,000
5	(Famicom / NES)	Nintendo	1,000,000+
6	IBM PC		850,000
7	Intellivision Mattel		750,000
8	Atari 400 / Atari 800		500,000
9	Apple II	Apple Inc.	420,000
10	NEC PC-88 / PC-98 NEC		360,000

Top selling global hardware 1984(thousands of units)

1	Famicom / NES)	2,940,000
2	Commodore 64 (C64)	2,500,000
3	IBM PC	2,000,000
4	TI-99/4A	1,000,000+
5	Apple II Apple Inc.	1,000,000
6	NEC PC-88 / PC-98 NEC	470,000
7	Apple Macintosh	370,000
8	MSX ASCII Corp.	350,000
9	Coleco Adam	255,000
10	Sega SG-1000	240,000

Top selling global hardware in 1985(thousands of units)

1	Famicom Nintendo	6,500,000
2	Commodore 64	1,500,000 to 2,500,000
3	IBM PC / IBM PC-JR	1,400,000
4	Atari 2600 Atari Console	1,000,00
5	Apple II	900,000
6	Commodore 128	500,000
7	NEC PC-88 / PC-98 NEC	430,000
8	ZX Spectrum	390,000
9	Sega (Master System)	280,000
10	Amstrad CPC / PCW	250,000+

Top selling global hardware in 1986 (thousands of units)

1	Nintendo Famicom	6,900,000+
2	Commodore 64 (C64)	2,500,000
3	Famicom Disk System	2,000,000
4	Commodore 128	1,000,000
5	Apple II	700,000
6	NEC PC-88 / PC-98 NEC	510,000+
7	Sega Master System	405,000+
8	Apple Macintosh	380,000
9	Amiga Commodore	200,000
10	Atari ST Atari Corp.	200,000

Top selling global hardware in 1987 (Thousands of units)

1	Nintendo Famicom	5,080,000+
2	Commodore 64 (C64)	1,500,000
3	Sega Master System Sega	935,000
4	IBM PS/2(Model 30/50)	658,000
5	PC Engine (TGrafx-16)NEC	600,000
6	Apple Macintosh	550,000
7	NEC PC-88 / PC-98 NEC	540,000+
8	Apple II	500,000
9	Atari ST	400,000
10	MSX ASCII Corp.	340,000+

Top selling global hardware in 1988 (Thousands of units)

1	Nintendo Entertainment System	8,590,000+
2	Master System	1,435,000+
3	Commodore 64 (C64)	1,250,000
4	IBM (IBM PC)	1,229,000+
5	Apple Macintosh	900,000
6	PC Engine (TGrafx-16)NEC	830,000
7	NEC PC-88 / PC-98 NEC	795,000+
8	Sega Mega Drive Sega	400,000
9	Amiga Commodore	400,000
10	Compaq PC Compaq	365,000+

Chapter 16 - What went wrong?

Sadly, a bright idea or a great concept may not be enough to make it a success. Often some wacky or even a brilliant idea but unfortunately at the wrong time will render the computer a commercial failure. Many poorly implemented products are successful today, not because the product is great but because of price or advertising. Apple told us that the Apple II was the biggest selling computer in the world. It wasn't and it never was.

Had the Enterprise 64 arrived a year earlier, had the Acorn Electron made its Christmas launch, had the Commodore plus4 been priced at £99 then things have been different. Had Clive Sinclair produced a ZX Spectrum that the public wanted rather than the QL or C5 electric trike then undoubtably Sinclair would have become a force to be reckoned with in 1986, but his passion was elsewhere.

Computers had become almost disposable in the late 1980s, only a handful of commercially successful machine were still on sale by 1989. The Commodore 64 and 128. The Spectrum +2/3 and machines made by Amstrad and bringing up the rear were Atari and Acorns BBC Micro. Many other manufacturers were completely ignored by retailers. By now the 16-bit machines were on sale and prices were falling fast

Should you walk into a computer shop or WHSmith for example, you would be greeted with a display of Spectrum, Commodore 64, and Amstrad software neatly displayed on shelves.

In the corner you may find BBC Micro / Electron and possibly an MSX game or two. You would be unlikely to find any TI99, ORIC, Enterprise or Sam Coupe titles. What is worse? To be late, to provide a poor product or to try and add as much as possible to make something amazing? A cautionary tale would be that of the Acorn Electron, the ORIC and many others but did companies heed this and take note? Possibly and possibly not. Advanced systems are always going to be troublesome.

SAM Coupé is an advanced 8-bit computer that has a compatibility mode for the popular Sinclair ZX Spectrum 48K and later 128K. Advanced graphic modes, colours and sound make the SAM Coupe more of a Super Spectrum than just a spectrum copy, or clone. In some ways the SAM had many features of the advanced 16BIT computers that Commodore and Atari would launch in 1985.

MGT gave constant and ever moving release dates for the SAM, eventually being released in April 1989 for the retail price of £149.95 (inc. VAT) the SAM Coupé was launched in the last quarter of 1989 by MGT just in time for Christmas. MGT was already known in the ZX Spectrum world for a range of hardware that they sold. The SAM was their pride and joy, and unfortunately to be their downfall.

The SAM name comes from a working name in the early design phases of 'Some Amazing Machine' (or 'Some Amazing Micro' or even 'Spectrum Advanced Machine' depending on who you talk to). The 'Coupé' was a nickname from two sources: one being an ice cream sundae called the "Ice Cream Coupé" and the other because the machine resembles a fastback car in profile with the feet as the wheels. The Prototype and production PCB is marked 'M.G.T. Plc Coupé'.

The case design of the SAM Coupé was produced by the Nick Holland Design Limited in Cardiff with the keys set back from the edge of the casing to provide a support for the wrists.

This was the era when the 16-bit machines, the Atari ST and the Amiga, were really starting to take off. Sales in computers such as the Spectrum were in rapid decline.

The Sam was aimed to fill this gap, as a powerful 8-bit machine with specifications that often outperformed those of the 16-bit machines, but at an 8-bit price. It was hoped that current 8-bit owners, particularly Spectrum owners, would jump on the nicely priced Sam rather than a more expensive 16-bit machine. Software companies, such as US Gold, threw around comments like the now infamous "Strider in 2 weeks" quote - "If, as with Strider, we've already produced a game across all common formats, all we have to do is simply take the code from the Speccy version and the graphics from the ST and sort of mix them together. This should take one bloke around two weeks at most." - needless to say, Strider never appeared on the Sam. Unfortunately, the Sam arrived too late. Some initial problems, and a lack of software meant that the interest just never took off. Some commercial games were initially converted, but the poor sales were enough to put most companies off. The bulk of Sam's software catalogue comes from small companies, set up specifically to support the Sam. Although these managed to gain some impressive licenses, such as Prince of Persia and Lemmings, it just wasn't enough.

MGT, finally went bankrupt, Alan Miles and Bruce Gordon then set up a new company called SamCo to continue producing Sam software and Bruce starting a separate venture SamTek to produce new hardware. Some magazines started giving the Sam negative press. SamCo struggled on for 2 years, and just as things were starting to look hopeful, they too went in liquidation with SamTek following shortly after.

West Coast Computers briefly appeared as a potential savior of the company, presenting ambitious plans for its future. However, after a period of relative silence, the company's fortunes declined. According to David Ledbury, approximately 12,000 Sam's were sold worldwide.

- Dragon 32

Dragon Data Ltd was a Welsh manufacturer of home computers during the early 1980s. These computers, the Dragon 32 and Dragon 64, exhibited a striking resemblance to the Tandy TRS-80 Colour Computer ("CoCo"), both of which adhered to a standardised Motorola datasheet configuration.The trajectory of Dragon Data Ltd during the period 1982–84 was marked by a series of ups and downs. Initially established by the Toy Company, Mettoy, the company experienced promising sales and appeared poised for a successful future.

At its peak, Dragon Data Ltd. engaged in negotiations with Tano to establish a North American branch. However, financial difficulties subsequently arose, casting a shadow over the company's future before it was spun off as a separate entity. Several factors contributed to this decline, including the delay in introducing the 64K model, inadequate colour support with a maximum of four colours displayable in "graphics mode" and only two colours in the highest 256 x 192-pixel mode, the late introduction of the external disk unit and the supporting OS-9 based software. These circumstances resulted in a loss of market share for Dragon Data Ltd.

In response to this challenge, under the guidance of GEC, Dragon Data Ltd. commenced the development of the next generation of Dragon computers, collectively known as Project Alpha (or Dragon Professional) and later, Project Beta. These systems progressed to the prototype stage prior to the company's receivership and subsequent acquisition by the Spanish startup Eurohard SA in 1984. Regrettably, Eurohard also encountered financial difficulties and subsequently entered receivership a few years later.

Mettoy Director Tony Clarke commissioned PA Technology Centre, Cambridge to construct a new microcomputer, leading to the formation of a new division within Mettoy. *(Source: Popular Computing Weekly - July 1982)*

October 1981

Ian Thomson Bell at the PAT Centre, Cambridge designs the prototype of the Dragon as part of project SAM. *(Source: Popular Computing Weekly - August 1982)*

"We chose Microsoft BASIC because the timescale dictated an off-the-shelf interpreter. The 6809 chip was selected because it is the best 8-bit processor. As far as the CPU is concerned, the design was relatively straightforward. With the 8-bit, the SAM chip and the 6847 you have virtually a home computer in three chips. The difficult parts of the design were the Microsoft driver and the video conversion."

The Microsoft driver was developed by Duncan Smeed at the University of Strathclyde. "When Duncan brought it down," Ian remarked, "we attempted to ascertain the reason for its comparatively slow performance. After all, the 6809 is a highly efficient chip. We examined the Tandy TRS-80, which also utilises the same chip, and discovered that it exhibited similar slowness. Initially, we designed a for/Next loop from 1 to 1000, which took two seconds to execute. Initially, we believed that the Microsoft BASIC was somehow cross assembled from the Z80 BASIC. Subsequently, we hypothesised that the internal clock might be the issue. However, neither of these explanations proved to be accurate. We subsequently analysed the time spent scanning the keyboard. Of the 2ms allocated in each iteration of the loop, 0.7ms was dedicated to checking whether any key strike, such as Break, had been registered. We approached this problem as a logical issue rather than scanning each key sequentially. Instead, we designed it to ascertain whether any key had been depressed. This modification significantly enhanced the software's performance, which is why the Dragon is so efficient.

Several (at least 20) 16K prototypes were built manually and used cases made from dental material - these were sent out to reviewers and developers. All the prototypes of "Pippin" and indeed the initial production run of 10,000 dragons were built as 16K machines as the decision to move to 32K came too late to change the initial production run. As a result, all 10,000 dragons in the 1st production run had to have a 16K "Piggy-Back" board added at the factory to bring them up to 32K. The decision to move from 16K to 32K was reportedly due to Sinclair launching both the 16K and 48K ZX Spectrum in April of 1982.

The Dragon 32 goes into full production with RACE Electronics assembling the circuit boards, Mettoy using their existing suite of 200 plastic injection moulding machines to make the cases and Dragon Data Ltd. The Dragon 32 is released at a retail price of £199.50 and a production capacity of between 30,000 and 35,000 machines for the rest of this year but Mettoy appear seem to be in some financial trouble.

Already the company is in financial difficulty and Managing Director, Mr. Tony Clarke, persuades financial institutions into a re-finance of Dragon Data. This left Mettoy with only a 15.5% shareholding after the Welsh Development Agency bought 23% and Pru-tech (Prudential Insurance) the largest holding with 42%. With new money being ploughed in, Dragon Data would be able to contract out work (to Race Electronics who also manufactured BBC computers for Acorn), enabling them to build up the production rate to come closer to meeting the high demand for their product.

As part of the finance deal with the Welsh Development Agency, Dragon Data would prepare to move to a larger factory with increased manufacturing capacity compared to the current site within Mettoy - this being the infamous factory at Kenfig near Port Talbot.

The move to the new premises was complete and 5,000 Dragons rolled off the production line every week, and this was to be increased to 10,000 units - Dragon Data believing that sales would continue strongly during the summer as they had on the run-up to Christmas. Although extra capacity did allow Dragon Data to extend its range, and a formidable hardware expansion was planned for the rest of '83.

By mid-1983 40,000 Dragon 32s had been sold, Dragon Data had become the largest privately owned company in Wales and high-street shops were queuing up to stock the popular machine; Dixons, Comet and Spectrum joining Boots as a Dragon retailer though the stationers like WH Smith and John Menzies both refused to stock the machines, stating that they had enough ZX Spectrums, Commodore 64s and ORICs already in stock.

But then suddenly an announcement is made and the promised disc drive, OS-9 operating system, and the Dragon 64 will be delayed.

Another announcement is made soon after, saying that the Dragon 32 would be launched in the US that year, and after discussion with three interested American companies it would be manufactured in the US for economic reasons as a joint venture with the chosen US company. By choosing a U.S manufacturer it became a lot easier to expand but would the Dragon affect Tandy colour computer (CoCo) sales? Tandy denied claims that they were planning legal action against Dragon Data (for its similarity of the 32 and the Colour Computer).

In 1983 a 64K upgrade board for the Dragon 32 became a main board swap at an increased cost of £75, the board also being used in the newly announced Dragon 64 which was to be priced at £250-300 but with extras such as an RS232 interface included.

June 1983

Dragon Data were now offering a mainboard swap for the 32K system to upgrade it to the full 64K upgrade but this would now be a full Dragon 64 main board with RS232 interface and second BASIC ROM onboard, service agents would also change the bottom half of the 32's moulding (adding an extra hole), at a total cost of £100 for the upgrade; the Dragon 64 was now expected to cost less than £275.

In August 1983, the Dragon 64 was launched on the 26th with a retail price of $399 in the United States and £225 in the United Kingdom, where it could be purchased from early September.

September 1983

Tano's production of the Dragon commenced. The optimistic expectation that sales would persist through the spring and summer at the same level as during the Christmas period proved to be highly unrealistic. Consequently, it was unsurprising that industry analysts were consulted when the shareholders requested the resignation of Managing Director Tony Clarke. It was reported to the press that he had previously communicated to the board his intention to resign for personal reasons.

The shareholders asked GEC (the largest electrical company in the UK) to provide a senior executive to become the new chief executive of Dragon Data on "temporary secondment".

Tano's production facility was around 48,000 square feet in the new plant where the Dragon was to be built. Rumours of a Dragon 128 are heard for the first time and possibly featuring dual 6809 processors, a numeric keypad, 128K ram and OS9 selectable ROMS.

However low sales and looming financial problems were on the horizon.

Could this be the end of the Dragon?

- Tangerine ORIC

The ORIC was conceived by John Tullis while he had been employed as a financial consultant at Tangerine. He came up with the idea for a home micro and decided they would have to develop a machine at the very low-cost end of the market. Cleverly sticking with the 6502 processor because it is the world's best-selling chip. The ULA went completely to plan, and they had the first ORIC working in August, using TTL emulators instead of the finished gate arrays. It worked first time! With the success of the Sinclair ZX Spectrum, Tangerine's financial backers had suggested a home computer and Tangerine formed ORIC Products International Ltd to develop and release the ORIC-1 in 1983. The ORIC is rumoured to be named after the computer, Orac from the BBC science-fiction series Blakes7. According to the December 1982 edition of Practical Computing magazine anyway but does anyone remember Blakes7?

The ORIC-1 improved over the Spectrums hardware with a solid chiclet keyboard design an improvement over the Spectrum's renowned "dead flesh" one. In addition, the ORIC had a true sound chip, the programmable GI 8912, and two graphical modes handled by a semi-custom ASIC (ULA) which also managed the interface between the processor and memory.

Like the Spectrum, the ORIC-1 suffered from attribute clash — albeit to a lesser degree in HIRES mode, when a single row of pixels could be coloured differently from the one below in contrast to the Spectrum, which applied foreground and background colour in 8 x 8-pixel blocks.

As it was meant for the home market, it had a built-in television RF modulator as well as RGB output and works with a home audio tape recorder to save and load data. According to ORIC, about 160,000 ORIC-1's sold in the UK.

On the 27th of January 1983 ORIC Products International Ltd. held the official launch party for the ORIC-1 computer. It took place at their headquarters at Coworth Park Mansion, Sunninghill, near Ascot, England. Peter Harding, the Sales Director, announced six major deals with High Street stores for the supply of over 200,000 units, and added "We're going to beat Clive Sinclair by offering much more for much less money".

The ORIC-1 was announced in the August/September 1982 edition of the Tansoft Gazette, which included a priority voucher valid until the 1st of November. ORIC International was launched with £1250 of capital. The name, incidentally, was an anagram of the last four letters of 'micro', and had nothing to do with Aurac, the computer in the contemporary television series 'Blake's Seven' as many people thought at time.

The shareholding was split five ways between the directors, who were:

- Managing director - John Tullis
- Sales director - Peter Harding
- BCA financial director - Ted Plumridge
- Tangerine directors - Paul Johnson and Barry Muncaster

The backer was British Car Auctions, thanks to the friendship between John Tullis and BCA managing director and chairman David Wickens. Tangerine ceased trading and Tansoft was formed with Paul Kaufman as Managing Director.

A 16k ORIC would have cost you £129, a 48k £169.95. A modem priced at £79.95 was also announced.

First into print with a review of the new machine was Popular Computing Weekly on the 13th of January 1983. Headlined (appropriately for those times) "ORIC-1 - not just a Tangerine dream", it advertised as the first colour micro to cost less than £100. That was the 16k version, of course. The Centronics printer port was "unusual, even unique, for a machine at this price". The early temporary manual was criticised, as was the lack of a program editor in the review machine.

Perhaps the most sensible conclusion was reached in the What Micro? review of February,1983.

"The ORIC is sound, simple to get along with and offers great expansion potential. It's not an earth-shattering novelty but is very good value indeed". The launch was not to be without its problems. Personal Computer World printed a full bench test in its April 1983 edition: "The appearance of the ORIC-1 has demonstrated once again the almost comical inability of British micro manufacturers to launch a new machine properly. Funded by British Car Auctions and utilising the considerable experience of Tangerine Computers, the ORIC is aimed at the fastest growing sector of the micro market - the sub-£200 home computer.

The delivery difficulties that dogged both the BBC and the Sinclair Spectrum should have alerted ORIC to the pitfalls ahead, but the new company observed their rivals' mistakes, then promptly went out and repeated them. Adverts inviting customers to send off their cheques began appearing in October. 30,000 orders were received in the first two months and ORIC was confident that large numbers would be delivered in time for Christmas. But delivery of ROM chips was delayed, and it became apparent that ORIC's deadlines were hopelessly optimistic... It's unfortunate that ORIC should have set about marketing its product in this unprofessional and slapdash way - it can do the company's reputation no good and, what is worse, it's liable to be reflected in the consumer developing a distrust of the computer that it really does not deserve."

The ORIC-1 was almost immediately exported to France, a country which was to prove a very successful market. "In 1981 we looked for a French product to distribute, without success. So, we looked in Great Britain, a country that was becoming an example to Europe. We spent 6 months analysing products there, and in August 1982 we started talking with ORIC."

"The proposed quality, technical standards and performance of their machine impressed us. The company's manufacturing, financial and marketing plans were well thought out. They envisaged producing 50 to 60,000 machines in the year to the 30th of June 1983, but in fact the total was 130,000." To match or even beat Sinclair, the ORIC was slashed in price to £99.95 for the 16k model, and £139.95 for the 48k this included a £40 printer voucher. The reality was that sales had just not happened as predicted, and they were now clogging the shelves of both dealers and ORIC themselves.

Significantly, shops like Rumbelows were advertising the VIC

284

20, Commodore 64, Texas TI994A and Spectrum to a buoyant market, but few retailers were pushing the ORIC.

ORIC were now in financial trouble. It was at this point that Edenspring Investments stepped in with a proposed cash injection of £2.25 million, with a commitment of up to £5.85 million - on condition that ORIC achieved pre-tax profits of £2 million for the two years ending June 30th, 1985.

"Sales are expected to reach 350,000 in the first year, a 600% increase on initial projections. ORIC exports in large quantities to France and other European countries and has recently set up joint ventures in Japan and Singapore to cover the Asian and Australasian markets."

In October, the ORIC-1 won the Best Home Computer Award in France and was the top-selling computer there but not in the UK. Software was being written, produced, and sold in France and the ORIC was the Sinclair Spectrum of France. Unfortunately, though, the French were not buying the enormous numbers of computers that were being sold in the English market.

In Home Computer Weekly magazine (11th October 1983) there was a hint of what was to come:

"ORIC is planning changes to its computer to add new BASIC commands and improve reliability. Barry Muncaster would only say no decision had been made on when or whether to introduce it. He did say that two or three software houses had seen samples because ORIC were endeavouring to ensure that existing software would not be affected.

ORIC sales boss Peter Harding said that the company would be launching a new computer in late spring. He said, "It's going to be the Electron and Commodore 64 beater!"

On the 13th of October 1983, the ORICs factory (Kenure Plastics) in Berkshire, where the ORIC-1 was manufactured was burnt to the ground in a suspected arson attack. The factory was rebuilt but huge stocks of parts had been lost (including 15,000 ROMs) that went to make up the ORIC-1. Amazingly production was restarted within 24 hours in a new factory. However, a neighbouring warehouse also went up in flames soon after. Police suspect that the arsonist got the wrong building first time around...

At a shareholder meeting on Friday, 18th November 1983 Edenspring approved the acquisition of ORIC for shares. The net effect was that the ORIC shareholders (John Tullis, Barry Muncaster, Peter Harding, Paul Johnson, British Car Auctions, and IEM Singapore) exchanged their shares for shares in Edenspring, who in return made up to £4 million available to fund expansion.

From its take-over by Edenspring Investments plc and subsequent Over the Counter (OTC) sales of shares, ORIC Products International Ltd has raised approximately £4 million in working capital to fund expansion and product diversification. After just ten months' trading to October 1983, the company has shipped 120,000 of its ORIC-1 8-bit 16K and 48K microcomputers and is looking at a first-year turnover more than £10 million: putting ORIC in the top league of British home computer makers. In addition to sustaining growth in the volatile home computer market.

The Atmos was a British designed and built machine and was the successor to the ORIC 1. Released in 1984, the Atmos had major improvements over the ORIC 1 like adding a true keyboard and smart new case, also installing an updated V1.1 ROM to the motherboard of the ORIC, which had some unfortunate bugs in its code. Otherwise, the machine is identical to the 48K version of the ORIC 1.

Soon after the Atmos was released, a modem, printer, and 3-inch floppy disk drive originally promised for the ORIC-1 were announced and released by the end of 1984. Unfortunately, the Atmos was no more reliable that the original machine. A voltage regulator that got extremely hot, and despite getting a new heat sink, it was not enough to stop it from failing. A buggy ROM and it still had problems loading from cassette.

It failed to turn around the fortunes of the brand, with stiff competition from Sinclair and Commodore, plus the new Amstrad CPC and the lack of software, meant that interest was fading fast.

Despite the hardware problems, the machine did sell reasonably well initially, especially in the Netherlands, but it was not enough to stop the parent company of ORIC international Eden Spring being sold to the French Company Eureka. The company would develop but not release the ORIC Stratos.

- MSX

MSX is a standardized home computer architecture, announced by Microsoft and ASCII Corporation on June 16, 1983. It was initially conceived by Microsoft as a product for the Eastern sector, and jointly marketed by Kazuhiko Nishi, then vice-president at Microsoft. Microsoft and Nishi conceived the project as an attempt to create unified standards among various home computing system manufacturers of the period, allowing the same software to run on various computers from different manufacturers.

MSX systems were popular in Japan and several other countries. Eventually, 9 million MSX units were sold worldwide, including 7 million in Japan alone but they never made much of an impact in the UK or USA for one reason and that was Commodore. Jack Tramiel had warned his inner circle that the Japanese were coming in early 1983 and it was Commodore's job to stop them and by that he meant simply by controlling the market price with the Vic-20 and Commodore 64.

Jack Tramiel knew that Japanese computers would be initially expensive to import into the US and if Commodore could control the higher and lower end of the market then there would be less of an opportunity for the MSX to sell. Despite Microsoft's involvement, few MSX-based machines were released in the United States. The very first commercial MSX for the public was a Mitsubishi ML-8000, released on October 21, 1983, thus marking its official "release date".

The meaning of the acronym MSX remains a matter of debate. In 2001, Kazuhiko Nishi recalled that many assumed that it was derived from "Microsoft Extended", referring to the built-in Microsoft Extended BASIC (MSX BASIC).

Others believed that it stood for "Matsushita-Sony". Nishi said that the team's original definition was "Machines with Software eXchangeability. Before the success of Nintendo's Family Computer, MSX was the platform for which major Japanese game studios such as Konami and Hudson Soft produced video games. The Metal Gear series, for example, was first written for MSX hardware.

Metal Gear is a stealth action game designed by Hideo Kojima who more famously went on to develop Metal Gear Solid on the first PlayStation. Metal Gear was developed and first published by Konami in 1987 for the MSX2 home computer and revolves around a special forces operative codenamed Solid Snake who carries out a one-man covert mission into hostile territory to destroy Metal Gear, a bipedal walking tank capable of launching nuclear missiles from anywhere in the world.

The game itself is top-down walk, search and shoot type game in a similar style to Commando but with far more puzzles to solve and missions often involve sneaking past enemy soldiers rather than engaging in combat. Metal Gear isn't the only good game on the MSX system, far from it but it is perhaps the most famous.

The MSX range spawned four generations of computers. The first three, MSX (1983), MSX2 (1985), and MSX2+ (1988), were all 8-bit computers based on the Z80 microprocessor. The MSX2+ was exclusively released in Japan as by then Japan was the main market.

In comparison with rival 8-bit computers, the Commodore 64 is estimated to have sold 17-30 million units worldwide, the Apple II sold around 6 million units, the ZX Spectrum over 5 million units, the Atari 8-bit sold at least 4 million units, the Amstrad CPC sold 3 million units, and the Tandy TRS-80 Model 1 sold 250,000 – 500,000 units.

These figures are estimated and are from various sources and are probably also wrong, but they are just a guide. We will never know the exact figures.

Manufactures did not publish exact sales figures or if they did then they were often embellished in an effort to show a larger user base. Apple is the perfect example of this, according to Apple they had the largest selling computer in 1978/79 but in truth they were way behind Tandy in sales (USA)

Sinclair were the biggest seller in the UK with its ZX80/81 and Spectrum until the mid 1980s when the Commodore 64 finally caught up and achieved global dominance of the home computer market here in the UK and the USA but this would be short lived as by 1987/8 the 8-bit market was already showing signs of regression as the 16-bit computers were becoming popular.

Chapter 17 - Games!

No matter how much you told your parents that computers were for school or college, we all knew that they were for games. Perhaps you might try programming in BASIC or some other language, you might even keep a list of your cassette tapes on a database, but it was always games for most people.

Even after the collapse of the American video game market in 1983, caused by the sheer amount of poor-quality software available on the Atari 2600 VCS, the video game industry was still worth an estimated $400 million dollars*. While the UK and Europe were much less affected by the disastrous failure of the American market it did have an impact here in the UK. Manufacturers disappeared, advertised games never appeared and new hardware cancelled as people thought that maybe, the craze of video games was over. Lasting from late 1983 until 1985, the video game crash shook a then-booming video game industry and led to the bankruptcy of several high-profile companies producing home computers and game consoles. It would take Nintendo to recover the situation and prove that games could sell and make money but here in the UK we suffered much less. The impact was mainly felt by those trying and failing to expand into the USA or home-grown American companies withdrawing from the market completely. This allowed homemade systems to expand into the void left by such companies as Texas Instruments, Mattel and others but other companies also saw an opportunity to capture more market share, like Commodore and Atari.

However, software in the UK never seemed to suffer from the chaos of the USA. This primarily because the UK had a large software base at that time, with our own developers and publishers who did not venture in to or rely on the USA at all.

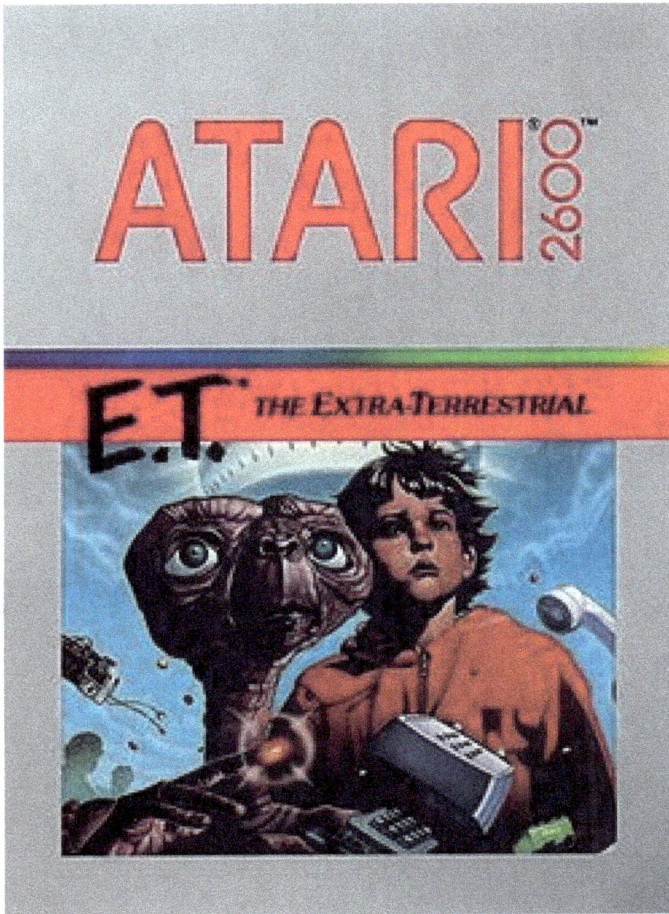

If one game encapsulates the whole sorry saga of the American games crash, it is probably ET from Atari. Written by Howard Scott Warshaw in just five weeks or so as Atari wanted the game released before Christmas 1982 to maximise profits.

The result was a game that was rushed and played poorly, was it the worst game ever made? Well of course not, nor was it the cause of the 1983 American games crash but these lofty titles have been bestowed upon it. Was it a bad game? Well, yes, awful and Howard Scott Warshaw even alludes to that in various interviews.

THE FUTURE OF LAW ENFORCEMENT HAS ARRIVED.

Detroit has seen better days. A gang of ruthless hoods has overrun the city, and crime is out of control. Attacks on the streets. Drug trafficking. Corruption and cop killing. It's so bad a private firm, O.C.P., now runs the police department.

As RoboCop, your job is simple—clean up the city. Armed with a heavy-duty arsenal of weapons, including

RoboCop's Special Issue Auto-9, make your way past street thugs, the notorious Clarence Boddicker and the powerful ED-209 to your final battle with Dick Jones.

Serving the public trust, upholding the law, and protecting the innocent was never so challenging, never so dangerous, and never so much fun as this.

With great graphics and great game action, the future of law enforcement is *ROBOCOP.* From Data East.

Now available for Commodore 64. Coming soon on IBM Amiga and Atari ST personal computers.

Data East USA Inc., 470 Needles Drive, San Jose, CA 95112 (408) 286-7074

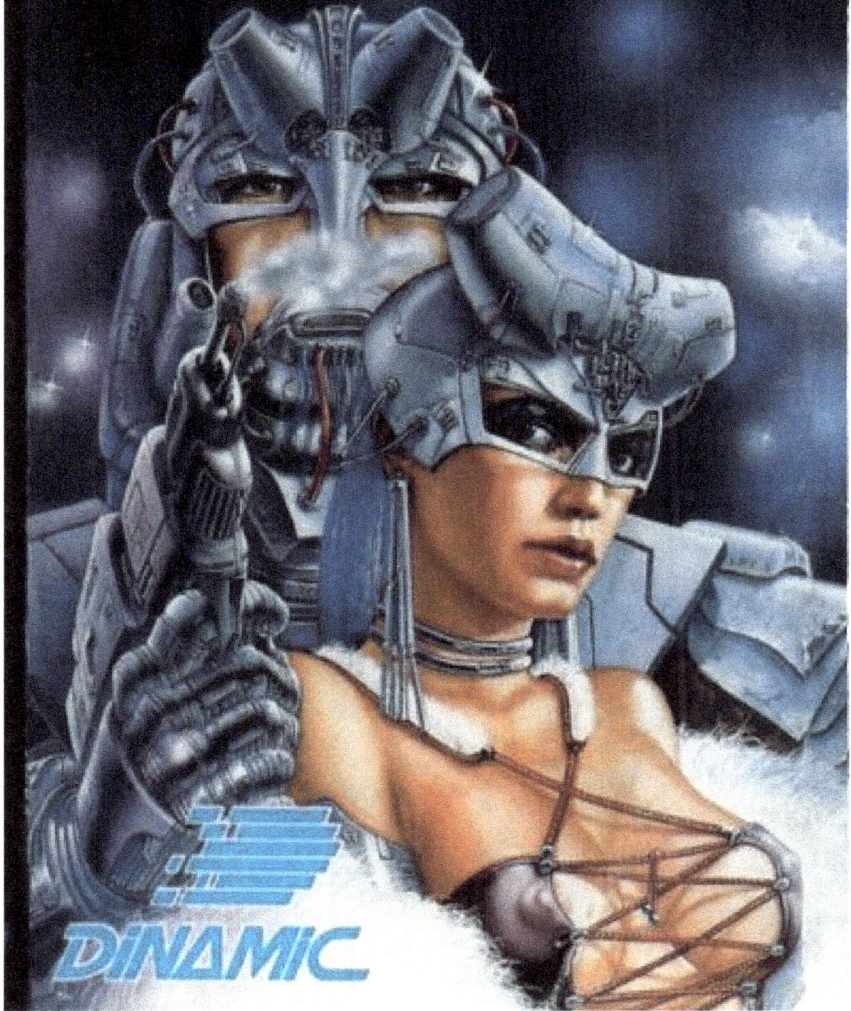

Raid Over Moscow – US GOLD

The Wild Bunch – Firebird

Kikstart by Mastertronic

My dear friend John has some recollections.

I was recently pondering the games I own over many platforms, either in Digital or physical form and it occurred to me that I have only ever twice owned more than one version of the same game, just so I could play it on another platform. The first time I owned two versions of the same game would be "The Black Crystal" for the ZX81 and ZX Spectrum but it wouldn't be until the best part of 40 years later that I would do it again with "The last of us" for the Sony PlayStation 3 and 4.

Looking back over my relationship with games and the computers and consoles I played them on over the last 40 years, this is quite a statement, I think! Let me explain…

I'm fortunate enough to have come into the world in 1971, so by the time I was 11 or 12, home computing and gaming was in its infancy, which means I have first-hand experience of Space Invaders, Pac Man and Galaxian arcade machines when they were new and shiny when they arrived in my particular part of North Clydebank in the old freezer room of the local grocer, but more than that, the pinnacle of my imagination and dreams would be a home computer that could play these types of games on, in my own space and safety from the punk loonies that would bully us just for being in the vicinity of those Arcade machines, even if we could afford to play them (which more often than not we couldn't and were most of the time merely enthusiastic supporters of the older kids who could afford to play them). It would be at this point that Sinclair would release the ZX81 and my parents managed to get one for me for Christmas 1981, just before I would start High School the following summer.

The ZX81 was a comparatively cheap computer but was still a stretch for us as a family to afford one just for me, given I had three other siblings, but my mum (since my dad left those things to her) managed to swing it anyway. It was the most amazing thing I ever experienced in my young life and I've yet to experience something akin to that initial emotion at receiving such a thing. I still remember the smell of that machine as I unboxed it and the amazement of my dad that I could connect it myself to our rented TV and make it work by tuning it in. These things were all quite exceptional back in the day.

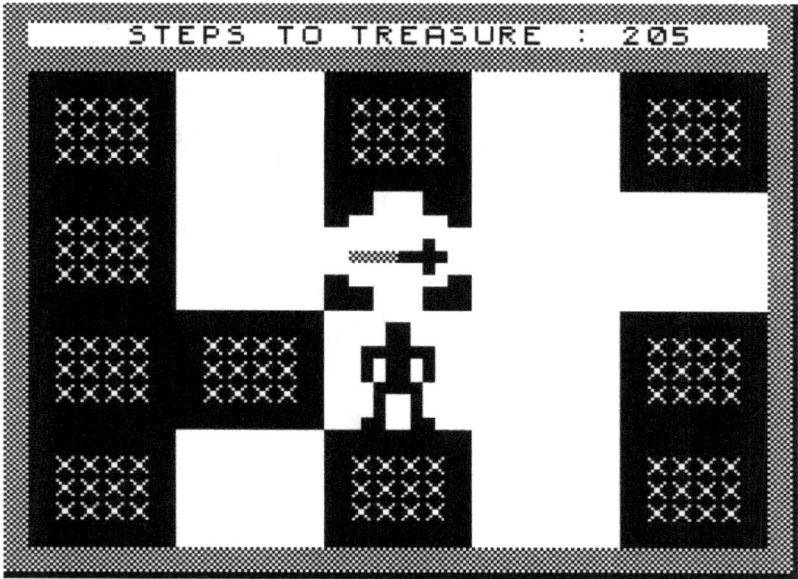

Maziacs, written by Don Priestley ZX81 16KB.

Moving on a couple of months it would become clear that for me to do more with this awesome wee machine, I would need the 16KB RAM PAK expansion, so I managed to plead my case enough that my mum managed to get this for me.

At this point I was programming my own games through magazine listings and fixing them so they worked but now I could have my own commercial games with this new expansion and the first of these would be Quicksilver's Defenda. This was a brilliant clone of Williams' "Defender" which to this day I'm amazed played on a ZX81 at all! It wouldn't be until a friend at school told me about "Black Crystal" and how amazing it was, I thought I simply had to have this game and experience it for myself, so again I managed to convince my mum that I would do anything to pay for it, and again, bless her soul she managed to get it for me.

Black Crystal was it. It triggered the dawning of realisation within me that Computers could really take gaming to the next level. This was a game that used the diminutive ZX81's character set to map out locations and show you in real time where castles were, where land boundaries were and where the alliances and "baddies" lived, and allow you, again in real time to defend yourself from attack by pressing keys on that lovely membrane keyboard to attack and defend (depending on what was happening). In this game, you really felt you were on a quest because if you got the timing wrong in an attack – you were dead!

Whilst playing this game (and most games of that era), my own imagination played a big part in visualising what was happening, with the screen simply representing the physical elements. This was at a time when movies like the amazing John Boorman's Excalibur and Clash of the Titans would be aiding my imagination for this type of game.

John McDermott 2021.

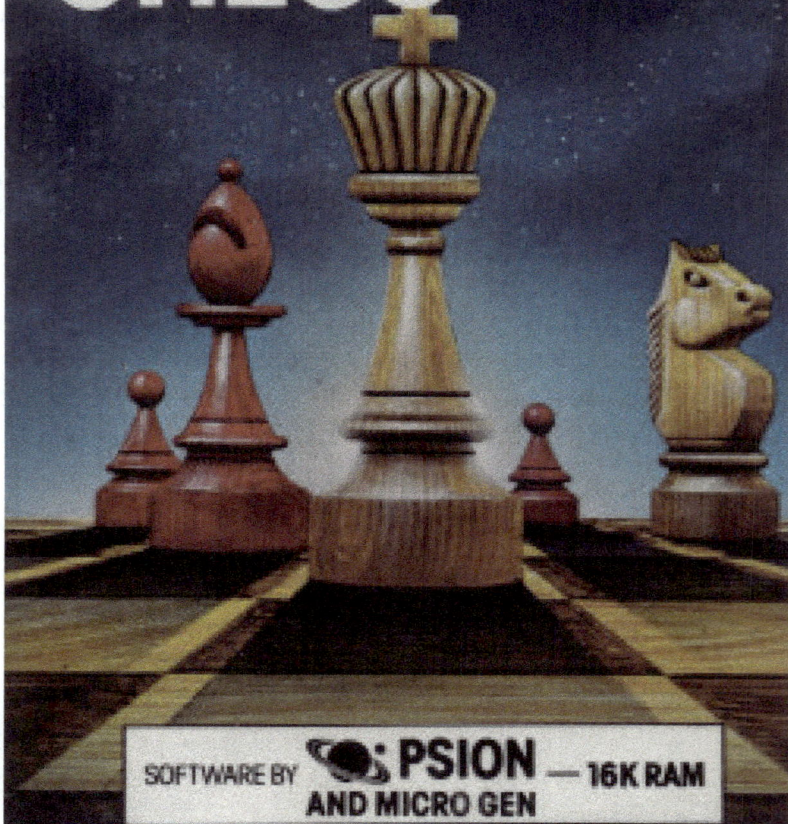

sinclair
ZX81
CHESS

SOFTWARE BY PSION — 16K RAM
AND MICRO GEN

298

But what is a game?

The very first video games were created on mainframe computers in the 1950s and 1960s, often at research centres or universities. The most famous of these is probably Spacewar! A space combat video game developed in 1962 by Steve Russell, Martin Graetz, Wayne Wiitanen, Bob Saunders, Steve Piner, and others. It was written for the newly installed DEC PDP-1 minicomputer at the Massachusetts Institute of Technology. Obviously, most people would never play or even see this.

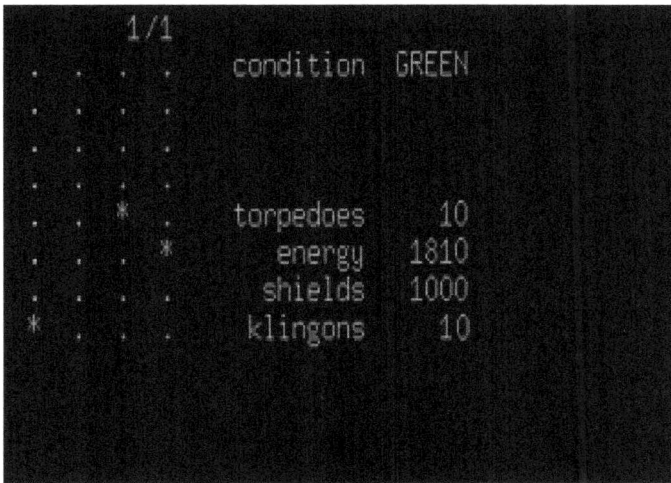

Image source: Gabe Newell's Favourite-Ever Game Is... | Rock Paper Shotgun

Some games created worlds with the written word, much like a book and others created an on-screen display by simply using those same letters but cleverly arranging them to look like graphics.

Star Trek lxxxviiiis a text-based strategy video game based on the U.S Star Trek television series (1966–69) and originally released in 1971.

In the game, the player commands the USS Enterprise on a mission to hunt down and destroy an invading fleet of Klingon warships. The player travels through the 64 quadrants of the galaxy to attack enemy ships with phasers and photon torpedoes in turn-based battles and refuel at starbases.

Mike Mayfield wrote the game in the BASIC programming language for the SDS Sigma 7 mainframe computer with the goal of creating a game like Spacewar! (from 1962) that could be played with a teleprinter instead of a graphical display. He then rewrote it for the HP 2000C minicomputer in 1972, it was included in Hewlett-Packard's public domain software catalogue the following year. It was then picked up by David H. Ahl, who ported it with Mary Cole to BASIC-PLUS and published the source code in the Digital Equipment Corporation Edu newsletter. It was then republished with other computer games in his best-selling 101 BASIC Computer Games book. Bob Leedom then expanded the game in 1974 into Super Star Trek. Apple Star-Trek, or Star-Trek for the Apple 1 was written in 1976 in Integer BASIC by Robert J. Bishop and released by McPheters, Wolfe & Jones. A more stripped back game but with only 8k on the Apple 1 it a good approximation.

What was the first home computer game?

When the Tandy TRS-80 was popular, Tandy really did not grasp the idea of gaming at all, their solution as to why kids would need a computer was perhaps to solve a math problem.

Tandy's earliest games were backgammon and blackjack and not very exciting. Most of the software listed for the computer was mainly mortgage and taxation programs. Hardly edge of the seat entertainment but then we didn't know what a computer was for did we? and this was seen as a perfectly acceptable way to use a computer at home.

Temple of Apshai[lxxxix] by Automated Simulations, 1979 TRS-80

Things changed when Temple of Apshai arrived, it was also known as Dunjonquest: Temple of Apshai. It is a dungeon crawl role-playing video game developed and published by Automated Simulations, who later became the well-known Epyx software in 1979. Originally released on the TRS-80 and Commodore PET, it was followed by several updated versions for other computers between 1980 and 1986. Yes, it has simple graphics by today's standards but with some imagination this can become a very enthralling game.

Text adventures were popular as well, as were simulations and almost anything else you can think of, but character defined graphics would quickly replace the more basic looking ascii style of display.

One genre that would go against that trend for a while, was the text adventure.

Go North

I Can't do that!

Go South.

Wander[xc] is probably the first video adventure game, written by Peter Langston in 1974 in BASIC and then rewritten and coded on a mainframe university computer. The game was considered lost until an archived version was found in an email from 1980. It wasn't just a game though, it had a toolkit to create games, somewhat like a very early version of infrom7 development kit that we use today. The original description refers to itself as "a tool for writing non-deterministic fantasy stories." The game was distributed in Langston's PSL Games collection for Unix.

The game comes with an included story, called "a3", along with instructions for new authors to author their own stories. The plot has the player take the role of a First Under-secretary to the Ambassador for an organisation called Corps Diplomatique Terrestrienne (CDT). Sent by Mr. Magnan to the mysterious country Aldebaran III, the player's mission to prevent up uprising against Terran nationals in a limited time.

The game was initially created in HP BASIC at Evergreen State College, probably on an HP2000 minicomputer. Langston rewrote the game in C in 1974 while at Harvard University and released it to other users of the mainframe system and he maintained the game through the rest of the decade, with a release in 1980 as part of his PSL Games Collection package of games for Unix.

```
Elliot was nearby, lying in the
rubble. There was blood on his
clothes. Feebly, he beckoned
Harper closer.

'Listen! Rigellians have
Doomsday Device. Will devastate
planet if they lose war! Go
east across town. Cross
no-man's-land. Find Device,
disarm it... but beware android
guard...'

His voice grew weaker, yet more
urgent.

'Find my light-guide - buried in
copse - use it to...'

With these words on his lips,
Elliot died.

anykey
```

The adventure game was still popular in 1987, Rigels Revenge from Mastertronic was a graphic text adventure in a similar vein to the Hobbit by Melbourne House.

Colossal Cave Adventure is also one of the earliest text adventure games or IF (interactive fiction) as they are known today. Developed in 1975 and into 1976 by Will Crowther for the PDP-10 mainframe computer, it was expanded later and improved upon by Don Woods in 1977 before going on to become the most well-known and copied adventure ever. Artistically and physically, this game is on every computer ever! Or so it seems.

The game starts with the player exploring a cave system, rumoured to be filled with treasure and gold. The game world is maze of dozens of rooms or locations, and the player moves between these areas and interacts with objects in them by typing in single line commands like "Go North" or "Go South" The game is based on Will Crowther's maps which he used while caving in Mammoth Cave in Kentucky, the longest cave system in the world. Don Woods expanded the game, increased the amount of fantasy elements featured in it, such as a dragon and magic spells.

The game directly inspired the creation of numerous adventure games, including Adventureland (1978), Zork (1979), Mystery House (1980), Rogue (1980), and Adventure (1980), which went on to be the foundations of the early interactive fiction scene.

More details are here:

https://ahopeful.wordpress.com/2015/04/22/wander-1974-a-lost-mainframe-game-is-found/

Due to the limited capabilities of early computers the adventure game was perfect to not only exploit its lack of power but also showcase the writing and creative skill of game developers.

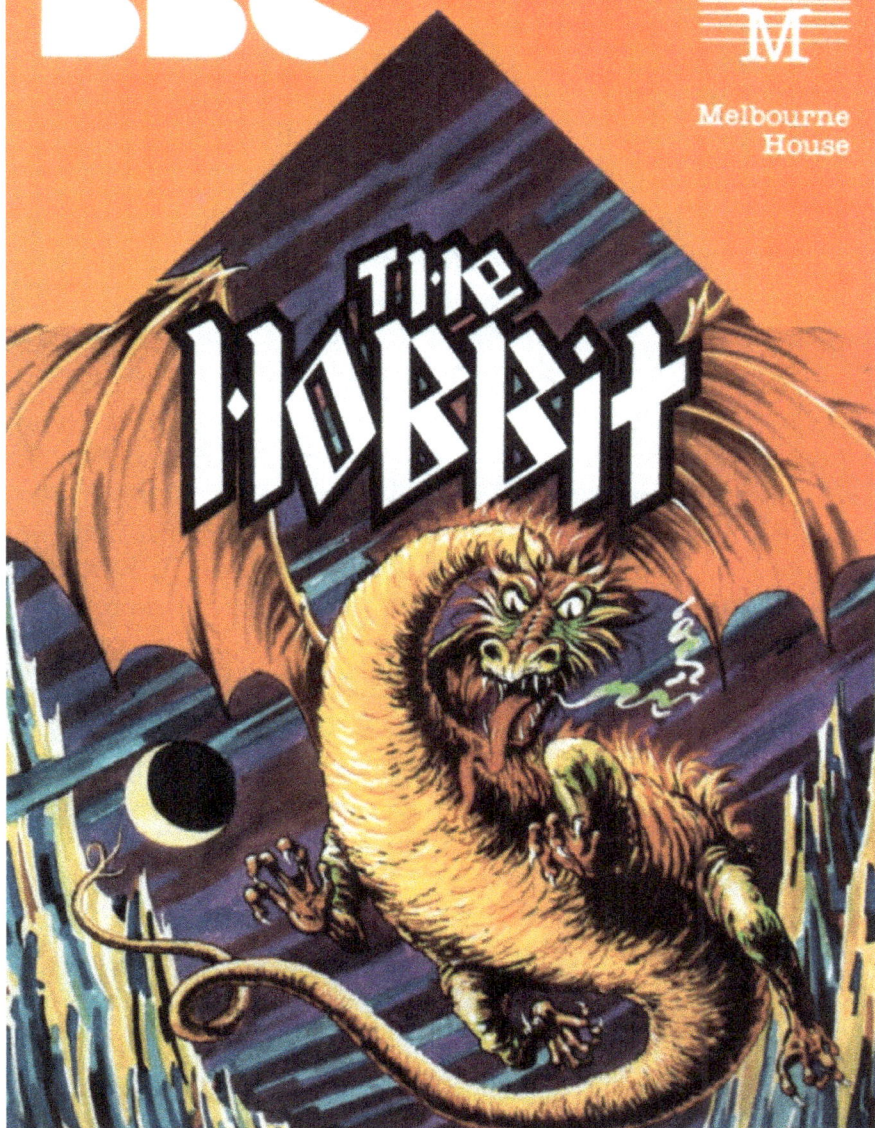

Early computers like the Commodore PET, Tandy TRS-80 and Apple II were swamped with text adventure almost from the initial release of the systems.

The games became so popular that even as more advanced computers arrived like the Atari 800 or Commodore 64 came along, the popularity of these mini stories didn't falter one bit, in fact the machine were swamped with these types of game.

Every computer has a text adventure of some kind, most likely a clone of Colossus cave or Adventure itself but as the 1970s moved in to the 1980s the quality and depth of these games increased hugely. With the birth of companies that specialised in text adventure, the adventure craze exploded in a big way.

Level 9 was a British software developer of computer software, active between 1981 and 1991. Founded by Mike, Nicholas and Pete Austin, the company produced software for the BBC Micro, Nascom, ZX Spectrum, Commodore 64, ORIC, Atari, Lynx 48k, RML 380Z, Amstrad CPC, MSX, Amiga, Apple II, Memotech MTX, and Enterprise platforms and is best known for its successful text adventure games until a general decline in the text adventure market forced their closure in June 1991.

Level 9's first release was an extension to Nascom BASIC called Extension BASIC. The first game, also for the Nascom, was called Fantasy. Level 9 devised their own interpretation language, A-code, around 1979. It was very memory efficient, mainly due to the advanced text compression routines which could compress text to about 50%. Level 9 created a whole catalogue of games from 1983, on many computers.

- Colossal Adventure (1983)
- Adventure Quest (1983)
- Dungeon Adventure (1983)
- Lords of Time (1983)
- Return to Eden (1984)
- Emerald Isle (1985)
- The Secret Diary of Adrian Mole Aged 13¾ (for Mosaic Publishing, 1985)
- The Archers (for Mosaic, 1985)
- The Price of Magik (1986)
- Knight Orc (1987)
- The Growing Pains of Adrian Mole
- Gnome Ranger (1987)
- Time and Magik trilogy (for Mandarin Software, 1988)
- The Price of Magik
- Lancelot (for Mandarin, 1988)
- Scapeghost (1989)

Adventure International (Scott Adams) were huge on the Commodore Vic20, releasing five of the companies' games for the launch of the Vic20 in 1980.

Following on from Adams' first text adventure, Adventureland, other games followed rapidly, with Adventure International releasing about two games a year.

In 1980, five of the company's games were ported to the Commodore VIC-20. Developer Neil Harris recalled: "Our sales guys could not figure out what they were going to do with them. 'What are these games? It's all words on the screen. There's no graphics! What kind of a video game doesn't have video?' they became the best-selling cartridges for the VIC-20!"

In 1982, Adventure International began releasing Scott Adams Graphic Adventures for computers like the Apple II, while continuing to sell text-only games for less powerful computers such as the VIC-20 and TI 99/4A. Graphic adventures like The Hobbit increased expectations of such games, however, and Adventure International's graphic adventures were inferior to others resulting in a rapid loss of market share. At its peak in late

1983/early 1984, Adventure International employed approximately 50 staff and published titles from over 300 independent programmer/authors. In Europe, the "Adventure International" name was a trading name of Adventure Soft and other games were released under the name that were not from Adventure International in the US.

https://en.wikipedia.org/wiki/Adventure_International

Gameography.

- Adventureland
- Pirate Adventure (also called Pirate's Cove)
- Secret Mission (originally called Mission Impossible)
- Voodoo Castle
- The Count
- Strange Odyssey
- Mystery Fun House
- Pyramid of Doom
- Ghost Town
- Savage Island parts I & II
- The Golden Voyage

Mystery House is an adventure game released in 1980 by Roberta and Ken Williams for the Apple II. It is remembered as one of the first adventure games to feature computer graphics and the first game produced by On-Line Systems, the company which would evolve into Sierra On-Line.

The game starts near an abandoned Victorian mansion. The player is soon locked inside the house with no other option than to explore. The mansion contains many interesting rooms and seven other people: Tom, a plumber; Sam, a mechanic; Sally, a seamstress; Dr Green, a surgeon; Joe, the gravedigger; Bill, a butcher; and Daisy, a cook.

At the end of the 1970s, Ken Williams sought to set up a company for enterprise software for the market-dominating Apple II computer. One day, he took a teletype terminal to his residence to work on the development of an accounting program. Rummaging through a catalogue, he found a program called Colossal Cave Adventure. He and his wife Roberta, both played it all the way through and their encounter with this game would have a strong influence on video-gaming history.

Having finished Colossal Cave Adventure, they began to search for something similar but found that the video game market had nothing like it. Roberta Williams liked the concept of a textual adventure very much, but she thought that the player would have a more satisfying experience with images and began to think of her own game. She thus conceived Mystery House, the first graphical adventure game, a detective story inspired by Agatha Christie's and Then There Were None.

Ken spent a few nights developing the game on his Apple II using 70 simple two-dimensional drawings done by Roberta. The software was packaged in Ziploc bags containing a 5¼-inch disk and a photocopied paper describing the game and was sold in local software shops in Los Angeles County. To their great surprise, Mystery House was an enormous success, quickly becoming a best-seller at a first-release price of US$24.95. Eventually, it sold more than 10,000 copies, which was a record-breaking phenomenon for the time.

Though Ken believed that the gaming market would be less of a growth market than the professional software market, he persevered with games. In 1980, the Williams founded On-Line Systems, which would become Sierra On-Line in 1982.

HAUNTED HOUSE
Cat. No. 26-1910
Radio Shack
TRS-80 MICRO COMPUTER SYSTEM
GAMES
A Thrill-Packed Game of Mystery and Adventure For Your 4K Level I or II TRS-80™ Microcomputer

Jim Bagley recalls

"My first job in the games industry was working with none other than Mike Singleton. I was thrown in at the deep end! That was for a company called Consult Computer Systems.

My love of games inspires me to create them. Sadly, in the old days we never got any feedback from the players but later some people got hold of my email and I surprised how much people liked them. Obviously at retro events I get to meet and to talk to gamers."

The Hobbit[xci] was the first licensed video game based on Tolkien's work, being the first part of The Tolkien Trilogy. The game was considered large at the time of its release and included 80 locations, of which 30 were illustrated. The game was released by Melbourne House for Amstrad CPC, BBC B, Commodore 64, Dragon 32, MSX, ORIC-1 and ZX-Spectrum.

The 1982 adaption of The Hobbit (1937) turned into the Interactive Fiction format, written by Philip Mitchell and Veronika Megler of Beam Software, and published by Melbourne House for the ZX Spectrum, and later ported to the Commodore 64 (1983), IBM Personal Computer (1983), and several other home computers.

Their ambition was to cram all the events and places of Tolkien's Middle Earth into a machine with 48K of memory. But they failed in such bold and interesting ways that the game still feels futuristic today.

Every character and object in the world are simulated simultaneously, with non-player characters pursuing their own goals under their own AI the computer does not know which character is the player and applies its rules impartially to all. This can unfortunately lead to chaos. Plot-critical characters are killed before you meet them. Thorin stops and begins to sing about gold while surrounded by the murderous goblins. Hobbit on the BBC Micro.

Hobbit BBC Micro

Hobbit on the MSX

a comfortable tunnel like hall

Hobbit on the Amstrad CPC

Infocom games were written using a programming language called ZIL (Zork Implementation Language), itself derived directly from MDL (programming language), that compiled into a byte code able to run on a standardized virtual machine called the Z-machine. As the games were text based and used variants of the same Z-machine interpreter, the interpreter had to be ported to new computer systems, rather than porting each game. Each game file included a sophisticated parser which allowed the user to type complex instructions to the game. Unlike earlier works of interactive fiction which only understood commands of the form 'verb noun', Infocom's parser could understand a wider variety of sentences. For instance, one might type "open the large door, then go west. With the Z-machine, Infocom was able to release most of their games for most popular home computers simultaneously: Apple II, Atari 8-bit family, IBM PC compatibles, Amstrad CPC/PCW (one disc worked on both machines), Commodore 64, Commodore Plus/4, Commodore 128, Kaypro CP/M, Texas Instruments TI-99/4A, Macintosh, Atari ST, Amiga, TRS-80.

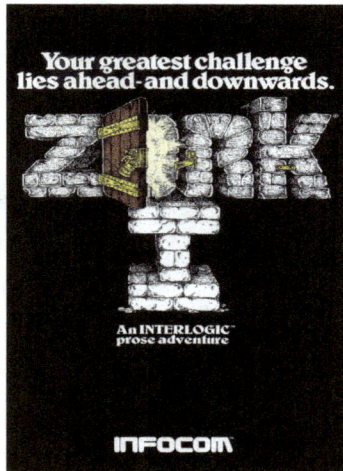

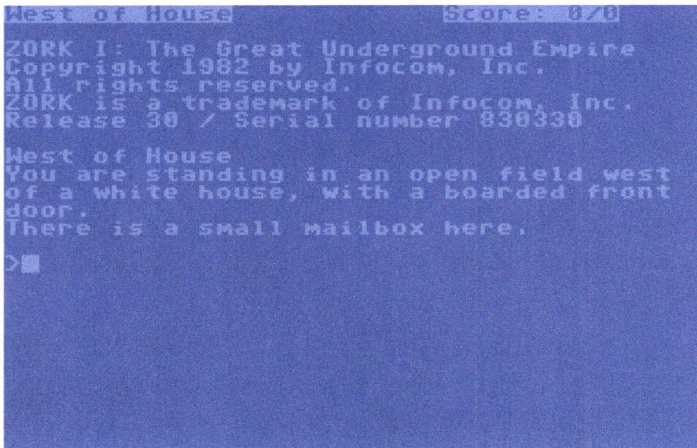

Zork[xcii] I was Infocom's first product. This screenshot of Zork I is representative of the sort of interaction a player has with Infocom's interactive fiction titles. Here it is depicted running on a modern Z-machine interpreter.

Inspired by Colossal Cave, Marc Blank and Dave Lebling created what was to become the first Infocom game, Zork, in 1977 at MIT's Laboratory for Computer Science. Despite the development of a revolutionary virtual memory system that allowed games to be much larger than the average personal computer's normal capacity, the enormous mainframe-developed game had to be split into three roughly equal parts. Zork I was released originally for the TRS-80 in 1980.[6] Infocom was founded on June 22, 1979; the founding members were Tim Anderson, Joel Berez, Marc Blank, Mike Broos, Scott Cutler, Stu Galley, Dave Lebling, J. C. R. Licklider, Chris Reeve, and Al Vezza.

Lebling and Blank each authored several more games, and additional game writers (or "Implementors") were hired, notably including Steve Meretzky.

Other popular and inventive titles included several sequels and spinoff games in the Zork series, The Hitchhiker's Guide to the Galaxy by Douglas Adams, and A Mind Forever Voyaging.

In its first few years of operation, text adventures proved to be a huge revenue stream for the company. Whereas most computer games of the era would achieve initial success and then suffer a significant drop-off in sales, Infocom titles continued to sell for years and years.

The popularity of adventure games continued for much longer that was foreseen, the demise of text style games was muted as early as 1982, but games still appeared on much more capable machines like the Atari ST, Amiga and Macintosh, well into the 1990s. As popular as text-based games were, the arcade games were where the action was, and people loved arcade game conversions on their home computer or at least they did initially. The arcade machine quickly outgrew the 8-bit limitations of the 8-bit home micro and the humble home computer was left to try its best to create an approximation of the game or at least to try.

After Chess, Checkers, Start Trek and possibly hunt the Wumpus, came Space Invaders and then everything changed!

Space Invaders is a 1978 arcade video game developed by Tomohiro Nishikado. It was manufactured and sold by Taito in Japan and licensed to the Midway division of Bally for overseas distribution. The mission is to simply shoot all the aliens on screen as they descend towards you. You have three destructible bases which offer limited protection and as the aliens descend the screen, row by row.

Unfortunately for us, the little aliens speed up as they get nearer to the player but how did the home computers cope with such a game? As it turns out, rather well as most of the home computers had similar speed and audio capabilities to the arcade machine. Exceptions were the ones with no audio features i.e. ZX80, ZX81 and TRS-80 for example.

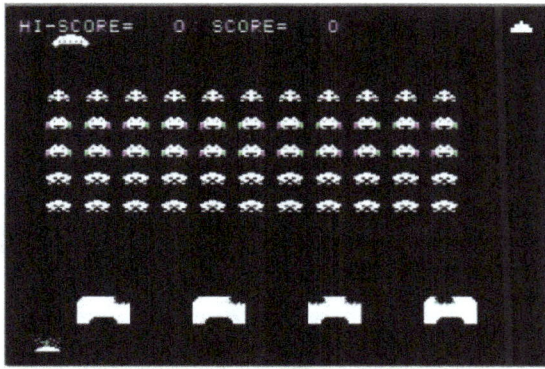

Apple II Invaders 1979

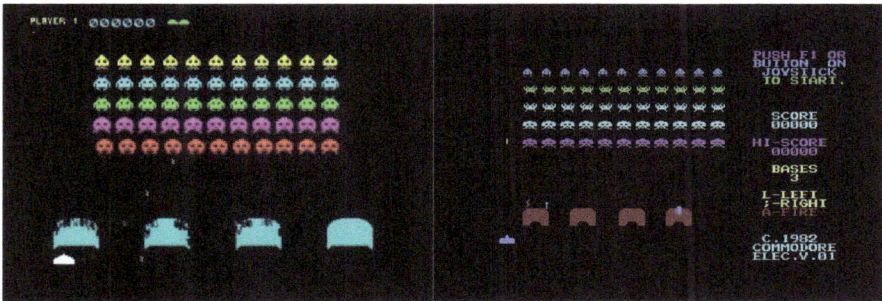

1982 ZX Spectrum Invaders & Space invaders by Commodore.

While it's fair to say that Space Invaders is not much of a challenge for our 1980s 8-bit computer systems, in fact most of the arcade machines of the late 70s and early 80s used very similar hardware to the home computers of the time.

What was the best 8-bit era version of Space Invaders? For me it was the Ti99/4a. Colourful graphics and great sound, it even included a bonus round that I have seen on any other system. Perhaps we should look at a more complex game and see how our home computers hold up in comparison to the arcades. Let's look at this 1983 hit, Spy Hunter.

Spy Hunter was developed by Bally Midway and released in arcades during 1983. The game is inspired by the James Bond films and was originally supposed to carry the James Bond name but Bally could not secure the licence and so it became Spy Hunter. So how did the home computers stand up to a more advanced arcade game? A mixed bag, the ZX Spectrum lost the famous Peter gun theme music. It had jerky scrolling with blue trees for some reason and then some, although it had limited colour clash. The Commodore 64 version was a much better affair with-in game music, sound effects and nice graphics. The Apple II thankfully dispensed with the theme music after the title screen – it is awful.

The Apple version is a simpler looking game with less action than the previous versions although better looking graphics than the Sinclair Spectrum. The BBC micro had a version too, which was mostly green looking, and the car jerked about wildly on screen as you move left to right. Almost in character squares, but it had in game music that didn't make your ears bleed unlike the Apple II version. The best version to play, is probably on the Atari 800. Of course, picking faults with arcade conversions is an easy thing to do and while it does show strengths and weaknesses in our home computer systems it does not tell the whole story. The Sinclair Spectrum is not known for its audio quality, neither is the Apple II. The Commodore 64 sufferers from medium resolution fat graphics and it has an affinity for the colour brown. The BBC micro has odd graphic modes and while powerful at the time, it was quickly abandoned by the game's publishers of the 80s.

Spy Hunter - Arcade 1983 & Spy Hunter - Commodore 64.

Spy Hunter : ZX Spectrum 48k & Amstrad CPC 64k.

Even by the early 1980s, arcades had surpassed home computers in terms of graphics, speed, and audio fidelity. Why was this the case? Well, arcades were constantly seeking the next groundbreaking innovation to captivate teenagers and alleviate their financial constraints. Twin CPUs, vector graphics, stereo sound, speech samples, and even video were all features that home computers lacked.

The advent of Don Bluth's Dragons Lair in 1983 revolutionized the arcade industry, introducing laser disc full motion video and immersive soundscapes. Former Disney animator Don Bluth took the world by storm and created a video game that shook the world. The game itself was rather uninteresting and not so long ago would have been called a Quick-Time event style of game. The gameplay consisted of nothing more than moving the player left, right, up, or down when arrows appeared on screen, but this was masked by beautiful hand drawn computer graphics and breathtaking speech and audio.

Could home computers match the capabilities of the ZX Spectrum? Of course not. They lacked the necessary storage capacity, graphics, and audio. For instance, the ZX Spectrum could store 48KB of data, while the Commodore 64 had 64KB, and the Atari 800 and Apple II also had 48KB. The BBC micro and Dragon32 had 32KB of RAM, respectively. Most home computers processed data at 1 or 2 MHz, while the ZX Spectrum managed 3 MHz Additionally, most machines could display 8 or 16 colours.

Dragons Lair – Commodore 64 & Dragons Lair – ZX Spectrum

Dragons Lair – Arcade

As we can see the home ports of Dragons Lair are almost undisguisable from the arcade original…

Arcade: Z80 4mhz, GI stereo sound.

Laserdisc Player - Pioneer LD-V1000 or Pioneer PR-7820

So, are the home computers now doomed as they can no longer keep up? No not at all. As the arcades raced ahead the home computers found their niche in variations of arcade games or obscure creations that would never see an arcade and to honest some of these were the best games to play. You don't play Outrun or Space Harrier on an 8-bit computer and expect and amazing experience, you won't find one. But if you look around and dig into a home computers games library, I'm sure you will find it fun and enjoyable and I for one – still enjoy games that I don't remember from back in the 80s. Obviously, games companies are and will always be trying their absolute best to provide the best entertainment, won't they? Surely no one would release sub-standard, poorly made, or incomplete games to the public. It's all the home computer's fault, they aren't powerful or colourful enough!

Sadly, the pocket money of many a child and of course adult were taken or in some cases almost stolen by game companies that not only provided inferior quality but often supplied the wrong game or even supplied unfinished games. In the days before patches, updates on online bug fixes, a released game was just that – released. How many of you bought Robocop for the Commodore 64? Or Thundercat's? Perhaps Transformers. Only to find that they were utter rubbish.

The Commodore 64 version of the Robocop game by Ocean was clearly rushed during development or at least in the final stages to capture the film's hype. The game sold well, topping the chart for almost a year in the UK and becoming the biggest selling game of the 1980s. Ocean had the idea of creating a good game I don't doubt and the music by John Dunn is fantastic, graphics offer colourfully detailed sprites. So far, so good. But after you play the game for some seconds, you suddenly find that the difficulty level is set way too high. You just have one life not three which is the arcade game norm at this point and your energy runs out quickly as soon as you get hit by on-screen enemies. Add to that, a timer that is impossible to beat and not forgetting level 7 which is unplayable as it is a graphical mess. It is so bad that you cannot see anything but coloured blocks on screen. In short, a mess of a game. But... What about BATMAN? Or The untouchables? Well unfortunately almost all of Oceans film games used the same formula – Platform walking or jumping, mixed with a mini game of some sort and then back to platform walking or jumping. Changing the main sprite meant that any film character could be stuck on a dull platform game.

Clive Townsend recalls.

"In 1983, I visited Durrel Software in Taunton, Somerset. During my visit, I had the opportunity to meet with Robert James Durrel White, who was impressed by some of my homemade games, including Citadel.

While there, he introduced me to the inaugural Durrel game for the ZX Spectrum, titled Jungle Trouble. He challenged me to circumvent the copy protection measures, which I successfully accomplished by hacking the game's loader. This achievement left a lasting impression on him, and I was granted permission to visit Durrel during the school holidays. During my time there, I had the privilege of meeting one of the pioneering programmers, Mike Richardson, who was responsible for coding the classic games Turbo Esprit and Thanatos."

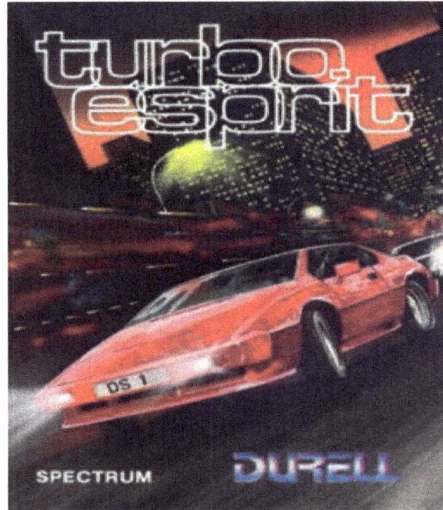
Turbo Esprit ZX Spectrum.

The first open world driving game? GTA on the ZX Spectrum maybe?

Was the 8-bit era all about blocky games with horrible sound effects? No of course, not and some of the games of back then are still around today on the Xbox and PlayStation. Not all the popular games made the transition from 8bit to 16bit, but many did.

So, what were the better games on the 8bit machines? That's a hard question but here are a few of the good ones.

- Commando
- Raid Over Moscow
- Maniac Manson
- Pirates!
- Turrican
- Defender of the crown
- Prince of Persia
- Beach Head
- Lode Runner
- LeaderBoard
- Mayhem in Monsterland
- Rescue on Fractalus!
- Dropzone
- International Karate
- Head Over Heels
- The Great Escape
- Atic Atac
- Project Firestart
- Rebel Star
- Summer games / Winter games

While these games may have been great on one system, they may well be awful on another system.

Chapter 18 - End of an Era.

The sales of 8-bit computers didn't just end in 1990, no they continued to sell, and some sold very well indeed and into the mid 1990's by which time almost all manufacturing of 8-bit machines had stopped. Atari, The Commodore 64, ZX Spectrum and Amstrad models all continued to be piled high in stores across the land, but sales had now slowed down. Slowly bit by bit the market started to shrink away in the early 1990s, the pull of the more powerful 16bit computers and the game consoles from Nintendo and Sega all split the software and hardware developers.

One advantage of the continued 8-bit sales was that the hardware was now ridiculously cheap to manufacture, allowing families on a budget to buy the likes of the ZX Spectrum 128k +2 or +3 or the Commodore 64, which was now selling for around £149.99 with a light gun. Compare this the Amiga A500 which cost £369.99 in 1990. The Sinclair Spectrum +2 was £119.99, and the Atari 520ST was £299.99. All of these were beaten by the Nintendo NES at £79.99 or even the Atari XE65 for the regal sum of £49.97*. (Curry's-September 1990*).

Software continued to be released and some of the best games ever created on the 8-bits were released in the late 80s and early 90s, but all of this would come to a rather abrupt end in about 1993/4 when computer magazines stopped being published and the games slowly disappeared as stores moved to the 16-bit computers and consoles or even the PC. Almost all manufacturers had stopped production of 8-bit computers in around 1994. The march of time had finally caught up. Software became a mixed bag with some amazing and a great deal of utter rubbish being released.

By 1990 the PC was managing to do something that the 8-bit home computers had never managed to achieve, they were accepted into businesses and as prices started to fall, they were welcomed into the home as well. Perhaps some 8-bit models had managed this to a lesser degree like the Commodore 64 or the Apple II but they were never going to compete with the unstoppable march of the clone PC. The PC was everywhere in the early 90's and with that came lots of software, from games to Desktop Publishing to art and spreadsheets. The PC had it all but at a higher cost than either Atari or Commodore machines.

The start of 1992 followed what would be the last great Christmas for 8-bit computer sales. Commodore had once again shot itself in the foot by releasing what would have been a great console in 1984 but not now 1992, the Commodore 64GS (game system). It was so outdated by 1992 standards that it was almost comical. In fact, it was so bad that almost no one bought it, Commodore allegedly took back unsold stock and stripped them down to fit in to the (now budget) C64 computer. Yet another costly mistake for the ailing company. Although the GS did resurrect cartridge sales for the C64, but they were only popular for a year or so.

The Amstrad Spectrum +2's was now bundled the James Bond game pack; the pack included a light gun and a compilation of three James Bond video games developed and published by Amstrad. The Commodore 64's equivalent was the Light Fantastic pack, which included four exclusively programmed games for the light gun to use.

Commercially the games scene started to change as the computers became cheaper and so did the people buying them – in so much as the age group fell. In the mid-1980s a teenager or young adult bought the Atari 800, ZX Spectrum or Commodore 64 by 1991/2 the demographic had changed to a younger consumer. Older users had mostly moved on to the ST or Amiga. This meant that while full priced disk games were available – most of the best sellers were now budget cassette games aimed at younger buyers with games being sold at pocket money prices.

Even the famous games magazines of the era started to suffer from the ever-present lack of content. The heady days of new hardware and dozens of big arcade titles to be reviewed had now almost dried up. Bizarrely Future Publishing's - Commodore Format magazine was launched in September 1990 just as the 8-bit scene was starting to die on its feet. Crash magazine and Zap64's Newfield publications filed for liquidation at the end of 1991. Zap64 and Crash would return phoenix like under new publishers Europress for a relatively brief period soon after.

Globally, meanwhile Apple's Macintosh was also doing well, rising from 1.3 million units in 1990 to its all-time high of 4.5 million units in 1995. The Macintosh market share peaked at 12% in 1993. It was a boom time for Apple, with the future looking bright but not necessarily for the Apple II. Other companies were not so lucky. Atari itself fell into a severe cashflow crisis as Nintendo had taken almost all its console market share in the U.S and Europe. The Atari ST computer range (including TT & Falcon) had been cancelled. The Atari 8-bit line was finally dead as a marketable product. Atari Inc. officially dropped all support of the 8-bit computer line in 1992 (about the same time as they dropped the 16-bit line to concentrate finances on the failed Jaguar games console. The company was sold to hard drive manufacturer JTS. The venerable Commodore 64 sales also fell sharply, dropping from 1.25 million units in 1989 to only 175,000 units in 1993. This sudden loss of revenue hurt the ill managed Commodore hugely. By 1991 the Sinclair name was all but finished on computers as Amstrad concentrated on the PCW range. Discontinuing all of its 8-bit Amstrad CPC and Sinclair machines in late 1992.

Signing off.

The rolling raster lines have finally finished flashing their hypnotic dance on my TV set, and the game has loaded at last …damn it!

R Tape Loading Error.

….Well! That is another five minutes of my life that I will never get back.

What was it called? Super Trolley or something like that on the ZX Spectrum. Never mind, I think I will give it a miss, perhaps another time. So, you might ask, is that the end of the 8-bit era? Most of the founding companies have gone bankrupt, the once great halls of these companies have long since closed their doors and the windows have been boarded up. The manufacturing plants have been sold off or demolished and the staff have all moved on.

Some of the people involved in these stories have passed away. Some have moved on to other professions and have never returned to the funny little computers of our youth. Unfinished games that were never finished are left semi-complete on cassettes and disk drives across the land. Ideas, plans and ambitions have all faded in the intervening years.

It's not the end of course, yes, the last commercial game available on the high street was sold years ago, the monthly magazines have all but gone, dumped into the nearest garbage bin long ago. The Cassette tapes have all been melted down and turned into Peloton pedals. But the computers are mostly still working and willing but is the audience?

Does anyone still care about the old computers, creaky old disk drives and food spattered keyboards? Does anyone really care about the squeaky audio and shrill 8-bit music anymore?

The answer is a solid yes, they do! And new software and hardware is being developed, seemingly every day. Innovative technology is making its way to our beloved 40-year-old hardware. Video signal enhancers of the ZX81, storage devices for the Electron and WIFI for the Commodore 64 to name but a few of things that have appeared in the last few years. Gone are the days of cassette loading and watching your life ebb by, minute by minute.

The glory days of the 1980s may be long gone now but this is not the end. New games are still made, and new computer systems are being made too. The 8-bit era will never end.

I must go now but I hope to see you soon in 16-bit Stories!

Michael J Nurney, December 2023.

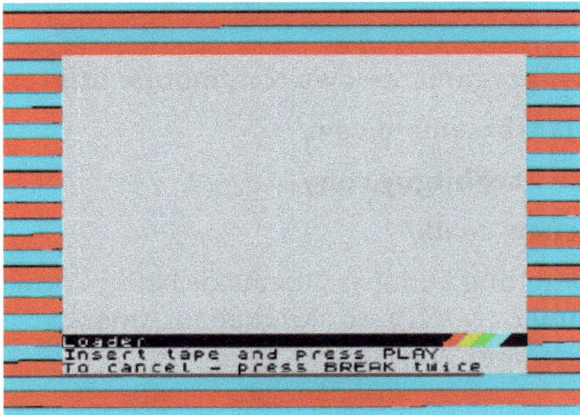

Further Reading.

The retro scene as it now called is alive and kicking, we have new magazines, YouTube channels and Instagram post aplenty these days. Books and even films which catalogue, dissect and deep dive into our hobby. Not to forget the wealth of websites and blog posts showing how to repair and collect or beloved machines.

Repair videos are essential to any collector and Adrians digital basement is almost compulsory viewing. LGR (Lazy game reviews), David Murray at 8-bit guy and 8-bit show and tell offer in depth reviews and history on hundreds of computer systems in the USA. Here in the UK, we have Nostalgia Nerd and Paul Jenkinson's Spectrum show among hundreds of other shows to watch at your leisure.

Magazines are seemingly more popular than ever with great articles and interviews; books are also on the rise with almost every popular YouTube stars offering their own unique look at the past. You won't go far wrong by checking out these sites and YouTube of course.

http://www.lazygamereviews.com/mobile.html

https://adriansbasement.com/

https://www.the8bitguy.com/

https://zxrenew.co.uk/

And not forgetting Dimitris Giannakis better known as **Modern Vintage Gamer** (MVG), an Australian-American programmer ,vintage gamer and YouTuber.

https://www.pixel.addict.media/shop/

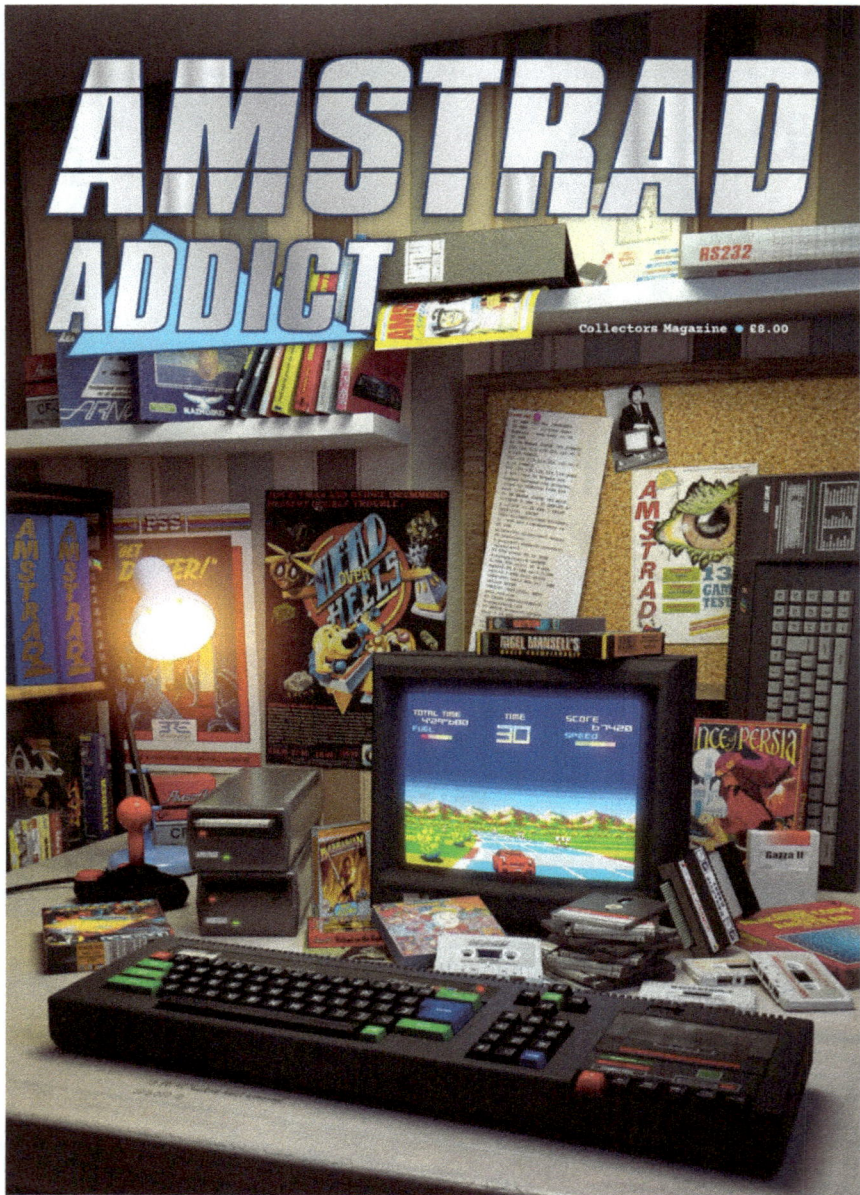

https://www.pixel.addict.media/shop/

RetroPassion

PUTTING THE PASSION BACK INTO RETRO

Atari ST • STE • STFM • STF Servicing

Recapping • Servicing • Upgrades

Latest from RetroPassion

Heretic II for AmigaOS 4 PPC

28 MAR 2024

We have stock of Heretic II for AmigaOS 4. This stunning full retail boxed version comes with manual, 2 CD's. A real classic! Requirements. Available here READ MORE

Individual Computers products added!

25 MAR 2024

We are super excited to now offer a selection of Individual Computers products to our store! If you don't know Individual Computers is a German computer company company specialising retro computer accessories for the Commodore 64 ... READ MORE

www.retropassion.co.uk

The Commodore Story

Changing the world 8-bits at a time

https://www.thecommodorestory.com/

The UK's No.1 Retro Gaming Podcast!

RETRO ASYLUM

AN RA PRODUCTION No. 283

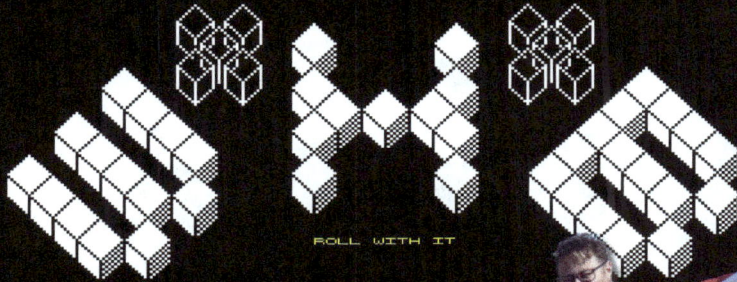

ROLL WITH IT

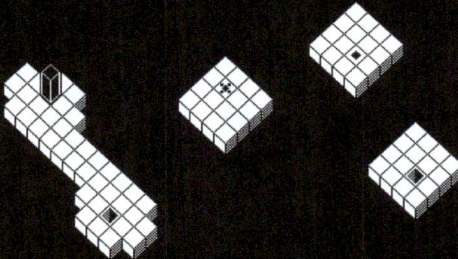

IN THIS EPISODE

Why Hate Boris? Which Hover Bike? No, it's got to Be Welsh Hairy Bloke! Join Dean, Chris, and Mads as they explore the wonderful ZX Spectrum puzzle game that is W*H*B.

LOVE THE SHOW?
Please leave us an iTunes review

http://retroasylum.com/

https://retroasylum.com/

Hugely enjoyable podcast focusing on gaming for all vintage platforms.

ZX Omni   XBerry Pi   Hermit Retro   ByteDelight   ULAs   Commodore 64

ZX Spectrum Replacement Cases (only)   Keyboard Membranes   ZX Spectrum Faceplates

ZX Spectrum Keyboard Mats   ZX Spectrum (glow in the dark) Mats   ZX Spectrum Extras   Storage solutions

ZX81 Parts   Composite mods   Vectrex

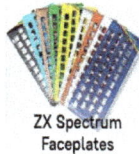

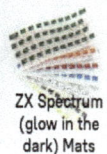

https://zxrenew.co.uk/

https://zappedtothepast.com/

One of the best podcasts in the UK, focused on the Commodore 64 gaming scene as reviewed by the UK magazine ZZap64.

MVT Computers presents, The A-PET.

Welcome to MVT Computers, retro meets modern!

Modern handmade steel computer cases, styled to look like the Commodore PET from the 1970s/80s.

A hinged lid reveals a modern PC with PCI expansion or a Commodore A500 or even an A1200 AGA motherboard. 15-inch IPS LCD panel with 4:3 mode for authentic vintage gaming.

www.mvtcomputers.com

Index

1

1541, 60, 118, 188, 194, 196

16bit, 14, 20, 135, 245, 327

2

264, 157

5

520ST, 186, 197, 208, 223, 229, 232, 234

6

600XL, 136, 147, 174, 177

6128, 197, 215

6502, 14, 15, 18, 70, 77, 126, 164, 194, 217

65C12, 217

8

800XL, 42, 136, 147, 148, 186, 189, 194, 199, 215, 229

8080, 13, 137

8-bit, 11, 14, 15, 16, 70, 71, 112, 119, 160, 166, 189, 197, 212, 215, 216, 228, 229, 232, 237, 240, 243, 246, 249, 255, 275, 278, 286, 288, 289, 314, 316, 317, 323, 327, 328, 329, 330, 331

A

Acorn, 15, 16, 26, 42, 59, 60, 62, 68, 77, 85, 89, 101, 103, 113, 120, 132, 139, 147, 149, 155, 156, 161, 165, 177, 181, 184, 185, 186, 187, 188, 189, 191, 196, 197, 198, 200, 202, 204, 211, 217, 221, 224, 241, 242, 243, 259, 274, 279

Acorn Atom, 77, 101

Activision, 180, 233, 243

ADAM, 183, 252

Alan Shugart, 18

Alan Sugar, 167, 193, 197, 208, 221, 222

Alan Turing, 17

Alex Reid, 189

Alphatronic, 169

Altair, 13, 15, 68

Amiga, 52, 60, 65, 113, 189, 203, 205, 206, 211, 216, 221, 223, 225, 226, 229, 230, 232, 233, 241, 245, 246, 249, 250, 271, 275, 306, 314, 316, 327, 328

Amstrad, 43, 52, 59, 62, 66, 113, 164, 167, 177, 190, 191, 193, 197, 200, 203, 208, 212, 213, 215, 216, 222, 223, 224, 225, 226, 227, 228, 232, 235, 240, 242, 243, 245, 250, 253, 255, 270, 274, 287, 289, 306, 311, 314, 327, 328

Apple, 15, 16, 19, 28, 31, 32, 52, 53, 57, 59, 67, 68, 75, 76, 102, 112, 113, 118, 127, 133, 134, 147, 157, 166, 193, 200, 204, 215, 225, 229, 230, 242, 243, 268, 269, 270, 271, 272, 289, 300, 306, 307, 308, 309, 314, 317, 318, 328, 329

Apple 1, 19, 300

Apple II, 19, 31, 32, 53, 67, 68, 76, 112, 113, 118, 147, 157, 166, 225, 242, 243, 268, 269, 270, 271, 272, 289, 306, 307, 308, 309, 314, 317, 318, 328

Aquarius, 42, 65, 143, 177

Atari, 11, 15, 16, 18, 21, 22, 23, 32, 36, 38, 40, 42, 44, 45, 52, 53, 54, 60, 66, 67, 68, 69, 70, 71, 102, 112, 113, 119, 125, 127, 130, 133, 135, 136, 139, 143, 144, 147, 148, 149, 156, 157, 160, 177, 182, 186, 188, 189, 193, 194, 197, 199, 200, 203, 208, 213, 215, 223, 224, 225, 228, 229, 232, 234, 236, 240, 241, 242, 243, 244, 245, 246, 249, 250, 267, 268, 270, 271, 272, 274, 275, 289, 290, 306, 314, 316, 327, 328, 329

Atari 1450XLD, 39

Atari 400, 32, 69, 70, 71, 113, 119, 125, 267, 268

Atari 800, 32, 40, 71, 119, 125, 130, 147, 157, 267, 268, 306, 328

Atic Atac, 326

Atmos, 154, 155, 174, 177, 286, 287

AY-3-8910, 159

AY-3-8912, 168, 218

B

Bandersnatch, 64, 149, 160, 184

Barrie Wills, 170

BBC, 38, 40, 42, 60, 64, 77, 83, 85, 86, 87, 88, 89, 106, 113, 120, 125, 127, 130, 134, 135, 136, 138, 139, 144, 147, 148, 152, 155, 156, 159, 160, 161, 163, 165, 177, 180, 181, 185, 186, 188, 189, 191, 196, 198, 199, 200, 202, 204, 211, 216, 217, 223, 224, 232, 237, 252, 254, 255, 259, 260, 261, 262, 274, 282, 284, 306, 311, 312, 318

Beach Head, 326

Ben Dalglish, 118

Bruce Gordon, 246, 276

C

C10, 190

C128, 15, 65, 119, 157, 186, 188, 194, 195, 199, 200, 202, 203, 205, 206, 216, 221, 223, 234, 236, 256

C128D, 206, 221, 236

C16, 15, 158, 166, 176, 179, 194, 199, 202, 204, 205, 223, 252, 256

C5, 180, 190, 197, 200, 201

calculating machine, 17

Canon, 158

Cascade, 127

Charles Babbage, 17

Chris Curry, 19, 42, 181, 189

Chris Kaday, 223

Chuck Peddle, 18, 19

Clive Sinclair, 19, 103, 157, 165, 180, 181, 195, 197, 201

CoCo, 167

Codemasters, 118, 243

Coleco, 133, 157, 178, 183, 267, 268, 269

Commando, 326

Commodore, 11, 12, 15, 16, 17, 19, 20, 23, 24, 26, 31, 32, 38, 40, 42, 52, 53, 58, 59, 60, 62, 64, 65, 66, 67, 68, 76, 90, 103, 106, 111, 112, 113, 114, 115, 118, 119, 125, 126, 130, 132, 133, 134, 135, 137, 143, 144, 147, 148, 149, 155, 156, 157, 158, 160, 161, 165, 166, 167, 168, 171, 172, 174, 175, 176, 177, 178, 179, 181, 182, 186, 188, 189, 193, 194, 195, 196, 199, 200, 202, 203, 204, 205, 206, 213, 215, 216, 221, 223, 224, 225, 227, 228, 229, 230, 232, 233, 236, 240, 241, 242, 243, 245, 246, 249, 250, 251, 252, 253, 254, 256, 257, 258, 260, 261, 265, 266, 268, 269, 270, 271, 272, 274, 275, 280, 285, 287, 289, 290, 301, 306, 307, 311, 314, 317, 318, 319, 322, 323, 327, 328, 329

Commodore Business Machines Ltd, 17

Compucolor, 67

COMX35, 137

CP/M, 102, 119, 149, 157, 161, 168, 169, 170, 186, 190, 193, 194, 197, 199, 200, 215, 216, 227, 235, 236, 314

CPC464, 193, 197

Cypher, 17

D

David Whittaker,, 118

David Ziembicki, 112

Defender of the crown, 326

digital watch, 18

Domark, 180, 228, 232

Donkey Kong, 23, 45

DOS, 24, 204

Douglas Engelbart, 18

Dragon, 125, 127, 130, 132, 134, 144, 145, 158, 161, 163, 165, 170, 171, 177, 213, 252, 277, 278, 279, 280, 281, 311

Dropzone, 326

E

Edward Goldwyn, 83

Einstein, 172, 198, 227

ELAN, 149

Electron, 16, 42, 62, 120, 132, 139, 145, 147, 149, 155, 165, 174, 177, 181, 184, 185, 186, 187, 188, 189, 196, 199, 200, 202, 242, 243, 259, 274, 285

Enterprise, 12, 100, 145, 149, 171, 179, 183, 184, 185, 186, 187, 188, 199, 223, 274, 300, 306

Eugene Evans, 149

F

FLAN, 149

floppy disk, 18, 65, 158, 287

FORTH, 28, 123

Frogger, 23, 176

G

Gary Bracey, 247

H

Head Over Heels, 326

Herman Hauser, 189, 221

Horizons, 107

Hyperion, 166

I

Ian Weatherburn, 149

IBM, 18, 24, 42, 52, 75, 165, 166, 200, 224, 226, 230, 240, 268, 269, 270, 272, 311, 314

Intel, 13, 15, 24, 25, 226, 241

International Karate, 326

J

J. Presper Eckert, 17

Jack Kilby, 17

Jack Tramiel, 16, 17, 52, 58, 112, 160, 182, 186, 189, 203, 208, 232, 236, 287

James D Sachs, 126

Jeroen Tel, 118

Jim Bagley, 311

John Gibson, 149

John Marshall, 27

John Mauchly, 17

Jupiter Ace, 123, 241

Jupiter ACE, 42, 130

JVC, 158, 170

K

Ken Olson, 26

Kenneth Kendall, 136

Kevin Toms, 163

KIM1, 20

Kray, 13

L

LeaderBoard, 326

Lode Runner, 326

Logic5, 23

Lord Reith, 86

LSI, 25

lynx, 149

Lynx, 27, 42, 120, 127, 130, 148, 149, 165, 180, 306

M

Manfred Kapp, 17

Maniac Manson, 326

Manic Miner, 61, 62, 115, 139, 156

Martin Galway, 118

Master, 202, 204, 211, 216, 217, 223, 224, 229, 249, 270, 272

Mastertronic, 167, 202, 225

Mattel, 42, 65, 143, 177, 229, 241, 267, 268, 290

Matthew Smith, 61, 62, 115

Mayhem in Monsterland, 326

MC-10, 42, 166, 167, 177

memory, 11, 12, 13, 16, 23, 28, 43, 46, 62, 65, 73, 80, 93, 108, 109, 135, 139, 145, 147, 148, 155, 156, 159, 175, 190, 199, 211, 212, 215, 217, 218, 223, 241, 245, 246, 249, 253, 254, 257, 258, 262, 282, 306, 311, 315

Memotech, 42, 135, 177, 199, 232, 306

Merlin, 23

MGT, 62, 66, 241, 246, 275, 276

Michael Wise, 18

Microdrive, 120, 130, 134, 145, 151, 153, 184, 188, 211, 219, 235, 236

Microfair, 103, 161

Microsoft, 27, 31, 38, 57, 136, 159, 170, 278, 287, 288

Mike Fischer, 27

Mike Glover, 149, 184

Mike O'Regan, 27

Mike Richardson, 224

Mitsubishi, 158, 170, 288

MK14, 19, 28, 29, 42

MOS, 14, 15, 18, 19, 24, 25, 26, 70, 89, 112, 160, 217

MOS6502B, 70

Motorola, 13, 14, 15, 16, 18, 24, 25, 145, 157, 182, 241

MSX, 59, 113, 136, 144, 158, 159, 166, 170, 171, 178, 179, 199, 228, 232, 243, 252, 269, 272, 274, 287, 288, 306, 311

N

Namco, 24

Nascom, 27, 28, 306

Nintendo, 15, 22, 23, 95, 227, 229, 242, 249, 250, 267, 268, 269, 270, 271, 272, 288, 290, 327, 329

Nolan Bushnell, 18, 53

O

Ocean, 180, 181, 196, 197, 225, 228, 246, 247, 249, 323

Olivetti, 189, 197, 202, 217, 221, 224

Oric, 12, 42, 127, 130, 135, 144, 154, 155, 158, 163, 168, 177, 186, 188, 189, 213, 241, 274, 280, 282, 283, 284, 285, 286, 287, 306, 311

P

Pac-Man, 11, 24, 75, 156

PASCAL, 28

PC10, 205, 234

PC20, 205, 234

Pet, 15, 28, 67, 166, 233

Pirates!, 326

plus4, 12, 161, 176, 199, 204, 223, 274

Plus4, 15, 60, 161, 166, 174, 175, 176, 179, 189, 194, 199, 202, 205, 223

Pong, 22, 60

PONG, 22

Prince of Persia, 326

Project Firestart, 326

Psion, 107

Psyclaps, 149

Q

QL, 145, 151, 152, 157, 158, 161, 164, 165, 174, 177, 178, 182, 186, 187, 188, 189, 191, 195, 198, 201, 202, 206, 216, 218, 222, 223, 226

Quantum Leap, 151

Quicksilva, 139

Quiz Wiz, 23

R

Raid Over Moscow, 326

Rebel Star, 326

Rescue on Fractalus, 326

Research Machines, 27, 68

retro, 163, 311

Richard Altwasser, 108, 123

RM, 27

Rob Hubbard, 118

Robert Noyce, 17

Robert Russell, 112

Robert Yannes, 112

Ron Wayne, 19

Roy Williams, 85

S

SAM Coupe, 66, 241, 275

SC3000H, 176

Science of Cambridge, 19, 28, 73

Scramble, 23

Sega, 23, 95, 176, 178, 229, 242, 249, 269, 270, 271, 272, 327

Shutgart, 181

Sinclair, 11, 12, 16, 18, 19, 24, 26, 28, 38, 42, 52, 53, 54, 58, 59, 60, 62, 64, 65, 66, 67, 72, 73, 78, 79, 80, 87, 90, 102, 103, 105, 106, 107, 108, 109, 110, 112, 113, 114, 120, 122, 124, 125, 130, 132, 134, 135, 139, 144, 145, 151, 152, 153, 157, 158, 161, 164, 165, 166, 167, 168, 170, 171, 172, 176, 177, 178, 180, 181, 184, 185, 186, 187, 188, 189, 190, 191, 195, 196, 197, 198, 200, 202, 203, 204, 206, 211, 213, 216, 217, 218, 219, 221, 222, 223, 224, 225, 226, 227, 229, 232, 235, 236, 237, 240, 241, 242, 245, 246, 253, 256, 258, 259, 262, 267, 270, 275, 279, 282, 284, 285, 287, 295, 318, 327

Sinclair's, 16, 65, 66, 73, 106, 109, 110, 122, 157, 158, 165, 184, 195, 200, 201, 203, 217, 222, 235, 238, 262

Sony, 52, 57, 66, 158, 170, 190, 288, 295

SORD M-5, 121

Space Invaders, 23, 68, 75, 295, 316, 317

Speak and Spell, 23

Spectrum, 11, 15, 28, 38, 40, 42, 43, 44, 53, 59, 60, 61, 62, 64, 65, 73, 90, 103, 105, 106, 107, 108, 109, 110, 113, 114, 115, 120, 124, 125, 127, 130, 132, 135, 137, 139, 144, 145, 148, 151, 153, 155, 156, 157, 158, 163, 166, 168, 174, 177, 178, 180, 181, 184, 185, 186, 187, 188,

189, 195, 198, 199, 200, 202, 203, 206, 216, 217, 219, 221, 223, 224, 225, 226, 232, 235, 240, 242, 243, 245, 246, 250, 253, 254, 255, 256, 257, 258, 259, 260, 261, 262, 263, 265, 270, 274, 275, 279, 280, 282, 284, 285, 289, 295, 306, 311, 317, 318, 327, 328, 330

Sphere Computers, 18

ST, 113, 189, 197, 200, 203, 208, 215, 224, 225, 226, 229, 232, 236, 241, 245, 246, 249, 250, 271, 272, 275, 276, 314, 316, 328

Star-Trek, 11, 100, 300

Steve Jobs, 19

Steve Wozniack, 19

Summer games / Winter games, 326

SX-64, 119

SX64, 119

SX64, 174

SX64, 221

T

tandy, 68

Tandy, 28, 37, 42, 67, 68, 76, 165, 166, 167, 177, 213, 226, 280, 289, 300, 306

Tatung Einstein, 172

Team17, 118

TED, 176, 194, 205

Ted Dabney, 18, 53

Texas Instruments, 11, 16, 20, 41, 43, 44, 50, 58, 59, 60, 67, 74, 91, 93, 94, 95, 133, 134, 135, 136, 142, 143, 177, 241, 259, 290, 314

TEXET, 132

the Chips are Down, 83

The Great Escape, 326

Ti99, 14, 32, 40, 42, 43, 44, 45, 46, 47, 48, 50, 51, 58, 60, 64, 67, 91, 92, 93, 94, 95, 113, 125, 130, 134, 138, 139, 163, 213, 252, 259, 317

Ti99/4, 14, 32, 67, 92

TI99/4, 20, 74, 95

TI-99/4A, 64, 91, 94, 133, 267, 269, 314

Ti99/8, 64, 134, 139

Tim Berners-Lee, 20

TMS-5220, 136

TMS9900, 14

TMS-9918A, 177

Toru Iwatani, 24

Tramiel, 16, 160, 203, 288

Triumph Adler, 169

TRS, 15, 61, 67, 76, 102, 163, 166, 167, 242, 243, 252, 289, 300, 301, 306, 314, 315

Turrican, 326

U

UK101, 31, 102

V

VCS, 21, 32, 36, 60, 70, 102, 267, 268, 290

VFD, 22, 23

VIC-20, 20, 23, 42, 60, 62, 106, 111, 112, 125, 132, 133, 134, 135, 139, 144, 149, 176, 177, 252, 267, 307

VisiCalc, 19

W

W. H. Smith, 80

Wafadrive, 184

WARGAMES, 137

Welchi, 18

WH-Smiths, 11

World of Commodore, 12

World War 2, 17

Y

Yamaha, 158, 170

Z

Z80, 14, 15, 24, 28, 73, 109, 121, 135, 136, 157, 161, 164, 166, 169, 177, 187, 193, 198, 212, 218, 232, 236, 288

Z-8000, 189

Z80A, 27, 68, 105, 159, 227

Zilog, 13, 15, 73, 109, 133, 135

ZX80, 11, 15, 24, 26, 42, 55, 67, 72, 73, 77, 79, 80, 102, 105, 106, 113, 122, 188, 252, 316

ZX81, 11, 40, 42, 50, 54, 60, 62, 73, 76, 79, 80, 87, 102, 105, 106, 113, 122, 125, 127, 130, 132, 134, 135, 139, 144, 158, 163, 166, 177, 186, 241, 246, 251, 252, 295, 297, 316, 331

Source material.

[i] https://en.wikipedia.org/wiki/ZX81

[ii] https://en.wikipedia.org/wiki/Cray-1

[iii] https://en.wikipedia.org/wiki/Altair_8800

[iv] https://en.wikipedia.org/wiki/Intel_8080

[v] https://en.wikipedia.org/wiki/Zilog_Z80

[vi] https://gunkies.org/wiki/MOS_Technology_6502

[vii] https://spectrum.ieee.org/the-inside-story-of-texas-instruments-biggest-blunder-the-tms9900-microprocessor

[viii] https://en.wikipedia.org/wiki/MOS_Technology

[ix] https://plato.stanford.edu/entries/computing-history/#Bab

[x] https://plato.stanford.edu/entries/computing-history/#UTM

[xi] https://en.wikipedia.org/wiki/John_Mauchly

[xii]https://www.chiphistory.org/integrated-circuit-invention-history-1958#:~:text=First%20conceived%20in%201952%20by%20Geoffrey%20Drummer%3B%20then,idea%20that%20the%20modern%20Integrated%20Circuit%20was%20invented.

[xiii] https://en.wikipedia.org/wiki/Commodore_International

[xiv] https://www.gearrate.com/en/mouse/history/#:~:text=The%20first%20prototype%20of%20the%20computer%20mouse%20was,is%20a%20horizontal%20wheel%20and%20a%20vertical%20wheel.

[xv] https://en.wikipedia.org/wiki/Alan_Shugart

[xvi] https://en.wikipedia.org/wiki/Nolan_Bushnell

[xvii] https://en.wikipedia.org/wiki/Control-Alt-Delete

[xviii] https://www.commodore.ca/commodore-history/the-legendary-chuck-peddle-inventor-of-the-personal-computer/

[xix] https://appleinsider.com/articles/20/04/01/apple-was-founded-44-years-ago-on-april-1-1976

[xx] https://www.commodore.ca/commodore-products/commodore-pet-the-worlds-first-personal-computer/

[xxi] https://en.wikipedia.org/wiki/Sinclair_Research

[xxii] https://en.wikipedia.org/wiki/Dan_Bricklin

[xxiii] https://www.computinghistory.org.uk/det/49852/Texas-Instruments-TI-99-4/

[xxiv] https://www.computinghistory.org.uk/det/2535/Commodore-VIC-20/

[xxv] https://www.computerhistory.org/revolution/the-web/20/385/2109

[xxvi] https://uk.pcmag.com/games/142576/the-atari-2600-at-45-the-console-that-brought-arcade-games-home

[xxvii] https://thinksetmag.com/insights/digital-detective-pong

[xxviii] https://ithistory.org/db/hardware/tiger-electronics/tiger-quiz-wiz

[xxix] https://www.retrogames.co.uk/015964/Handheld/Logic-5-by-MB-Games-Boxed

[xxx]

xxxi https://archive.org/details/argos-autumn-winter-1980-1981/page/n231/mode/2up

xxxii https://en.wikipedia.org/wiki/ZX80

xxxiii https://en.wikipedia.org/wiki/Pac-Man

xxxiv https://en.wikipedia.org/wiki/Intel_4004

xxxv https://en.wikipedia.org/wiki/Nascom

xxxvi https://en.wikipedia.org/wiki/MK14

xxxvii https://en.wikipedia.org/wiki/Compukit_UK101

xxxviii https://www.pcworld.com/article/490655/history-atari-computers.html

xxxix https://www.pcworld.com/article/490655/history-atari-computers.html

xl https://en.wikipedia.org/wiki/Acorn_Atom

xli https://en.wikipedia.org/wiki/BBC_Micro

xlii https://en.wikipedia.org/wiki/TI-99/4A

xliii https://en.wikipedia.org/wiki/Evans_%26_Sutherland

xliv https://en.wikipedia.org/wiki/Magnavox_Odyssey_2

xlvi https://en.wikipedia.org/wiki/ZX81

xlvii https://en.wikipedia.org/wiki/ZX_Spectrum

xlviii https://en.wikipedia.org/wiki/Commodore_64

xlix https://en.wikipedia.org/wiki/Sord_M5

l https://en.wikipedia.org/wiki/DK%27Tronics

li https://en.wikipedia.org/wiki/Jupiter_Ace

lii https://en.wikipedia.org/wiki/Cassette_50

liii https://en.wikipedia.org/wiki/Coleco_Adam

liv https://www.cjemicros.co.uk/micros/individual/newprodpages/prodinfo.php?prodcode=ACO-BBC-TMS5220

lv https://en.wikipedia.org/wiki/Acorn_Electron

lvi https://en.wikipedia.org/wiki/Dragon_32/64

lvii https://www.computinghistory.org.uk/det/3959/Atari-800XL/

lviii https://en.wikipedia.org/wiki/ORIC

lix https://en.wikipedia.org/wiki/MSX

lx https://en.wikipedia.org/wiki/Amstrad_CPC

lxi https://www.telegraph.co.uk/cars/classic/uks-rarest-cars-1984-renault-11-txe-electronic-one-of-only/

lxii https://en.wikipedia.org/wiki/TRS-80_MC-10

lxiii https://en.wikipedia.org/wiki/TRS-80_Color_Computer

lxiv https://en.wikipedia.org/wiki/Dragon_Data

lxv https://en.wikipedia.org/wiki/Commodore_Plus/4

lxvi https://archive.org/details/your-spectrum-magazine-10/page/n105/mode/2up

lxvii https://www.c5owners.com/sinclair-c5-history#:~:text=The%20Sinclair%20C5%20was%20launched%20on%20the%2010th,too%20well%20on%20snow%20and%20ice%20covered%20roads.

lxviii https://en.wikipedia.org/wiki/Frankie_Goes_to_Hollywood_(video_game)

lxix https://www.express.co.uk/expressyourself/113527/Battle-of-the-Boffins

lxx https://en.wikipedia.org/wiki/Enterprise_(computer)

lxxi https://en.wikipedia.org/wiki/Atari_ST
lxxii https://en.wikipedia.org/wiki/Sinclair_Research
lxxiii https://www.theguardian.com/technology/2001/mar/08/onlinesupplement5
lxxiv https://en.wikipedia.org/wiki/BBC_Micro
lxxv https://en.wikipedia.org/wiki/Amstrad
lxxvi https://en.wikipedia.org/wiki/Commodore_128
lxxvii https://en.wikipedia.org/wiki/Sinclair_Research
lxxviii https://www.company-histories.com/Commodore-International-Ltd-Company-History.html
lxxix https://www.youtube.com/watch?v=sHJ6vVxJLlQ
lxxx https://www.computinghistory.org.uk/det/2666/Amstrad-CPC-6128/
lxxxi https://www.classic-computers.org.nz/collection/atari130xe.htm
lxxxii https://en.wikipedia.org/wiki/BBC_Master
lxxxiii https://www.computinghistory.org.uk/det/8239/Commodore/
lxxxiv https://en.wikipedia.org/wiki/ZX_Spectrum
lxxxv https://www.c64-wiki.com/wiki/C128DCR
lxxxvi https://en.wikipedia.org/wiki/SAM_Coup%C3%A9
lxxxvii https://en.wikipedia.org/wiki/Batman_(1989_video_game)
lxxxviii https://en.wikipedia.org/wiki/Star_Trek_(1971_video_game)
lxxxix https://en.wikipedia.org/wiki/Temple_of_Apshai
xc https://en.wikipedia.org/wiki/Wander_(1974_video_game)
xci https://en.wikipedia.org/wiki/The_Hobbit_(1982_video_game)
xcii https://en.wikipedia.org/wiki/Zork

For errors and omissions please contact the author directly via email.

mvtcomputers@hotmail.com

```
47 6f 6f 64 62 79 65 20 61 6e
64 20 74 68 61 6e 6b 20 79 6f
75 2e 20 49 20 64 6f 20 68 6f
70 65 20 79 6f 75 20 65 6e 6a
6f 79 65 64 20 72 65 61 64 69
6e 67 20 74 68 69 73 20 62 6f
6f 6b 2e
```

There are so many more stories to tell.

End.